Approaches to Teaching the Works of Eliza Haywood

Approaches to Teaching the Works of Eliza Haywood

Edited by

Tiffany Potter

The Modern Language Association of America
New York 2020

Library of Congress Cataloging-in-Publication Data

Names: Potter, Tiffany, 1967– editor.
Title: Approaches to teaching the works of Eliza Haywood / edited by Tiffany Potter.
Description: New York : Modern Language Association of America, 2020. | Series: Approaches to teaching world literature, 10591133 ; 162 | Includes bibliographical references. | Summary: "Offers pedagogical techniques for teaching novels, plays, and nonfiction by Eliza Haywood, including considerations of literary genres, gender roles, family dynamics, social class, and popular culture. Gives syllabus suggestions for undergraduate and graduate courses in eighteenth-century English literature, the history of the novel, women's writing, and general education"— Provided by publisher.
Identifiers: LCCN 2019039523 (print) | LCCN 2019039524 (ebook) | ISBN 9781603294621 (hardcover) | ISBN 9781603294249 (paperback) | ISBN 9781603294256 (EPUB) | ISBN 9781603294263 (Kindle edition)
Subjects: LCSH: Haywood, Eliza Fowler, 1693?–1756—Study and teaching. | Haywood, Eliza Fowler, 1693?–1756—Criticism and interpretation.
Classification: LCC PR3506.H94 Z57 2020 (print) | LCC PR3506.H94 (ebook) | DDC 823/.5—dc23
LC record available at https://lccn.loc.gov/2019039523
LC ebook record available at https://lccn.loc.gov/2019039524

Approaches to Teaching World Literature 162
ISSN 1059-1133

Cover illustration of the paperback and electronic editions: Jean-Honoré Fragonard, *The Love Letter*. Metropolitan Museum of Art, Jules Bache Collection, 1949.

Published by The Modern Language Association of America
85 Broad Street, suite 500, New York, New York 10004-2434
www.mla.org

CONTENTS

PREFACE

Every once in a while, a historical writer bursts into sudden critical prominence, providing exciting new opportunities for teaching and research; this volume seeks to build on the rapidly expanding scholarship on the works of Eliza Haywood to reflect upon the ways in which Haywood's work can be taught, in terms of critical approaches and classroom practices.

Influential in her time as a novelist, playwright, periodical essayist, and bookseller, Haywood has moved since the 1990s from relative obscurity to a prominent place in the canon of eighteenth-century English literature. During this same window, scholarship on women's writing has exploded and old-fashioned understandings of the "rise of the novel" in Daniel Defoe, Samuel Richardson, and Henry Fielding have been supplanted by a more historically informed recognition of the evolutions of prose fiction across the Restoration and the first half of the eighteenth century. Reflecting these shifts, Haywood's short fiction *Fantomina* is now widely reprinted in anthologies, which, as many have noted, is both a blessing and curse: Haywood's importance to eighteenth-century literature and culture extends far beyond *Fantomina*, and the singularity of its anthologization does as much to limit students' knowledge of Haywood as it does to facilitate it. Good, then, that several of Haywood's fictional works are already staples of courses in women's writing, the history of the novel, and eighteenth-century British literature. Beyond her fiction, Haywood's as yet underexamined place in theater history creates opportunities for innovation, and her periodical writing contributes an important female perspective on the essay genre so influential in her era, providing a wealth of insight into her cultural moment.

One goal of this volume is to share approaches to this broad pool of Haywood's works, inviting teacher-scholars to bring Haywood into a range of courses and conversations. Contributors provide background information, overviews of scholarship, module designs, and innovative classroom approaches for teaching Haywood in courses across college curricula. Several essays focus specifically on studying Haywood in core curricula, as part of survey courses, or with students who do not match the traditional stereotype of the English major. The essays collected here offer pedagogical frameworks for a wide variety of classrooms, from introductory courses and surveys (where the relative brevity of Haywood's works, combined with students' perceptions of their "relevance," makes them especially teachable) to advanced courses from an array of perspectives. Essays included here recognize Haywood's potential value to genre-based courses on the novel, theater history, fantasy, romance fiction, and protest literature, as well as thematically oriented courses engaging legal cultures, social rank, and other intellectual and artistic emphases. Within these contexts, contributors also share their strategies for what might seem like dangerous texts to teach—those whose treatment of rape, violence, and notions of difference may contradict our standards. Haywood wrote repeatedly on questions of power, status, sex, and consent, and she brought those issues into the discursive light; for us to silence her again three centuries later because we are nervous about teaching the subject matter would be a critical loss that several contributors agree can be addressed with specific teaching strategies.

Patrick Spedding's essay in this volume uses online resources to demonstrate that accessible editions of Haywood's works correlate directly (and perhaps causally) with critical attention and scholarship. The response to the survey of instructors taken for this volume would seem to confirm that the same pattern occurs in classrooms: accessible editions lead to teaching. The complication with Haywood is that she was both influential and extremely prolific in so many different genres and forms across four decades. Sorting this body of work into discussions that teachers will find valuable in their course design, facilitating high-impact learning, has been the central challenge in developing this volume. On balance, we have chosen to provide multiple approaches to the Haywood texts that are currently most frequently taught and also to provide discussions and strategies for lesser-known texts that have the potential to contribute significantly to students' understandings of the eighteenth century and its literatures.

In particular, this volume operates around one foundational principle: providing arguments, materials, and innovative teaching strategies that extend classroom discussion of Haywood's work beyond easy categorizations such as "women's writing" and "amatory fiction" and into questions around print culture, genre, the history of the novel, and the ways in which Haywood's texts concurrently interrogate and enforce several of the contested regulatory mechanisms of eighteenth-century London. We hope that our essays will help teacher-scholars to actualize the full range of potential pedagogies related to Haywood beyond the novel into theater, periodicals, secret histories, and fantasies.

Part 1 opens with an overview of the classroom editions that offer the best combination of editorial excellence, accessibility, and low cost, followed by a summary of scholarly resources that illuminate Haywood's work and the eighteenth-century literary environment. Good scholarship is at the core of nearly all good teaching, and the "Materials" section seeks to provide a guide for bringing the two together. Together, this section and the essays that follow in part 2 engage a range of critical approaches, including theoretical framing on gender and identity, queer studies, affect theory, and orientalism and colonialism, as well as critical approaches around genre through amatory fiction, fantasy, epistolarity, and the "rise" of the novel, alongside dramatic and nonfiction forms.

Part 2 of this volume, "Approaches," is divided into four sections that together create a foundation for teaching Haywood to students of all levels. First is "Backgrounds," which provides a brief overview of Haywood's life, her readership, and the print culture in which she was such an active and influential agent. Next is "Culture and Contexts," in which each essay focuses upon an issue that is broadly important in teaching Haywood, with brief engagements of a number of her works to show how the information provided might be used in a class on any one of several of Haywood's works. Essays in the third section, "Individual Works," focus on one or two works each, offering new approaches for widely taught texts like *Fantomina*, *Love in Excess*, and *The History of Miss Betsy Thoughtless*; providing teaching contexts for accessible, but often less taught, texts that have potentially important contributions to make to larger critical and classroom conversations; and establishing the ways in which Haywood's works can be brought into dialogue with cultural debates and with other writers, most notably Fielding, her off-and-on colleague and rival, but also Richardson, Defoe, Samuel Johnson, John Gay, and Joseph Addison and Richard Steele.

As editor, I offer my heartfelt thanks to the contributors to this volume: I am immensely grateful that such an outstanding cadre of scholars was also so generous and efficient throughout this process. I wish also to acknowledge the insightful work of the outside readers, as well as the support of the team at the MLA. I hope that together we have created a resource that will facilitate brilliant teaching and foster future generations of eighteenth-centuryists of all stripes.

Part One

MATERIALS

Texts for Teaching

Editions

It is possible now to teach a full course on Eliza Haywood from student-friendly modern editions that include extensive introductions, explanatory annotations, and helpful bibliographies. That said, a significant number of Haywood's many texts still await a modern editorial hand and must be taught from unedited scans of eighteenth-century prints, either online (for faculty members at institutions with the means to subscribe to services like Gale's *Eighteenth Century Collections Online* [*ECCO*]), in hard copy prints (those with the best provenance are available from Gale, but others from unscholarly publishers that generate scans of out-of-copyright texts are also for sale on *Amazon* and other sites); or photocopies or course Web sites, if one has appropriate permissions or access to original texts. Though frugal students often appreciate the no-cost availability of online scans of eighteenth-century documents like those on *ECCO*, teaching from scans creates challenges for many less experienced readers, while for others it presents opportunities for different kinds of analysis. Few of Haywood's texts are available in competing editions; however, regarding those that are, this volume cites those high-quality editions that are the most readily available in stand-alone volumes at a reasonable cost. Nearly all the editions discussed below are also available digitally from their publishers' Web sites or through services like *Kindle*, though prices are often not significantly lower than those of printed books. Some edited versions are also available through resources like *Google Books*. One particularly useful open-access online resource is Jack Lynch's "minimally edited transcription" of *Fantomina; or, Love in a Maze*.

Many teachers first encounter Haywood through *Fantomina*, which is also widely reprinted in the standard survey anthologies, including those by Longman, Norton, and Broadview. Beyond anthologies and beyond *Fantomina*, Broadview Press has made good industry of expertly edited, high-quality editions at a good price, and their format includes a selection of contextualizing documents by and about Haywood, as well as excerpts from other works that illuminate the issues and environments that frame each text. There are Broadview editions of *Love in Excess* (edited by David Oakleaf); *Fantomina and Other Works*, which includes *The Tea-Table* (edited by Alexander Pettit et al.); *Anti-Pamela*, with Henry Fielding's *Shamela* (edited by Catherine Ingrassia); *The Adventures of Eovaai, Princess of Ijaveo* (edited by Earla Wilputte); and *The History of Miss Betsy Thoughtless* (edited by Christine Blouch). Several university presses have also produced classroom editions, including Michigan State's collection of *The Distress'd Orphan*, *The City Jilt*, and *The Double Marriage*, published under the title *Three Novellas* (edited by Wilputte); Kentucky's The Injur'd Husband *and* Lasselia (edited by Jerry C. Beasley) and *The History of Jemmy and Jenny Jessamy* (edited by John Richetti); and Toronto's The

Masqueraders; or, Fatal Curiosity, *and* The Surprize; or, Constancy Rewarded (edited by Tiffany Potter). *The British Recluse* is included in Oxford's short anthology *Popular Fiction by Women, 1660–1730* (edited by Paula R. Backscheider and Richetti).

For a full course on Haywood, instructors would be well advised to consider Backscheider's *Selected Fiction and Drama of Eliza Haywood*, which includes the plays *A Wife to Be Lett* and *The Opera of Operas*; full texts of *The City Jilt* and *The Mercenary Lover*; and excerpts from *Eovaai*, *The Wife*, and *The Invisible Spy* (including the accounts of the Elizabeth Canning case discussed in Kathryn R. King's essay for this volume). Teaching *The Invisible Spy* or *The Female Spectator* can present something of a challenge in terms of text access. Both Carol Stewart's splendid edition of *The Invisible Spy* and King and Pettit's authoritative *Female Spectator* are prohibitively expensive. Selections are available from each in Patricia Meyer Spacks's *Selections from* The Female Spectator and in Backscheider's *Selected Fiction and Drama* (*Invisible Spy*), but they must omit more than they can possibly include, so instructors may need to supplement with additional selections.

In most of the examples listed above, the recommended teaching text is also the standard text for scholarly citation. The exceptions, however, are important and lie in King and Pettit's eight-volume *Selected Works of Eliza Haywood*, which includes the full text of *The Female Spectator*, *The Dramatic Historiographer*, *The Parrot*, *Epistles for the Ladies*, *The Wife*, *The Husband*, *The Young Lady*, and *Miscellaneous Writings, 1725–1743*.

Biographical and Bibliographical Materials

We have relatively little hard biographical information on Haywood, but there is excellent scholarship on what we do have. This has not always been the case, as earlier generations of Haywood biographies replicated innuendo and gossip in a way that fostered the "two Haywoods" narrative that this volume counters. Blouch's 1991 article "Eliza Haywood and the Romance of Obscurity" recounts the key elements of previous biographies by David Erskine Baker (1764) and George Frisbie Whicher (1915) and does away with several old errors, speculations, and canards. Building upon Blouch, King widens the lens through which Haywood's life is considered in her meticulous *Political Biography of Eliza Haywood*, now the biographical standard. King recognizes the near impossibility of writing a book-length biography, given the dearth of documentary evidence from Haywood's life; her account works to separate "those parts of the received account that are undocumented, patently false or highly suspect from claims that can be shown to have some foundation in the historical record," even as she recognizes that this process of necessity involves "a great deal of inference and inevitably some degree of guesswork" (5). The inferences, however, are firmly grounded in Haywood's social and political milieu, with documentation on the people and politics with whom we know she was involved at specific points in her life. King brings these resources into dialogue with Haywood's satirical and social writing, particularly in her periodicals and her conduct-literature-style work, in order to illuminate not her private life but her places and positions in the world in which she traveled.

Haywood's publication history has an initial murkiness similar to that of her biography, and the scholarly conversation is ongoing about the exact boundaries of her oeuvre. The first and still most definitive attempt to identify or exclude publications from the Haywood canon is Patrick Spedding's *A Bibliography of Eliza Haywood* (2004). In 2011 Leah Orr's article "The Basis for Attribution in the Canon of Eliza Haywood" argued for further exclusions based on a different methodological approach.

In these days of the online *MLA Bibliography*, there is little call for bibliographies of critical work on a given author, but both King's *Political Biography* and Spedding's Web site (patrickspedding.blogspot.ca) include discussion or complete transcription of several reviews of Haywood's work from before the twentieth century. Students seeking critical assessments of more recent published research (beyond full-length book reviews) can be directed to the annual overview in *The Review of English Studies* and the short reviews of books and articles in *The Scriblerian*.

General Background Reading

Teaching Haywood well requires a familiarity with the social and literary environments from which she wrote; this familiarity can be a lifelong journey, of course, but the short list below offers some paths to a strong starting position. Roy Porter's well-indexed and readable *English Society in the Eighteenth Century*, W. A. Speck's *Literature and Society in Eighteenth-Century England*, and James Sambrook's *The Eighteenth Century: The Intellectual and Cultural Context of English Literature, 1700–1789* are classic overviews of the social, political, and economic contexts of the eighteenth century. Charlotte Sussman's *Eighteenth-Century English Literature, 1660–1789* includes particularly useful chapters on national identity, female sexuality and domesticity, and print culture and the public sphere. For those interested specifically in women's history, the collection *Women's History: Britain, 1700–1850* (edited by Hannah Barker and Elaine Chalus) gathers essays on women and work, politics, education, religion, poverty, crime, the family, and the body. On conduct and legal status, see Kathryn Sutherland's "Writings on Education and Conduct: Arguments for Female Improvement" and Gillian Skinner's "Women's Status as Legal and Civic Subjects" in Vivien Jones's *Women and Literature in England, 1700–1800*; for specific examples, see Margo Collins's discussion of Haywood's *The Wife* and *The Husband*. In a pinch, the introductory chapters to the eighteenth century in the Norton and Broadview anthologies cover the ground concisely, and the Longman's introduction is very good (Greenblatt et al., Introduction; Black et al.; Sherman and Zwicker).

There are several recent overviews that support teaching Haywood within the specific framework of women's writing. An instructor looking for a concise group of current, readable essays would do well to begin with the *Cambridge Companion to Women's Writing in Britain, 1660–1789*, which includes Betty Schellenberg on the professional woman writer, Mark Towsey on women as readers and writers, and genre-based overviews of the early novel (Nicola Parsons), drama (Felicity Nussbaum), and periodical writing (Mary Waters). Around a slightly narrower chronology, Ros Ballaster's collection *The History of British Women's Writing, 1690–1750* is home to Kate Williams's chapter on women and the rise of the novel and to Karen O'Brien's "Woman's Place," a concise and useful introduction to the experiences of women in early eighteenth-century England and to that period's social, political, and philosophical thought. Another recent collection, Jennie Batchelor and Gillian Dow's *Women Writers, 1660–1830: Feminisms and Futures*, seeks, according to its cover, to map "the future of eighteenth-century women's writing and feminist literary history." Within this frame, E. J. Clery addresses Haywood specifically in her reflection upon political economies of women's writing in "Free Market Feminism." Batchelor and Manushag N. Powell's *Women's Periodicals and Print Culture in Britain, 1690–1820* collects an insightful series of essays on a neglected genre.

Those teaching Haywood within a survey or novel history course will undoubtedly already be aware of the seventy years of debate following Ian Watt's *The Rise of the Novel*, including Michael McKeon's *The Origins of the English Novel, 1600–1740*, Lennard J. Davis's *Factual Fictions*, and Nancy Armstrong's *Desire and Domestic Fiction*. The essays in Tom Keymer's *Oxford History of the Novel in English: Prose Fiction in English from the Origins of Print to 1750*, including Nicholas Hudson's overview, "Formal Experimentation and Theories of Fiction," enter and extend these discussions. Women's contributions to the early novel are also documented in Williams's "Women Writers and the Rise of the Novel" and Ballaster's "Women and the Rise of the Novel: Sexual Prescripts" in Jones's *Women and Literature in England*. A helpful overview for survey teaching comes in Richetti's chapter "Prose Fiction in the Early Eighteenth Century: Behn, Haywood, Defoe, Swift" in his *History of Eighteenth-Century British Literature*, and students can be directed to primary sources on early fiction collected in Cheryl Nixon's theoretically informed yet readable *Novel Definitions: An Anthology of Commentary on the Novel, 1688–1815*.

One contested element of the early novel discussion that is particularly relevant to teaching Haywood is the genre of amatory fiction. Ballaster's full-length discussion in *Seductive Forms* is engaged in Toni Bowers's essay "Sex, Lies and Invisibility" in *The Columbia History of the British Novel*, William B. Warner's "Formulating Fiction," Kathleen Lubey's "Eliza Haywood's Amatory Aesthetic," and Bowers's revisiting of amatory fiction in this volume. Bowers also expands her discussion in "Representing Resistance: British Seduction Stories, 1660–1800" in Blackwell's *Companion to the Eighteenth-Century English Novel and Culture.*

Beyond fiction, *The Cambridge Companion to British Theatre, 1730–1830*, edited by Jane Moody and Daniel O'Quinn, provides a well-organized environment scan that can be supplemented by essays on drama by Nussbaum in *The Cambridge Companion to Women's Writing* and by Jane Spencer in *The History of British Women's Writing, 1690–1750.* Ballaster frames Haywood within another genre in "A Gender of Opposition: Eliza Haywood's Scandal Fiction," and Shawn Lisa Maurer provides an overview of the periodical that can then be specialized using the essays in *Fair Philosopher*, discussed below, as well as Kristin Girten's "Unsexed Souls," which explores the treatment of natural philosophy in *The Female Spectator.* On Haywood's poetry, see Wilputte's "Eliza Haywood's *Poems on Several Occasions.*"

Critical Collections

Haywood is the focus of individual essays in a number of critical collections, but only three collections are dedicated to Haywood scholarship. Many of the core issues that are likely to be raised in undergraduate classrooms are brought together in the foundational collection on Haywood, *The Passionate Fictions of Eliza Haywood: Essays on Her Life and Work*, edited by Kirsten Saxton and Rebecca Bocchicchio in 2000. Here, Backscheider's "The Story of Eliza Haywood's Novels" sets the frame for the questions that early-adopter teachers might have had and raises the "two Haywoods" mythology. Her contextualization is further supported by Blouch's documenting of evidence for Haywood's readership in "'What Ann Lang Read.'" Richetti's "Histories by Eliza Haywood and Henry Fielding" offers a starting point on the Haywood-Fielding dialogue, examined through the frame of imitation and adaptation (which King both extends and refutes in her essay on Fielding and Haywood in the 2006 collection *Henry Fielding in Our Time*). On the novels themselves, the collection offers takes on the intersections of politics and desire in both *Love in Excess* (Bowers, "Collusive Resistance") and *Fantomina* (Croskery, "Masquing Desire"), and Andrea Austin looks into the implications of parody for readers of *Betsy Thoughtless*, alongside Oakleaf's consideration of Betsy's reflection on the pastoral and country life. Several of Haywood's less-often-taught texts also receive attention here, particularly in Bocchicchio's essay on *The British Recluse* and Saxton's on *The City Jilt. Passionate Fictions* also directs readers' attention to texts that are less known, notably Jennifer Thorn on Haywood's exotic tales and Ballaster on her scandal fiction.

Fair Philosopher: Eliza Haywood and The Female Spectator, edited by Donald J. Newman and Lynn Marie Wright in 2006, is an essential resource for those using Haywood's periodical writing either as its own focus or in dialogue with other work. Bibliographical and readership issues are addressed by Newman's "*The Female Spectator*: A Bibliographic Essay" and Spedding's "Measuring the Success of Haywood's *Female Spectator*, 1744–46," respectively, and the political work done by Haywood's longest-lived periodical is considered by King ("Patriot") and Wilputte ("'Too Ticklish'") in terms of both ideology and party. Eve Tavor Bannet ("Haywood's *Spectator*"), Nicola Graves, and Juliette Merritt ("Reforming the Coquet?") take on the complex and sometimes contradictory ways in which Haywood's periodical examines notions of female experience and education. The chapters in this collection encompass a wide selection from Haywood's four volumes of essays.

A 2014 special issue of the *Journal for Early Modern Cultural Studies* will be helpful particularly to teachers interested in engaging with Haywood's interest in issues of social justice, based, as editors Amanda Hiner and Patsy S. Fowler point out, on King's assertion that, though Haywood fearlessly criticized both ministerial and Tory factions, she "consistently aligned herself with those excluded from or out of power" (*Political Biography* 7). This special issue invites scholars to reconsider Haywood in light of King's *Political Biography* and includes Ingrassia's case for reflecting upon the heteronormative literary tradition by queering Haywood ("'Queering' Eliza Haywood"). Economic exclusionism and social policy in eighteenth-century England are discussed by Jennifer Buckley in her case study of Haywood's *Cleomilia*, which can be beneficially paired with Cheryl Nixon's essay "Regulating the Unstable Family." Also informative on the social environment surrounding Haywood's writing life is "The Pious Mrs. Haywood," in which King uses *Epistles for the Ladies* to reintegrate what she argues is Haywood's spiritual commitment. Rejecting old-fashioned ideas of any unsophisticated simplicity in Haywood's narrative forms, Rachel Carnell discusses the nuanced political and ideological work carried out by the often devalued genre of the secret history ("Eliza"), a discussion extended by Bannet on *The Invisible Spy* ("Narrator"), then taken still further in Wilputte's history of the Hardwicke Marriage Act in the context of *Dalinda; or, The Double Marriage* ("Haywood's Tabloid Journalism").

Criticism

The critical conversation around Haywood has evolved rapidly since the early 1980s, when the doors to modern Haywood studies first cracked open with Jean Kern's attention to the "fallen" woman and Mary Anne Schofield's "Exposé of the Popular Heroine." Recent criticism continues to engage with evolving understandings of gender, genres, and sexualities and extends into politics, economies, social practices, and ideological impositions, as well as theoretical approaches like affect and cognition. But since students' initial response to many of Haywood's works is to be surprised by their sexual elements, a good reading list on the topic might include the following works. Helen Thompson's essay "Eliza Haywood's Philosophical Career" in *Ingenuous Subjection: Compliance and Power in the Eighteenth-Century Domestic Novel* grounds women's sexuality and subjectivity within a wider context, and Deborah Nestor's "Virtue Rarely Rewarded" extends to the relationship between ideology and narrative form. Kate Parker examines the politics of attempted rape in Haywood, in an essay that pairs well with Susan Staves's germinal "Fielding and the Comedy of Attempted Rape." Jonathan Kramnick's "Locke, Haywood, and Consent" provides a philosophical framework within which to approach the topic, and Bowers's *Force or Fraud* connects resistance to seduction to larger social movements of resistance.

Mary Beth Harris's essay "Upsetting the Balance: Exposing the Myth of Masculine Virtue and Desire" provides a history of ideal masculinities, with specific engagement of *Philidore and Placentia*, but women take the lion's share of attention in gendered approaches to Haywood. These conversations often begin with the ways in which Haywood interrogates conventional constructs of the feminine, as in Shea Stuart on subversive didacticism and Kristine Jennings on femininity as fiction in *Betsy Thoughtless*. Helen Thompson's "Plotting Materialism" compares *Fantomina* with the Ephesian matron story, drawing attention to epistemologies of identity and what Thompson calls "feminine consistency." And what we might term "feminine inconsistency" is illuminated by Leslie Morrison's work on "serialized identities" in *Fantomina* and *Anti-Pamela*. Several essays draw attention to Haywood's importance to thinking about female speech, including Potter's "The Language of Feminized Sexuality: Gendered Voice in Eliza Haywood's *Love in Excess* and *Fantomina*," Powell's "Parroting and the Periodical: Women's Speech, Haywood's *Parrot*, and Its Antecedents," and Sonya Lawson Parrish's "'Obtain but Their Consent': Agency and Female Speech in Eliza Haywood's *Love in Excess* (1719)."

Haywood's engagement of emotion, passions, and affect as sensory, intellectual, and social processes is addressed by Emily Hodgson Anderson's "Performing the Passions in Eliza Haywood's *Fantomina* and *Miss Betsy Thoughtless*," Rebecca Tierney-Hynes's "Fictional Mechanics: Haywood, Reading, and the Passions," and James Noggle's "Unfelt Affect." Natalie M. Phillips takes a cognitive science approach in *Distraction: Problems of Attention in Eighteenth-Century Literature*, considering *Fantomina* and *Betsy Thoughtless* in conversation with Miguel de Cervantes, Jonathan Swift, Laurence Sterne, Samuel Johnson, Jane Austen, Fielding, and others.

Haywood criticism also foregrounds her representation of contemporary social practices. Robert Jones's "Eliza Haywood and the Discourse of Taste" intersects with discussions of Haywood's concurrent depiction and creation of popular culture, at times as part of what today we would call her "brand." Backscheider's "Paradigms of Popular Culture" discusses Haywood in these terms, as do Holly Luhning's "Writing Bodies in Popular Culture: Eliza Haywood and *Love in Excess*" and Potter's "Life in Excess: Eliza Haywood and Popular

Culture in *The Masqueraders* and *The Surprize*." Catherine Craft-Fairchild includes Haywood in her discussion of the social practice of the masquerade and its analogues in *Masquerade and Gender: Disguise and Female Identity in Eighteenth-Century Fiction by Women*, and Karin Kukkonen adds a cognitive studies element in discussing examples from Daniel Defoe, Frances Burney, Fielding, and Haywood in "The Minds Behind the Mask: Reading for Character in the Masquerade."

Miranda Burgess also draws attention to what is and is not seen in "Bearing Witness: Law, Labor, and the Gender of Privacy in the 1720s," on Haywood's *Mercenary Lover*. Legal practices are also the focus of Susan Paterson Glover's *Engendering Legitimacy: Law, Property, and Early Eighteenth-Century Fiction*, which engages with several of Haywood's short fictions of the 1720s. Property and the law also intersect in Haywood's representation of marriage across the chronology and generic range of her career. Aleksondra Hultquist compares *Love in Excess* with *Betsy Thoughtless* in "Marriage in Haywood," and Laura Thomason includes Haywood's periodical and conduct writing (alongside the works of Hester Chapone, Lady Mary Wortley Montagu, and Sarah Scott) in *The Matrimonial Trap: Eighteenth-Century Women Writers Redefine Marriage*. Wilputte's comparison of Aphra Behn, Haywood, and Fielding in "Wife Pandering in Three Eighteenth-Century Plays" foregrounds the staging of the legal and social norms and disruptions of marital arrangements.

Ingrassia's *Authorship, Commerce, and Gender in Early Eighteenth-Century England* establishes Haywood in London's economic sphere, and King's *Political Biography* remains the most important resource on Haywood's place in political realms. Haywood's literary engagements with Jacobitism are also addressed in Carnell's *Partisan Politics, Narrative Realism, and the Rise of the British Novel* and in Stewart's argument for *The Fortunate Foundlings* as a Jacobite novel. Marta Kvande expands into Haywood's political novels more broadly in "The Outsider Narrator in Eliza Haywood's Political Novels." David Diamond discusses Haywood's confrontation of the South Sea Bubble in *Memoirs of a Certain Island*, and Clery focuses on political economies specifically in "Free Market Feminism." Christopher F. Loar broadens Haywood's political context further in "The Exceptional Eliza Haywood: Women and Extralegality in *Eovaai*" and in the chapter "Violence, Reason, and Surveillance," focusing on *Eovaai* and *The Invisible Spy*, in his book *Political Magic*. Broader still is Jennifer Hargrave's "'To the Glory of the Chinese': Sinocentric Political Reform in Eliza Haywood's *The Adventures of Eovaai*."

Finally, as we think about teaching, many of us seek resources on reading Haywood in dialogue with other writers of the period. She is grouped among other female writers in the various volumes on women's writing discussed above. Haywood is read alongside Behn and Charlotte Lennox in Catherine Craft's "Reworking Male Models," and Matthew Rigilano's "Embodying the Invisible" examines materiality and subjectivity in Margaret Cavendish, Delarivier Manley, and Haywood. King documents links between Haywood and Fielding in

"Henry and Eliza: Feudlings or Friends," and Ingrassia focuses on *Anti-Pamela* and *Shamela* in her volume's introduction to the two parodies of *Pamela*. Nicholas Seager addresses Defoe, Haywood, and Richardson together on domestic fiction in "The 1740 *Roxana*," and Karen Lipsedge considers Haywood, Richardson, and Burney in *Domestic Space in Eighteenth-Century British Novels*.

Beyond the fiction, Wilputte brings together the plays of Haywood, Fielding, and Behn in "Wife Pandering in Three Eighteenth-Century Plays," and T. G. A. Nelson discusses Oliver Goldsmith, William Wycherley, and Haywood ("Stooping to Conquer"). Tassie Gwilliam examines links between theater and fiction in her comparison of Haywood and Hannah Cowley in "Disguise, Fantasy, and Misrecognition in *The Belle's Stratagem* and *Fantomina*." For fuller considerations of Haywood in dialogue with other cross-genre writers, see Ballaster's "Satire and Embodiment" on allegorical romance on stage and page and Anderson's *Eighteenth-Century Authorship and the Play of Fiction: Novels and the Theater, Haywood to Austen*.

Visual, Audiovisual, and Online Resources

There are no film or television versions of Haywood's works, and even her *YouTube* presence is, at the time of this writing, sparse, consisting of *LibriVox* audiobooks for *The Fortunate Foundlings* and *Betsy Thoughtless* and a video reading of *Fantomina*. There are also a handful of student projects, particularly film trailers and character performances, that hint at a potentially inspiring teaching approach. Fortunately, however, other online resources on the eighteenth century are abundant. Beyond *ECCO*, discussed above, two of the best Web sites for Haywood's readers are *Orlando: Women's Writing in the British Isles from the Beginnings to the Present* and *The Proceedings of the Old Bailey*. *Orlando*, begun at the University of Alberta and now housed with Cambridge University Press, is the single most valuable online resource around eighteenth-century women's writing, providing "entries on authors' lives and writing careers, contextual material, timelines, sets of internal links, and bibliographies" (orlando.cambridge.org). The site supports searching by name, chronology, or tags for infinite potential recombinations of material on authors' lives, works, environments, and contexts. Haywood's entry is fulsome, scholarly, and searchable, with material on her biography and entries on more than twenty-five of her works, all interwoven with links to other aspects of Haywood's life and career. *Orlando* is behind a paywall, however, so its access is limited by institutional subscription.

The Proceedings of the Old Bailey, happily, is open access and provides "a fully searchable edition of the largest body of texts detailing the lives of non-elite people ever published, containing 197,745 criminal trials held at London's central criminal court" between 1674 and 1913 (oldbaileyonline.org). In addition to the court records themselves, the site includes a well-organized and extensive set of short essays on crime, justice, and punishment; gender in courts;

the Old Bailey itself; and the city of London and the communities of people within the city. Each of these then breaks into a submenu of essays, through which students can follow links and threads to investigate a range of implications of geography, race, rank, procedures, and punishments. For example, "London and Its Hinterlands" further divides by chronology as it offers data on demographics, the built environment, social structure, occupations, culture, and politics, as well as information on currency and costs, which so often confuse student readers.

There are many more relevant sites than can be mentioned here, but, for students of Haywood with a particular interest in the history of sexualities, Rictor Norton's Web site on eighteenth-century homosexuality offers insight into nonnormative sexual practices and the emergence of private sexual communities in the era through links to documents and historical records available online (rictornorton.co.uk/eighteen). Finally, students can access instantly through *Locating London's Past* (locatinglondon.org) the sort of data that used to involve spending months in the archive. The open-access site facilitates integrated search across fifteen major electronic resources (and links to several databases) and then invites students to map their findings through the site onto John Rocque's 1746 Survey of London, Westminster, and Southwark.

A more traditional resource, William Hogarth's prints offer a visual hint of the social practices and dangers that Haywood's fiction and essays reflect and interrogate. Hogarth's work is nicely annotated and authoritatively presented on Tate Britain's Web site (www.tate.org.uk/art/artists/william-hogarth-265), but individual images are easily found with *Google Images*. To guide students in reflecting upon what characters might have looked like, direct them to the Victoria and Albert Museum's excellent introduction to fashionable dress across the eighteenth century, with full-color photos (vam.ac.uk/content/articles/i/introduction-to-18th-century-fashion). Finally, Celia Barnes provides a less formally curated but wonderful collection of visual materials and links to scholarly and popular sites on eighteenth-century literature and culture (www.pinterest.com/celiabee/eighteenth-century-literature-and-culture). Online resources expand constantly (and occasionally contract), so instructors should always perform a search during course design to confirm links and to discover emerging resources.

Survey and Classroom Contexts

The survey of instructors conducted for this volume made clear that Haywood's works are taught in a broad array of environments, from freshman "core," composition, and introduction-to-literature courses to sophomore surveys and senior specialist and graduate courses. *Fantomina* is taught more often than any other text, though several others are reported to be taught regularly—*Betsy Thoughtless*, *Love in Excess*, *Anti-Pamela*, and *Eovaai* in particular. There is, however, a widely expressed interest in expanding that canon, especially into Haywood's periodical and dramatic works and shorter narrative pieces that can be effectively taught in limited classroom hours. Survey respondents expressed strong interest in seeing new classroom editions of more of Haywood's work, not least in response to the ubiquity of *Fantomina* in anthologies and the concern that just that one short piece should stand in for Haywood's enormously varied and complex oeuvre. Academic publishers might take note of repeated requests for inexpensive critical classroom editions of *Epistles for the Ladies* and *The Female Spectator*, as well as *A Wife to Be Lett*, perhaps in conjunction with substantive excerpts from *The Dramatic Historiographer*. All these works are included in the Pickering and Chatto *Selected Works of Eliza Haywood*, which makes them accessible to scholars with extensive university libraries but less available to students and to teachers at smaller institutions.

Most survey respondents reported spending one to two class hours on a short piece like *Fantomina*, three to four on mid-length works like *Love in Excess*, and four to nine on a long novel like *Betsy Thoughtless*. This flexibility appears to be one reason that respondents report using Haywood frequently and in a variety of contexts. Specific courses in which respondents reported teaching Haywood include variations of the British literature survey and surveys of eighteenth-century literature and theater, as well as courses on women writers and on the novel. Still more specific courses have focused on satire, libertinism, aesthetics and Enlightenment philosophy, work and labor, and the history of desire and sexuality, as well as courses on social reporting and secret histories. Courses on urban identities, the city of London (pairing the expansion of the city with the emergence of the novel), the gendering of public space, eighteenth-century style, experimental literatures, property law and economic history, and masquerade and theories of identity all likewise benefited from the inclusion of Haywood's work, as did one on the history of the periodical and one—sure to intrigue undergraduates—called Sex and the City. *Eovaai* has been taught in courses on the history of science fiction, fantasy, and fairy tales.

Respondents reported using Haywood's work in dialogue with a vast range of other eighteenth-century publications. Several mentioned contextualizing Haywood with conduct literature for both men and women; with social essayists and periodicals of various stripes, from Richard Steele to blog culture; and with philosophical work on the self, neo-Platonism, and identity, including Thomas Hobbes, John Locke, Lord Shaftesbury, and David Hume. Others mentioned teaching units that put together specific texts written in explicit contest with one another (*Pamela*, *Shamela*, and *Anti-Pamela*; *The Spectator* and *The Female Spectator*; *The Beggar's Opera*, *The Tragedy of Tragedies*, and *The Opera of Operas*; *Evoaai*'s satire alongside *The Dunciad* and *Gulliver's Travels*) or those that create less explicit but clearly significant groupings (*Fantomina* and

Defoe's *Roxana* or *Moll Flanders*; *Eovaai* and other "choice of life" novels like *Candide* and *Rasselas*; or, in plays, *A Wife to Be Lett* and Fielding's *The Modern Husband*, both putative comedies that deal with the finances of adultery). There are clear benefits to teaching Haywood in conversation with other women writers with whom she was associated in her day: the rest of the "Fair Triumvirate of Wit," Behn and Manley, as well as Mary Astell and Jane Barker, and then later female writers like Sarah Fielding, Charlotte Lennox, Mary Wollstonecraft, Burney, and Austen. One respondent recommends pairing some of Haywood's identity-fluid characters with Charlotte Charke's *A Narrative of the Life of Mrs. Charlotte Charke* in order to raise questions of gender destabilization and performance.

Asked to list the most important critical conversations to which Haywood can contribute, respondents frequently listed issues of gender, sexuality, love, and desire, the topics with which Haywood and her fellow female writers are most often associated. Respondents used these categories only as a starting point, however. Each listed other conversations as well: cognitive studies, the history of the mind, and the theory of the passions; the connections between eighteenth-century theater culture and the "new" form of fiction; print culture and the circulation of text, art, and knowledge; identity theory, disguise, and masquerade culture; genre fiction (romance, children's literature, science fiction, fantasy, philosophical fiction); orientalisms; satire and comedy; popular culture; rank, status, class, and social order; and the place of women in the new economic systems emerging in the eighteenth century.

Respondents chose both traditional and innovative modes of assessment of students' engagements with Haywood. For many of us, inviting students to participate in our discipline as scholars in training means assigning critical research essays, including engagement with the existing scholarship, close reading, and analytical argumentation of the sort that we engage in ourselves. Others foreground different traditional skills in requiring annotated bibliographies, metacritical review essays, or in-class presentations (with or without *PowerPoint*, *Prezi*, or a written paper). As several of the essays in this volume report, active learning is another frequent strategy, ranging from five-minute pair-and-share break-out groups and full-class team debates to extended projects like role-playing games and mock trials. Many also report using free online resources as part of their pedagogy, including wikis, blogs, and class *Facebook* pages, as well as class sites on *Pinterest*, where students are invited to post images of engravings, paintings, maps, or other visual materials. One respondent described an assignment drawing attention to literary and print communities: students use the *English Short Title Catalog* (*ESTC*) to find works with similar qualities as the Haywood text (same author, publisher, year, keywords, etc.); they then look up the similar works using *WorldCat* and other resources to piece together a short report on publication context. Others report using *Google Docs* to collaborate on annotating a passage from a Haywood text that does not exist in a modern edition. The essays on teaching Haywood with digital humanities in this volume go further still in describing how free, open technologies can invite new approaches to student engagement with Haywood.

Chronology of Haywood's Publications

The attribution to Haywood of some works is under debate. All texts listed here are attributed to Haywood in at least one of the two primary bibliographies of her works; a significant number of the publications attributed to Haywood in Spedding's foundational *Bibliography of Eliza Haywood* are also listed as "confident" or "probable" by Leah Orr ("Basis for Attribution"). Publications marked with an asterisk are accepted by Spedding but described as "possible" or "doubtful" by Orr.

1719 *Love in Excess; or, The Fatal Inquiry* (parts 1 and 2; part 3 published in 1720)

1721 *Letters from a Lady of Quality to a Chevalier* (translation)
The Fair Captive

1722 *The British Recluse; or, The Secret History of Cleomira, Suppos'd Dead*
The Injur'd Husband; or, The Mistaken Resentment

1723 *Idalia; or, The Unfortunate Mistress*
A Wife to Be Lett
Lasselia; or, The Self-Abandon'd
The Rash Resolve; or, The Untimely Discovery

1724 *Poems on Several Occasions*
*A Spy upon the Conjurer; or, A Collection of Surprising Stories . . . Relating to Mr. Duncan Campbell**
The Masqueraders; or, Fatal Curiosity (part 2 published in 1725)
The Fatal Secret; or, Constancy in Distress
The Surprize; or, Constancy Rewarded
*The Aragonian Queen: A Secret History**
La Belle Assemblée; or, The Adventures of Six Days (translation)
Memoirs of a Certain Island Adjacent to the Kingdom of Utopia (volume 2 published in 1725)*
*Bath Intrigues: In Four Letters to a Friend in London**
*Memoirs of Baron de Brosse**

1725 *The Lady's Philosopher's Stone; or, The Caprices of Love and Destiny* (translation)*

The Unequal Conflict; or, Nature Triumphant

The Tea-Table; or, A Conversation between Some Polite Persons of Both Sexes

*The Dumb Projector: Being a Surprizing Account of a Trip to Holland made by Mr. Duncan Campbell**

The Fatal Fondness; or, Love Its Own Opposer

Mary Stuart, Queen of Scots

Fantomina; or, Love in a Maze

The Force of Nature; or, The Lucky Disappointment

1726 *The Mercenary Lover; or, The Unfortunate Heiress**

*Reflections on the Various Effects of Love**

*The Distress'd Orphan; or, Love in a Mad-House**

*The City Jilt; or, The Alderman Turn'd Beau**

*The Double Marriage; or, The Fatal Release**

*The Secret History of the Present Intrigues of the Court of Caramania**

*Letters from the Palace of Fame**

Cleomelia; or, The Generous Mistress

1727 *The Fruitless Enquiry: Being a Collection of Several Entertaining Histories*

The Life of Madame de Villesache

Love in Its Variety: Being a Collection of Select Novels (translation)

Philidore and Placentia; or, L'Amour Trop Delicat

*The Perplex'd Dutchess; or, Treachery Rewarded**

1728 *The Agreeable Caledonian; or, Memoirs of Signoriora de Morella* (part 2 published in 1729)

Irish Artifice; or, The History of Clarina

The Disguis'd Prince; or, The Beautiful Parisian (translation; part 2 published in 1729)

1729 *The City Widow; or, Love in a Butt*

Persecuted Virtue; or, The Cruel Lover

The Fair Hebrew; or, A True, but Secret History of Two Jewish Ladies

Frederick, Duke of Brunswick-Lunenburgh

1730 *Love-Letters on All Occasions Lately Passed between Persons of Distinction*

1733 *The Opera of Operas* (coauthored with William Hatchett)*

1734 L'Entretien des Beaux Esprits*: Being the Sequel to* La Belle Assemblée (translation)

1735 *The Dramatic Historiographer; or, A Key to the Play* (retitled as *A Companion to the Theatre* in 1736; reprinted as volume 1 of the two-volume *A Companion to the Theatre; or, A View of Our Most Celebrated Dramatic Pieces* in 1747)

1736 *The Adventures of Eovaai, Princess of Ijaveo: A Pre-Adamitical History* (reprinted as *The Unfortunate Princess; or, The Ambitious Statesman* in 1741)

1741 *Anti-Pamela; or, Feign'd Innocence Detected* (also known by the alternate title printed at the top of the first page, *Anti-Pamela; or, Mock-Modesty Display'd and Punish'd*)

1742 *The Virtuous Villager; or, Virgin's Victory* (translation)

1743 *The Sopha: A Moral Tale* (translation, with William Hatchett)

The Memoirs of an Unfortunate Young Nobleman

*A Present for a Servant-Maid; or, The Sure Means of Gaining Love and Esteem**

1744 *The Fortunate Foundlings**

The Female Spectator (4 volumes, 1744–46)

1746 *The Parrot. With a Compendium of the Times**

1747 *Memoirs of a Man of Honour* (translation)

1748 *Life's Progress through the Passions; or, The Adventures of Natura**

Epistles for the Ladies (November 1748–May 1749, monthly)*

1749 *Dalinda; or, The Double Marriage*

1750 *A Letter from H—G—g, Esq.**

1751 *The History of Miss Betsy Thoughtless* (4 volumes)*

1753 *The History of Jemmy and Jenny Jessamy* (3 volumes)*

1755 *The Invisible Spy* (4 volumes)*

1755 *The Wife**

1756 *The Husband. In Answer to the Wife**

*The Young Lady**

Part Two

APPROACHES

Introduction

Tiffany Potter

The stories Eliza Haywood tells depict the experiences, practices, and perceptions of both men and women of the eighteenth century and provide unmatched perspectives on the intersections and interactions among popular consumer cultures and privileged notions of elite culture and high art, illuminated by engagements with the author's religious, economic, and ideological contexts. Across the genres, her works give particular voice to the concerns and circumstances of women, but Haywood was not then and is not now a "women's writer." Her vast productivity—literary, theatrical, and periodical—exemplifies and engages with contemporary social debate on women, of course, but equally extends codes of masculinity and social rank, fiscal economies, legal systems and social regulation, faith, violence, sexuality and desire, and the potential for self-fashioning in both the individual and the nation. This collection addresses all these social and literary narratives and also seeks to renegotiate the conventional discursive narrative of Haywood herself: echoing the corrections to Haywood's biography made by Christine Blouch and Kathryn R. King, an important piece of this volume's work is to interrogate the long-standing "two Haywoods" account of her career, by which her early novels were associated with a dissolute culture of scandal and her later works with a narrative of reform of both author and genre. Effective teaching of Haywood's works requires thinking that breaks free from such imposed narratives to articulate for students the importance of her writing across a startling array of cultural and literary contexts of her century.

The essays collected here provide historical analysis, critical materials, and specific pedagogical strategies to help teachers move classroom discussion of Haywood's work into these sorts of conversations, well beyond the enclosed critical spaces of "amatory fiction" and "women's writing." Together, the contributors to this volume illuminate the ways in which the variety in Haywood's work and the breadth in reader responses—both eighteenth-century and contemporary—are suggestive of a range of contested art forms and ideologies that provide a number of potential classroom approaches.

This volume's four sections are organized around a usage model that aims to support those planning to teach a specific Haywood text, as well as those hoping to find and teach a new text. The essays in "Backgrounds" introduce readerships and print culture as well as bibliographical issues concerning the evolving Haywood canon. Essays in "Culture and Contexts" provide teachers with the information needed to teach Haywood in the context of her historical moment. Each essay in this section focuses on an issue of textual specificity with wider implication, providing discussion of a group of Haywood's texts in order to illuminate a range of contexts in which the provided critical information might be used, including how it can be brought into conversation with other eighteenth-century literary and cultural texts. Teachers can use the essays in this section to support course modules on specific texts or as the source of strategies for connecting individual Haywood texts to larger threads when examining specific themes, surveying different national literatures, or reading across eras.

Essays in "Individual Works" offer a detailed approach to teaching one or two specific works. The combination of multiple essays on the more frequently taught novels, plus additional essays on those less frequently taught, is informed by both the philosophical reasons of scholarship and the depressingly practical ones of online essay banks. Essays in this section document ways in which Haywood's works can be brought into dialogue with the works of other writers, including Aphra Behn, Henry Fielding, Samuel Richardson, Daniel Defoe, and Samuel Johnson. There are also essays that demonstrate the important cultural and literary work done by Haywood's longer novels, making the case for giving a lengthy text like *The History of Miss Betsy Thoughtless* the time it would require in our densely packed syllabi. The three essays in the final section, "Digital Approaches," offer methodologies for using digital humanities and online technologies in the teaching of Haywood. These essays describe a series of approaches for using digital humanities in the classroom but keep their dependence on specific sites, tools, or apps to a minimum so that the suggested pedagogical strategies can be used as technologies and tools continue to evolve.

From beyond that use-based structure, though, shine the wider connections and critical intersections among Haywood's works and the approaches that we propose for teaching them. Martha Bowden opens the discussion by pointing out the teaching opportunities created by Haywood's sudden ascent into the current canon of literature anthologies, while also recognizing the pedagogical and critical hazards created when a single text, like Behn's *Oroonoko* or Haywood's *Fantomina*, comes to represent an author in undergraduate courses, regardless of how nonrepresentative that text might be in the author's body of work. Bowden provides two paths for preventing "*Oroonoko* syndrome" in teaching Haywood: strategic teaching of *Fantomina*, illuminated by other excerpts and historical documents, and teaching different easily accessed Haywood texts that contribute to the survey courses typically served by the major anthologies.

Even when students are invited to think of Haywood in a broader context, though, different challenges arise, as students can be caught up in the deceptively obvious, but wrong, sense of Haywood's writing career as comprising an early period, focused on dissolute stories of scandal and smut; a chastening by critics, such as Alexander Pope; and a late-life resurgence as a conservative moralist writer of more artistically and socially worthy novels like *Betsy Thoughtless*. This reformation narrative is debunked by Aleksondra Hultquist, who examines the evolution of the "two Haywoods" mythology and then provides an approach to the teaching of *Betsy Thoughtless* as an account of forging subjectivity, not through the reformative internalization of moral precepts, but rather through a provocative "narrative of experience." Similarly attuned to the reformation mythology, Catherine Craft-Fairchild describes a course structure that pairs *Fantomina* with *Betsy Thoughtless*, in conversation with conduct and courtship narratives by Lord Halifax and Colley Cibber. Together, these two essays provide several strategies to help students recognize the degree to which continuity, more than correction, typifies Haywood's career.

Gender and Identity

To date, Haywood is most commonly read through the lenses of gender and identity. Kim Simpson sets up these approaches by capitalizing on students' immediate recognition of gendered transgressions of social norms in Haywood's early fiction. Simpson provides a way to help students build upon that simple recognition, using theories of gender performativity and materialist feminism in a classroom exercise that invites students to reflect upon their own public identities or "online selves" versus what they consider their private selves. The scholarship on identity and gender performance, especially in the "recovery project" phase of Haywood studies, has located her work consistently in the shadow of heterosexual courtship narratives. Catherine Ingrassia's essay encourages expanding the approaches to gender in Haywood studies to teach beyond the heteronormative. Her approach uses *Fantomina* as a case study that teaches students about the experimental nature of Haywood's early writing and about the ways in which those experiments encompass alternative, interrelated constructions of intimacy, gender formation, and narrative structures. Christopher Loar's essay similarly extends the traditional focus on the feminine in Haywood studies by addressing Haywood's interrogation of prescriptive modes of masculinity. Loar explores the "panoply of manhoods" depicted in *Betsy Thoughtless* as a touchstone in an eighteenth-century fiction course. His approach teaches the catalog of Haywood's men as replications and parodies of versions of manhood alongside Richardson's Mr. B., Fielding's Joseph Andrews and Tom Jones, and Defoe's pirates, con artists, and castaways, uncovering for students Haywood's manipulation of masculinities as a negotiation of larger political, ideological, and social issues.

Legal and Social Frameworks, Sexuality and Violence

Several of these questions engaging representations of gender are grounded in legal and cultural norms around property, sexuality, and violence. Many teachers shy away from teaching texts such as Haywood's amatory fictions (and even Behn's play *The Rover* and Richardson's masterpiece *Clarissa*) because of their complex and hazy depictions of seduction, rape, and sexual violence. Laura Alexander and Emily Dowd-Arrow provide strategies for teaching these sorts of "dangerous" texts so that the important cultural work that Haywood was doing in her day is not lost because of the reader discomfort that it so provocatively creates. Alexander offers a critical re-visioning of *Anti-Pamela*, declining the traditional reading of the novel as a celebration of a manipulative pleasure-seeker, and teaching it instead in the context of women's protest literature. Her role-play classroom assignment foregrounds Syrena's original victimization in being forced by her mother to become a child prostitute and then asks students to struggle themselves with the economic circumstances and cultural pressures that are beyond characters' control, but according to which they must make choices. Dowd-Arrow similarly emphasizes Haywood's recognition of the sexualized violence that could be tacitly facilitated by the entitled performance of masculine power and enforced requirements of female shame. By focusing on Haywood's discussions of consent, seduction, and rape in *The Female Spectator*, *Love in Excess*, and a tale from *The Invisible Spy*, Dowd-Arrow's approach gives students the critical vocabulary and legal and historical frameworks necessary for understanding the complex and contradictory implications of scenes of sexual coercion and violence in Haywood's work.

The ways in which these legal structures and cultural norms regarding gender and the family illuminate the content and structures of Haywood's early fiction are further outlined by Cheryl Nixon. Her essay describes teaching units that pair Haywood's shorter fictions with accessible eighteenth-century legal texts and conduct guides that address parallel issues of social and legal policing of behavior in public and domestic scenes. Kathryn R. King then takes on one of the most famous legal cases of the century, remodeling her classroom into a courtroom in order to examine Haywood's account of the Elizabeth Canning kidnapping case in her secret history *The Invisible Spy*, a publication that King typifies as Haywood's take on print culture and the "new world of print." Using this example of the collapsing of legal discourse into a pamphlet war—including volleys from Justice Henry Fielding—King has her students try the case themselves on the basis of broadsides, pamphlets, and legal documents like those now readily available from digital archives like *The Proceedings of the Old Bailey*. Her students analyze the intersections among law, politics, gossip, and moral regulation as they are informed by gender and social rank in Haywood's society (and her fictional versions of it). Those notions of rank were themselves evolving rapidly across the eighteenth century, however, and Nicholas Hudson illuminates the challenge of teaching texts where social differences that are of critical importance to characters and contemporary readers are nearly invisible to modern students. Hudson's discussion ranges from the early fiction through *Anti-Pamela* and *Betsy Thoughtless* to document Haywood's depiction of the slow and nuanced widening of the ruling ranks across the century.

Literary Conversations

In her consideration of these wider cultural questions, Haywood was part of several contemporary social and literary debates. Her work can serve as a brilliant vector in students' recognition that literature in the eighteenth century was not the work of the isolated, inspired artist but required ongoing public participation in contemporary discourse and occasionally even in outright factional war. Several of the essays in this volume offer ways to consider Haywood's works in conversation with other writers of her era. Beginning with literal conversation, Earla Wilputte's essay illuminates coterie culture in her approach to teaching *The Tea-Table*, Haywood's fictionalization of Aaron's Hill's literary circle, the Hillarians. Expanding focus to address a cross-century conversation, Cynthia Richards locates Haywood in the context of the early women writers survey, with a particular focus on the way that writers—from the men who penned the Bible to Mary Wollstonecraft—theorize the feminine and create the "bad girl" narrative. During the eighteenth century, social debates were often enacted in fiction, and Loar outlines the one on the nature of masculinity in a conversation that includes the narrative interventions of Defoe, Richardson, and Fielding.

Fielding in particular was Haywood's partner in a career-long series of intermittent conversations. Around the same time that Haywood was leading the market in short fiction in the 1720s, she and Fielding were also working in theater, sometimes for the same companies. Sarah Creel considers the staging of artistic debate through the dueling theatrical parodies *The Tragedy of Tragedies* (Fielding) and *The Opera of Operas* (Haywood). Robin Runia picks up their conversation as she examines the three-part social debate on virtue, gender, rank, and ambition among Haywood, Fielding, and Richardson during the *Pamela* controversy. And King's essay considers Fielding and Haywood in the period in which the two took opposing sides in the public scandal and politicized pamphlet war around the alleged kidnapping of the young servant Elizabeth Canning. This volume positions Haywood on equal literary terms with some of her most distinguished contemporaries and affirms that she need not be taught through her reactions to them or through theirs to her. Rather, we recognize the sites of conversational intersection, especially in the careers of Haywood and Fielding, and offer ways for teacher-scholars to examine the manner in which she contests literary and ideological terrain with some of the most influential writers of the era.

Genres

Toni Bowers opens the genre conversation with her call to reconsider traditional definitions of amatory fiction as the default generic framework for teaching Haywood's early work. Bowers proposes an approach where current critiques of the category of amatory fiction are used to teach the complexity of literary history and to interrogate the typically invisible cultural work performed by ostensibly neutral analytical categories. Epistolary genres are a source of Runia's approach to teaching the *Pamela* adaptations, as she invites students to consider the implications of epistolarity in the early novel through recognition of the relations between the narrative strategies of presumably truthful personal letters and the realistic novel. Haywood's fiction went beyond the realistic, though, and Ros Ballaster describes teaching Haywood's *The Adventures of Eovaai, Princess of Ijaveo* as an oriental tale in the burgeoning field of fantasy studies. Ballaster explains how, in a suite with Johnson's *Rasselas* and William Beckford's *Vathek*, *Eovaai* can be taught in a way that addresses temporal and geographical dislocations as opportunities to comment on contemporary culture, as well as on the questions of both gendered and cultural difference in the fantasy "choice of life" novel.

While Haywood is best known as a novelist, her importance in eighteenth-century studies is amplified by the fact that she was so successful in so many different literary genres. Creel's essay takes on the theatrical genres of the 1730s, examining Haywood's *The Opera of Operas* as a musical adaptation of Fielding's burlesque comedy *The Tragedy of Tragedies* (mediated by the generic innovations of John Gay's *The Beggar's Opera*), with particular attention to social satire and competition among the creators of ballad opera, a genre in vogue at the height of Haywood's theatrical period. And, while there were other female playwrights in Haywood's era, she is the only widely recognized female periodical writer of the time, offering a woman's voice in a genre dominated by men like Joseph Addison, Richard Steele, Fielding, and Johnson. In discussing a course module that fits in both gender studies and literature classrooms, Dowd-Arrow uses *The Female Spectator*'s story of Erminia at the masquerade as a case study in teaching Haywood's periodical writing. Dowd-Arrow demonstrates the ways in which these essays can be taught in historical and literary contexts, as significant publications on their own or as supporting material engaging with further works by Haywood and others.

Finally, Kirsten Saxton and Cassie Childs provide a very different approach for teaching *The Female Spectator* in a first-year or common core course focused on research methods and critical approaches to literature. Taking an intersectionalist feminist and cultural studies approach, their essay describes ways to teach *The Female Spectator* alongside modern periodical and blog culture, introducing the historically expansive legacy of social reading practices and inviting students to use the tools of digital humanities to participate in a rigorous critical analysis of gender, genre, and rhetoric in the essay form. The assignment outlined here pays particular attention to the ways in which Haywood's periodical models women's writing and reading and the sociability of reading a periodical text, communicating the important insight that reading practices in the eighteenth century were not limited to novels.

Current Media and Theory

Saxton and Childs are not the only contributors who argue that Haywood's work often looks forward in its interests and methodologies. While their essay suggests an assignment structure using digital media to engage students with the often-unloved genre of the eighteenth-century essay, Tonya-Marie Howe offers three other ways in which the ever-expanding availability of digital resources can allow students to recognize their current medium of choice as both an echo of and a doorway into the media of the eighteenth century. Whether using audio tools to replicate aurally the textual markers of intimacy, using optical character recognition software to discern the importance of the variants and textualities of eighteenth-century print, or analyzing the naturalization of critical hierarchies in ostensibly neutral reporting media such as *Wikipedia*, Howe's assignments and approaches invite students to engage actively with eighteenth-century print through new media and its tools. Laura Runge's related essay explains how to use digital humanities resources to teach Haywood and, reciprocally, how to use Haywood to teach students to use the digital corpora of the present in preparation for the digital tools of the future.

Haywood's work can be illuminated by modern technology and still more so by being brought into conversation with current critical theory. Simpson outlines a teachable path through the theoretical challenge of Judith Butler, Elizabeth Grosz, and Vicki Kirby, and Ingrassia's argument for the relevance of queer methodologies in teaching Haywood creates new critical questions for students and scholars. Stephen Ahern's engagement with the theory of affect similarly facilitates a whole new way of teaching Haywood's passionate scenes and impassioned critiques, using *Love in Excess* to blend current theory with historical documentation of eighteenth-century understandings of desire, interiority, and self-determination. This approach introduces students to the difference between modern ideas of emotion and the sense of the passions that dominated historical theories of human motivation and agency.

As Ahern makes clear, Haywood's fiction invites us into popular depictions of human emotional life; Paula R. Backscheider argues that in such representations, Haywood was one of the first self-conscious producers of popular culture in the eighteenth century and among the first to create what we would now recognize as a brand. Backscheider's essay suggests the ways in which current popular culture theory can be used to locate Haywood in a course on the eighteenth-century novel or used as the through line of a full course on Haywood. In the other direction, this essay also locates Haywood in a wider discussion of the popular, opening exciting doors to the relatively open critical field of historical situation of popular culture theory.

And this, of course, brings us to one of the great joys of teaching Haywood: inviting students into the pleasures of working on an understudied text or author. As one survey respondent described it, Haywood is one of a small group of now canonical authors about whom undergraduate students can conduct real, original research without undue burden. In offering approaches to teaching Haywood, the contributors to this volume provide ways to invite less experienced students into eighteenth-century studies and to guide more advanced students into their own capacity for original scholarship and potentially groundbreaking work.

Haywood and Her Readers: Eighteenth-Century Print Culture and the Literary Marketplace

Tiffany Potter

On the first page of *A Political Biography of Eliza Haywood*, Kathryn R. King declares Eliza Haywood an "uncooperative biographical subject," given the dearth of reliable sources of evidence on the details of her life. Even without explicit evidence of dates, appointments, and correspondents, however, teachers still have information that can be equally useful in the classroom: we can document Haywood's intellectual and social environments, some of the philosophical and social circles in which she traveled, and the print culture and ideological conversations to which she contributed. This essay begins with what we do know of Haywood's biography and then moves to a brief overview of her readership and the literary marketplace in which she published. Together, these backgrounds provide a common foundation for the essays in this volume and a short guide to the parts of her story most widely applicable in the classroom.

The opacity of Haywood's life is in part by her own choice: her first biographer, David Erskine Baker, recorded in 1764 that, "from a supposition of some improper liberties being taken with her character after death, by the intermixture of truth and falsehood with her history, she laid a solemn injunction . . . not to communicate to any one the least circumstance relating to her" (1: 216). Her request seems to have been observed, but other types of evidence show us a woman who was well known in the theater, who traveled in literary and intellectual circles to which most women did not have access, and who was sharply conscious, as both author and publisher, of the markets and the demands of popular culture and its audiences, especially women.

The best current evidence suggests that Haywood was born in 1693 to a merchant family named Fowler. She was married before the autumn of 1714, which we surmise not from church records but from her theatrical billing as "Mrs Haywood" at the Smock Alley Theatre in Dublin that year. We do not know anything about Haywood's husband, other than that he was *not* the clergyman Valentine Haywood (Blouch, "Eliza Haywood" 536–40). From a letter that she wrote in 1729, it appears that she had two young children at that time, but, other than Alexander Pope's 1728 reference to her as the mother of two bastards (*Dunciad* 2.149–50), there is no further record of Haywood's children; some biographers suggest that they died in childhood (King, *Political Biography* xii). The paternity of these children is also unclear: King disputes Christine Blouch's suggestion of Richard Savage as the likely father of the first child (*Political Biography* xii; "Eliza Haywood" 549n28). Blouch and Patrick Spedding both identify William Hatchett as the likely father of the second ("Eliza Haywood" 549n28; *Bibliography* 25), and Spedding argues that Hatchett and Haywood "lived together for most of their lives as a de facto couple" (*Bibliography* 26), but King calls Hatchett's paternity "wholly improbable" (*Political Biography* 6), arguing that Haywood and Hatchett were barely acquainted before 1728. Because Haywood became a well-known writer, her death on 25 February 1756 was reported, and she was buried in St. Margaret's churchyard, not physically far (but a huge reputational distance) from Poets' Corner in Westminster Abbey. Even given the scarcity of records for her private life, the literary record shows that Haywood was an active and recognized participant in London's cultural life, suffering the costs and enjoying the benefits of being that rare woman in the traditionally masculine world of letters. Both for her contemporaries and for generations to follow, Haywood's public image was influenced by her depictions in the works of two other writers: Pope's vicious attack in *The Dunciad* and a less angry but still trivializing staging as Mrs. Novel in Henry Fielding's play *The Author's Farce* (1730). Pope's apocalyptic satire includes a blistering portrayal of eighteenth-century literary culture in which Haywood, embraced by two illegitimate children, is famously objectified as the sexualized prize in a literal pissing contest between two publishers:

> See in the circle next, Eliza placed,
> Two babes of love close clinging to her waist;
> . . . .
> [she is a] Juno of majestic size,
> With cow-like udders, and with ox-like eyes. (2.149–56)

As "Martinus Scriblerus," the faux-editor of the *Dunciad Variorum* edition, Pope adds, "In this game is exposed in the most contemptuous manner, the profligate licenciousness of those shameless scribblers (for the most part of that sex, which ought least to be capable of such malice or impudence) who in libellous memoirs and novels, reveal the faults and misfortunes of both sexes, to the ruin or disturbance of publick fame or private happiness" (2.157n). Pope makes explicit what Haywood signified to some anxious literary contemporaries: the decline of some ostensibly pure, true culture as publishers abandoned classical values in favor of lowest-common-denominator morality to serve markets driven by consumers who were uneducated and undiscriminating.

As noted by Sarah Creel, Robin Runia, Christopher Loar, and King in this volume, Haywood and Fielding had a long rivalry (sometimes friendly, sometimes not), and it is perhaps not entirely surprising that Fielding established Haywood as Mrs. Novel, the figure of empty prose prattling, in *The Author's Farce*. Though Fielding and Haywood would later work collegially at the Haymarket Theatre, the character of Mrs. Novel is defined by her frivolous art, her deceitful sexuality, and her deluded romantic pursuit of the castrato Seignior Opera. Fielding's representation declines the dehumanizing cruelty of Pope's, but for forty-one nights in 1730 his wildly popular play circulated the caricature that would be attached to Haywood for 250 years: the facile woman who embraces sex for pleasure and profit and who misrepresents both herself and the very ideas of virtue and morality, making her merely the same as the female characters she created in certain of her fictions.

Haywood, however, defied such critics and throughout her career worked successfully and often concurrently in several media. She performed intermittently as an actress beginning in 1714 and composed a handful of plays, including the tragedy *The Fair Captive*, the comedy *A Wife to Be Lett*, and the musical *The Opera of Operas*. She published some forty short works of fiction and a dozen or more long novels over five decades,[1] starting with the breathtakingly successful *Love in Excess* in 1719: Haywood's first novel was among the most successful pieces of prose fiction published before Samuel Richardson's 1740 sensation *Pamela*, though the specific number of editions and copies is contested (see Luhning 165n3; Spedding, *Bibliography*). She also wrote in several nonfiction genres, publishing a theater history reference work, influential periodicals like *The Female Spectator*, and conduct manuals for both genders in *The Wife* and *The Husband*.

Haywood had a burst of spectacular productivity between 1719 and 1729, publishing more than three thousand pages that included three translations and at least twenty-five pieces of short fiction, several of which were among the most frequently reprinted publications of the decade. A period of reduced output followed as her attention shifted away from fiction toward theater. For a long time, the chronological coincidence of Haywood's shift to theater and the publication of Pope's attack in *The Dunciad* led to speculation that Haywood was shamed into silence, but the evidence provided in King's *Biography* supports a fiscally minded move toward the theater following the fortune made by John Gay's *The Beggar's Opera* in 1728 and extended by a period of moderately well-paid critical work on her 1735 theater history volume *The Dramatic Historiographer* (later expanded as *A Companion to the Theatre*). According to Blouch, Haywood was "not silenced by Pope, but capitalized on her post-*Dunciad* notoriety during the early years of the decade" ("Eliza Haywood" 541). Haywood returned to fiction in 1741 with *Anti-Pamela*, her vehement response to Richardson's conservative appropriation of the female voice in *Pamela*. *Memoirs of an Unfortunate Young Nobleman* (1743) then marks the beginning of the period of her life upon which a narrative of reform has often been imposed by readers and critics, famously including Clara Reeve's pronouncement in her 1785 overview of the romance genre that Haywood "repented of her faults, and employed the later part of her life in expiating the offences of the former" (1: 120). In Haywood's lifetime, her later novels, especially *The History of Miss Betsy Thoughtless*, were often read as tales of lessons learned by chastened willful women. However, as a large body of scholarship makes clear—including several of the essays in this volume—the implications of Haywood's long career arc are nowhere near that clear or that conservative.

After Reeve, there appears to be no substantive discussion of Haywood until the 1891 entry in the *Dictionary of National Biography* (*DNB*), apparently the first post-eighteenth-century account that takes Haywood's work seriously. Sidney Lee asserts that "[l]iterary enemies represented that her character was bad," but "her friends asserted" that she was an abandoned wife striving to support her children and that "her novels hardly suggest that their author was personally immoral. She owed her evil reputation to the freedom with which she followed the example of Mrs. Manley in introducing into her romances scandals about the leaders of contemporary society, whose names she very thinly veiled" (313). The entry adds new attributions to Haywood's canon and observes that "she wrote clearly and brightly, and her books sold rapidly" (314). Despite the invitation of the *DNB* format, Lee creates no reform narrative but rather addresses the influence of gossip and rivalry in Haywood's literary reputation. George Frisbie Whicher picks up Haywood's critical and biographical torch in 1915, though his account is the source of several of the biographical errors that haunted Haywood scholarship over the twentieth century. He argues for Haywood, not as an artist "who may yet come into her own," but instead on the basis that "even the weakest link in the development of a literary form is important" (vi–viii). His recalcitrant defense of Haywood and his uncomfortable-sounding engagements with her work brought her into the twentieth century, where she had an unfortunate meeting with Virginia Woolf in the *Times Literary Supplement* in 1916. In her unflattering review of Whicher's book, Woolf is generally uninterested in questions of morality or immorality but refers to Haywood's legacy of "unreadable journalism," decrees Haywood "a writer of no importance," and claims that "no one reads her for pleasure" ("Scribbling Dame" 78). Modern scholars have begged to differ, but for some two hundred years, Haywood existed generally under a cloud of devaluation, when she was noticed at all.

In her own day, though, she was famous and successful, and with her later work she experienced a significant shift in her perceived literary respectability.

Her reputation was further substantiated by her work as an essayist and publisher, as she created three different periodicals: *The Female Spectator*, *The Parrot*, and *The Young Lady*. The periodical essays offer insights on conventionally feminine topics (fashion, morals, courtship, domestic life) but also on publishing, politics, literature, and science. Together, these essays constitute an important complement to literary representations of her cultural moment (see Newman and Wright). In this later period of Haywood's life, her place in the literary world extended not just across genres, but also to the business side of print culture as the bookseller at a pamphlet shop in Covent Garden called the Sign of Fame. She sold several items published under her own imprint, including works of her own, such as *Anti-Pamela*, and those of such other writers as Susanna Centlivre and William Hatchett. Paula McDowell describes Haywood's multimodal engagement with print culture as a "synthetic" model, which unites not just readers and authors but also those involved in the physical production and distribution of literary products as part of a communications circuit that embodies the essential and symbiotic relationships among women as producers and consumers in the new reading economy (136). As Paula Backscheider's essay in this volume observes, Haywood models the variety of ways that profit comes about in eighteenth-century literary production: "author of . . ." title-page branding and the operating of her own print shop helped to foster successful follow-up texts and collections and bolstered less obviously popular publications.

The physical forms of Haywood's books reflect the variation in the broad cultural understanding of women's writing and its social and artistic worth. Some of her novels were published as prestige items and others as pulp with low production values and lower social valuation. For at least two of her early publications, there is bibliographical evidence that Haywood's work was being marketed to polite audiences of rank: Al Coppola has shown that both *Love in Excess* and *Letters from a Lady of Quality to a Chevalier* were printed on high-quality paper, with generous white space and elaborate ornamentation—qualities of "elegant production" that King suggests conveyed "suitability for a fashionable readership" ("New Contexts" 266). Haywood's other novels of the 1720s, though, were often printed in dense blocks of text on cheap paper. Just three years after the publication of *Letters*, its author was being criticized as a low scandalmonger even by those who only months before had been part of her close literary circle—a group of clever, ambitious young writers who called themselves the Hillarians. Though the reasons for this apparent shift from elegant young authoress to pulp writer are not yet fully understood, the early 1720s represents a period of marked change in the formal valuations of Haywood and her work (see King, *Political Biography* 17–34).

Regardless of how Haywood was being read at any given moment in her long career, she was indeed being read, especially as literate audiences expanded. Estimates vary, but Roy Porter suggests that by midcentury "almost all" English men in the middle and upper classes were literate, as were approximately half of men of the laboring ranks (167). According to John Brewer, perhaps one-third of English women could read by that time, and up to sixty percent of women in London as early as 1720, though, as R. A. Houston observes, the ability to read "did not mean that a person can necessarily be described as a reader" (192). Overall literacy rates favored men, but reporters such as Edward Gibbon and Samuel Johnson agreed that women read a great deal, perhaps even much more than men did. While some commentators like Joseph Addison and David Hume suggested that well-read women were an indicator of an enlightened society, there was also anxiety that too much reading could lead women to neglect their domestic duties, or that the wrong sort of reading—especially novels—could lead them to moral error (Towsey 22–23).

A long tradition has assumed Haywood's readers to be nearly exclusively female and typically uneducated. Pope and Fielding imply as much in the eighteenth century, and in the late nineteenth century Edmund Gosse asserted, "Eliza was read by servants in the kitchen, by seamstresses, by basket women, by 'prentices of all sorts, male and female, but mostly the latter" (162–63). By the 1960s Robert Adams Day was making similar unsubstantiated assumptions about a female readership, but he also suggested that, given book prices and usual wages, a wider range of readers must be recognized:

> [S]ervants would most naturally come by novels like Mrs. Haywood's when they were discarded by the gentry, rather than purchase, for her books were too expensive to be bought outright by those who worked for a living. . . . Doubtless Mrs. Haywood's wares were known to the more frothy minds of the polite world and to the daughters of middle-class trading families. (73)

In 2017 Leah Orr challenged Gosse's claim, using evidence of pricing and wages to argue that, "with the exception of chapbooks, most fiction was written for and marketed to an elite audience, regardless of its literary quality of content" (*Novel* 29). She observes a significant range in retail pricing of fiction, from five or six shillings for a long volume to three pence for a short chapbook, with price set, she suggests, not on any sense of value as a literary artifact, but rather on the costs of paper and production (35–36). Using data and analysis from the statistician Gregory King and the eighteenth-century studies scholar Robert D. Hume, Orr notes that families earning less than fifty pounds per year (about eighty percent of the English population) would not likely be able to purchase books in the three- to five-shilling range, but might well purchase the less expensive short publications (37–38), a grouping that could include works like Haywood's short narratives of the 1720s, as well as chapbooks and scandal stories.

Other scholars have confirmed some breadth of readership for Haywood's work in the eighteenth century, including Blouch's witty analysis "'What Ann Lang Read'" and King's work in her *Political Biography* on the varying places that Haywood occupied in the popular consciousness of her day, as well as William Warner's "Novels on the Market."[2] Haywood's work was read by women and men who were not at all "frothy-minded," including, as the evidence of their own novels suggests, Fielding and Richardson, as well as Savage, Aaron Hill, John Dyer, and Martha Fowke. Records of private libraries show that copies of Haywood's work were held by some families of rank, and that others consented to be named dedicatees of her publications. Far from Gosse's typification of Haywood's readers as "straggling nymphs" consuming disposable froth (163), it seems clear that Haywood's work was consumed across genders, ranks, and decades. Orr's table of the thirty-three "[n]ew works reprinted at least five times" between 1690 and 1730 documents that six of them were works of fiction by Haywood (despite their being published relatively close to the 1730 cutoff for the table): *Love in Excess*, *The Injur'd Husband*, *The Masqueraders*, *The Rash Resolve*, *The City Jilt*, and *The Distress'd Orphan*. Only one other writer has anywhere near so many reprinted texts in this time frame: Daniel Defoe, with six (Orr, *Novel Ventures* 187–88). James Raven indicates that this trend continued: even in the decade after her death, judging by the number of editions printed, Haywood was the most popular female novelist in Britain (14). These data, however, should be framed with the recognition that between 1690 and 1730, only a tiny percentage of the works published were fiction: from as low as 0.5% in 1710 (a year with a much larger than average number of total publications) to 2.0% in 1700 and 0.6% in 1730 (Orr, *Novel Ventures* 35).

The rush of pamphlets, newspapers, magazines, and books marks the eighteenth century as a time of an increasingly essential literacy, where reading emerged as an important component in understanding the events of one's community. By 1760 about a dozen daily or weekly newspapers were circulating in London, with some thirty-five more in towns beyond the city. The first London newspaper, *The Daily Courant*, began publication in 1702, followed by popular broadsheets like Steele's *Tatler* (1709–11) and Addison and Steele's *Spectator* (1711–12). These publications had significant influence on public discourse, providing news, gossip, and moral essays that could drive the day's conversation in coffeehouses and other gathering places and thus disseminate rapidly. This level of social influence might seem surprising, given that *The Spectator* had daily print runs of only about three thousand (London's population was some seven hundred thousand), but copies distributed in venues like the coffeehouse each found numerous readers. In fact, Addison suggested that his publication could expect twenty readers per print copy. His number was ambitious, but the implication of effect on popular tastes and understanding appears valid. Like *The Tatler* and *The Spectator*, early magazines like *The Gentleman's Magazine* (started in 1731) typically assumed a male readership, which led to the creation of periodicals aimed at other groups, notably the anonymously authored *The Female Tatler* (1709–10), issued Mondays, Wednesdays, and Fridays, balancing *The Tatler*'s Tuesday, Thursday, and Saturday publication schedule. Haywood's own *The Female Spectator* would be one of the most important of the feminocentric periodicals and one of the few that was definitively written by a woman.

This expansion of print culture occasioned changes to censorship and copyright laws and to other regulatory mechanisms. The 1662 Licensing of the Press Act (which required texts to be licensed before being printed) was allowed to lapse in 1695, and enforcement shifted from advance censorship to punishing libel and sedition after publication. This system was formalized in the 1710 Statute of Anne, which placed legal responsibility for content on authors and booksellers (in the eighteenth century the categories of "bookseller" and what we now consider "publisher" overlapped, with some booksellers publishing books under their own imprints and owning copyrights, some merely selling books, and some—like Haywood—doing both [see Orr, *Novel Ventures* 42–46]).

The first version of copyright was also established by the Statute of Anne: booksellers would purchase a text's copyright for fourteen years, with the option to extend for another fourteen if the rights holder was still alive after the first copyright expired. Traditionally uncopyrighted material, such as pamphlets and newspapers, was subsequently regulated by Queen Anne's Stamp Act of 1712, wherein a tax had to be paid on paper printings under approximately one hundred pages, with payment indicated by a stamp. The stamp tax raised significant sums for the government, creating for these ephemeral publications an institutional value beyond the exchange between author, printer, and reader. Government controls over literature were not done quite yet, though: the 1737 Licensing Act reeled in a critical and sometimes brutally satirical theatrical trend toward political drama by requiring that all new plays be approved by the Lord Chamberlain. The move effectively shut down the nonpatent theaters that had been flourishing and created a decades-long desert in the production and publication of new plays, perhaps nudging Haywood from her focus on the theater back toward fiction and driving other playwrights like Fielding toward the novel, creating the next step in the path for the near-theatrical voices of characters like Syrena Tricksy and Abraham Adams, Betsy Thoughtless and Tom Jones.

Haywood is in many ways not particularly typical of writers in the eighteenth century, but her long life, her range of genres, and the ways in which she was situated in the worlds of theater and fiction, periodicals and politics, licensing and scandal, and regulation and subversion make her a pivotal figure in teaching not just the history of women's writing but the broadest contexts of English literature and social history.

NOTES

[1]The numbers given here are intentionally vague. For more on the debate regarding the Haywood canon, see Spedding, *Bibliography*; Orr, "Basis for Attribution."

[2]On women writers and readers in the eighteenth century, see Turner, *Living by the Pen*; Colclough, *Consuming Texts*. For more recent short overviews suitable for students, see Schellenberg, "Professional Female Writer"; Towsey, "Women as Readers and Writers."

Haywood's Works: Availability, Editing, and Issues of Bibliography

Patrick Spedding

Two of the largest challenges facing those wishing to teach or study the works of Eliza Haywood have been access to Haywood's works in a convenient form, suitable for teaching and study, and access to a body of scholarship suitable to support the teaching and study of those works. In this essay, I examine the broad correlation between the increased access to Haywood works and the increase in the scholarship on those works, providing an account of the multiplying forms of access to Haywood's works over the last century and the increasing volume of scholarship that has become available on those works since the 1980s. While the broad correlation of access to scholarship is clear, it is, however, incomplete. For a handful of Haywood's works, increased access has not led to an increase in scholarship. My analysis of the distribution of scholarship suggests that the primary reason for the imperfect correlation of access to scholarship may be that there is a general bias among teachers, students, and scholars toward Haywood's prose fiction and periodicals over her drama, nonfiction, and many translations.

In 1915 George Whicher wrote *The Life and Romances of Mrs. Eliza Haywood* to counter the "inadequacy" of Haywood's critical recognition. In order to do so, he had to "ransack" half a dozen major American libraries, the British Museum, the Bodleian, and "several minor literary museums in England." He was obliged to travel from Urbana, Illinois, to Baltimore, Boston, Chicago, New Haven, New York, Providence, and—on the eve of World War I—London, because "no one library contains anything like a complete collection of Mrs. Haywood's innumerable books" (viii). The first modern reprint of a work of Haywood's did not occur until 1929, when John Lane published Mary Priestley's selection from *The Female Spectator*, and the second was not until 1963, when William McBurney edited *Philidore and Placentia* for the University of Nebraska Press. As a consequence, travels such as those undertaken by Whicher remained necessary until long after World War II for anyone outside London who wished to read or study more than a small fraction of Haywood's oeuvre.

Haywood wrote more than seventy works in a wide variety of forms: numerous works of prose fiction—both short and long—about a dozen works of nonfiction, a number of translations from the French, a handful of plays and periodicals, and a small quantity of verse. But, because much of what Haywood wrote was published anonymously or pseudonymously during her lifetime, there has been considerable confusion about the extent of her oeuvre. I attempted to end that confusion in 2004 by undertaking a lengthy analysis of the evidence that had been offered for all the works that had been attributed to Haywood up to that time (Spedding, *Bibliography*).[1] As I document below, access to the many works now attributed to Haywood began to improve only slowly for would-be readers. By the time *Philidore and Placentia* appeared in 1963, four of Haywood's plays had been reproduced in microprint in *Three Centuries of Drama: English, 1701–1750.*[2] Starting in the late 1960s, other Haywood items began to be reproduced in modest numbers in microfilm collections such as *Eighteenth-Century Sources for the Study of English Literature and Culture* (17 items) and *The Microbook Library of English Literature* (13 items). Starting in the late 1970s, a significant number of works by Haywood began to appear in collections such as *Early British Fiction: Pre-1750* (56 items) and *The Eighteenth Century* (182 items). Two dozen of Haywood's works were also printed in facsimile editions in the 1970s and '80s: a dozen of her novels appeared in Garland's Foundations of the Novel and Flowering of the Novel series from 1972 to 1975, and a dozen of her shorter works appeared in volumes in the Scholars' Facsimiles and Reprints and Augustan Reprint Society series from 1983 to 1995. In the mid-1990s Chadwyck-Healey issued more than a quarter of Haywood's oeuvre as e-texts on CD-ROM and made these texts available to subscribers to *Literature Online* (*LION*). In the following decade, digitization projects such as *Eighteenth Century Collections Online* (*ECCO*) began converting microfilm collections into subscription textbases of indexed electronic files. Soon after, large digitization projects, such as *Google Books*, *Internet Archive*, and *HathiTrust*, and smaller scanning projects, such as those indexed by *The European Library* and *Europeana*, made reproductions of many of Haywood's works freely available for the first time to readers outside the large institutions that subscribe to microfilm and facsimile series and online services such as *ECCO*.

Although many of Haywood's major works were becoming available on microfilm by the mid-1980s, none had been reprinted or edited for more than thirty years. This changed in 1986, with the publication of Dale Spender's edition of *The History of Miss Betsy Thoughtless*, and in 1993, with Gabrielle M. Firmager's selections from *The Female Spectator*, which became the first work by Haywood to be published in a form that was well adapted to undergraduate teaching, providing a helpful introduction and explanatory notes. The first complete major work by Haywood to receive this treatment, David Oakleaf's edition of *Love in Excess*, appeared the following year. Between 1993 and the end of 2004 large and prestigious publishers released for the teaching market ten individual works and eight collections of works by Haywood, many in low-priced paperback form. These eighteen volumes made available twenty-seven of Haywood's seventy-one surviving works, plus selections from a further two. Since the end of 2004, only four more works by Haywood have been issued in edited form for the first time, meaning that fewer than half of Haywood's works have been reprinted (i.e., thirty-three of seventy-one, or 46.5% of surviving works).[3] But as a result of the publishing activity that took off in the mid-1990s, for more than a decade instructors have had access to a wide range of inexpensive, reliable editions for use in teaching a variety of works by Haywood at the undergraduate level.

The evolving and steadily growing publishing activity outlined above continues to widen access to an increasing number of reproductions of the original editions of Haywood's works. By way of case study, *A Wife to Be Lett*—a popular play by Haywood—was printed four times (1724, 1729, 1735, 1757). Eighty copies of these four editions are held in fifty-seven libraries around the world (forty-five scattered across the United States, twenty-three in the United Kingdom, five in Europe, five in Australia, and two in Canada). The play has appeared in microprint (1953) and facsimile (1986) and on microfilm seven times (1983, 1983, 1985, 1986, 1989, 2000, 2006)—microfilms that began to appear online via *ECCO* in 2003; the full text was released on CD-ROM in 1994 and then to subscribers online from 1996; the prologue and epilogue were edited by Pierre Danchin in 1993; the whole play was edited by Paula R. Backscheider in 1999, by Derek Hughes in 2001, and by Michael Caines in 2004; and copies of the original editions appeared on *Google Books* and the *Internet Archive* in 2007, 2011, and 2013. What this means is that scholars no longer had to travel very far, if at all, to read one of the original editions of Haywood's play; from the early 1950s many scholars and advanced students had relatively easy access to a first edition of *A Wife to Be Lett* on microcard and, from the early 1980s, on microfilm; from the mid-1980s scholars and students at medium and large universities were able to borrow a copy of *A Wife to Be Lett* or—soon after—to print out copies of the microfilm to take home and study; from the mid-1990s it was possible for most university students to read, download, and edit electronic versions of the text for study; and from the end of the 1990s it rapidly became very easy to teach *A Wife to Be Lett* using an edited version of the text. Since 2003 most scholars and students have been able to consult various copies of digital facsimiles of the text, and since 2007 anyone with an Internet connection has been able to view or download digital facsimiles, plus increasingly reliable plain-text versions generated by optical character recognition. While these changes have benefited Haywood scholars, teachers, and students committed to reading or studying her works, they have also made it significantly easier for nonspecialists, prompted by a passing interest in the author or in one of her works, to investigate further. What might have required an intercity or crosstown excursion up until the 1970s became a trip to the library basement to view or print out a microfilm in the 1980s, to the computer lab in the 1990s, and to the library stacks by the end of the 1990s. Since the mid-2000s specialist and nonspecialist alike have been able to consult a significant proportion of Haywood's works with ease from a home computer or mobile device.

An account of increased access similar to the one above could be offered for many of Haywood's individual works. Well-known pieces, such as *The Female Spectator* and *Betsy Thoughtless*, were printed often: original editions are held in many libraries around the world, and these editions have been regularly reproduced in several forms. Most of Haywood's works have never been edited but have been reproduced. But some texts have never been reproduced or are not widely available in any form. For example, only two copies are known of

Haywood's *The Fatal Fondness*; the novel has never been reproduced in any form and is unavailable to anyone unable to travel to the University of Bristol or to Sir John Soane's Museum in London. Likewise, *Letters from the Palace of Fame*, while known in five copies, has never been reproduced in any form and is also currently unavailable to anyone unable to travel to London; Toronto; Boston; Bloomington, Indiana; or Columbia, Missouri. And while *The Young Lady* is now known in two copies (one in London, one in Chicago) and has appeared in a microfilm series (*Women Advising Women*), the series concerned is not widely held, and the text is currently unavailable in electronic form. Consequently, though it is increasingly easy for scholars, teachers, and students to read or consult many of Haywood's works, the lack of access to the remainder of her works remains an impediment to their study.

Just as Whicher wrote his scholarly account of Haywood in the hope of reversing her critical neglect among scholars, Spender appears to have been motivated to republish *Betsy Thoughtless* out of a desire to make it easier to read and teach Haywood's works and thereby to raise awareness of her works among teachers and students. While a causal relationship can't be established, there does appear to be a series of close correlations between scholarship, editing and publishing, and teaching. It is not very surprising that the works that have long been the focus of scholarship are those that are now readily available, and that those that are readily available are more likely to be taught in the hope of instilling the sort of understanding of and appreciation for works that may lead a student to undertake further study and contribute to scholarship. The pioneering Haywood scholarship of the 1980s and early '90s seems to have led to the unmistakable demand for more editions of her works in the mid-'90s—which is undoubtedly why seventeen of her works appeared in teaching editions between 1995 and 1999, with three different teaching editions of *Fantomina* appearing in 1996 alone. The ready availability of edited editions of Haywood's works appears to have significantly boosted the scholarship on those works, and this scholarship has made it easier still to teach those works.

Although the availability of an increasing number of Haywood's works in a form readily adapted to undergraduate teaching seems to have raised the number of critical studies of Haywood, those studies are limited to a relatively small number of Haywood's works. It remains the case that there are very few studies of many of Haywood's works, including those that have been published in edited form, while some studies have been published based on texts that are yet to be edited. This imperfect match between editing and scholarship suggests that academic publishers have overestimated the demand for some titles and underestimated it for others. The same evidence suggests, moreover, that the varied availability of original editions, microfilm, facsimile, and digital texts has protected scholars and students from a dependence on edited texts alone.

Table 1 provides a crude snapshot of the quantity of scholarship currently available. The data is taken from *Google Scholar*, which is by far the most complete citation index of literary scholarship now available.[4] The table includes

Table 1. Citations to works by Haywood

Title	Citations	1993ff	In title
Ab.26 *Fantomina*	388	360	19
Ab.1 *Love in Excess**	553	488	16
Ab.67 *The History of Miss Betsy Thoughtless**	381	362	10
Ab.60 *The Female Spectator**	588	519	8
Ab.53 *The Adventures of Eovaai, Princess of Ijaveo*	133	120	5
Ab.69 *The Invisible Spy**	126	112	5
Ab.9 *The Rash Resolve*	98	83	4
Ab.8 *Lasselia*	95	86	3
Ab.22 *The Tea-Table*	292	222	2
Ab.54 *Anti-Pamela*	234	213	2
Ab.59 *The Fortunate Foundlings*	161	120	2
Ab.68 *The History of Jemmy and Jenny Jessamy**	97	81	2
Ab.61 *The Parrot*	251	83	1
Ab.4 *The British Recluse*	190	171	1
Ab.58 *A Present for a Servant-Maid*	111	92	1
Ab.31 *The City Jilt*	85	81	1
Ab.5 *The Injur'd Husband*	84	73	1
Ab.12 *The Masqueraders*	78	66	1
Ab.64 *Epistles for the Ladies**	77	66	1
Ab.6 *Idalia*	165	149	0
Ab.17 *Memoirs of a Certain Island Adjacent to the Kingdom of Utopia* *	116	104	0
Ab.16 *La Belle Assemblée* *	99	76	0
Ab.7 *A Wife to Be Lett*	88	73	0
Ab.13 *The Fatal Secret*	83	61	0

columns for titles (and the title codes from my *Bibliography*); the total number of references to each work in the body of all articles indexed; the total number of these references since 1993 (when modern teaching editions of Haywood's works began to appear); and the total number of articles that mention individual works by Haywood in the title of the article concerned (this being a proxy for the frequency with which each work is the primary focus of an article).[5] The table shows that more than half the total number of all citations in each category pertain to between three and six titles, *Fantomina*, *Love in Excess*, *Betsy Thoughtless*, and *The Female Spectator* being the most frequently cited and discussed, followed by *The Tea-Table* and *The Parrot*. Depending on one's focus, arguments could be mounted for the precedence of many of the remaining titles as the focus of Haywood scholars in general: *The Adventures of Eovaai, Princess of Ijaveo*; *The Invisible Spy*; *The Rash Resolve*; and *Lasselia* often appear as the primary focus of scholarship, and *The Parrot*, *Anti-Pamela*, *The British Recluse*, and *Idalia* are frequently cited and discussed.

Given the obvious limits of this bibliometric approach, however—confined as it is to one inevitably incomplete and evolving index of literary scholarship—the precedence of individual titles within the table is less important than the precedence of this group of titles as a whole over the remaining titles in Haywood's oeuvre. While the list contains one-third of all titles attributed to Haywood (twenty-four of seventy-two) and has a fairly even distribution of earlier and later works (indicated by my item numbers), it is dominated by eight of her twelve longest works (marked with an asterisk)[6]—including six of her longest works of prose fiction (*The Invisible Spy*, *Betsy Thoughtless*, *The History of Jemmy and Jenny Jessamy*, *Love in Excess*, *Anti-Pamela*, and *Eovaai*)—and three of her four periodicals (*The Female Spectator*, *The Parrot*, and *Epistles for the Ladies*),[7] while only one of her five plays (*A Wife to Be Lett*) and one of her nine translations (*La Belle Assemblée*) make it into the group. More than half of Haywood's works appear never to have been the focus of an article, and a quarter have been mentioned fewer than eighteen times in all the books, articles, reviews, theses, and so forth indexed by *Google Scholar*. So, however the top two dozen titles might be arranged, it is clear that these two dozen works, primarily periodicals and longer works of original prose fiction, are the ones that loom largest in Haywood scholarship.

Notable for its absence from the table is Haywood's *Philidore and Placentia*, which was printed in 1963, 1964, and 1978. Although this work of prose fiction has been widely available to teachers and students for more than fifty years, it has thus far been the (minor) focus of only one essay published in 1998 and one in 2017, the first to see *Philidore and Placentia* as a primary subject (see Hicks; Harris). Nevertheless, of the twenty-six titles edited between 1993 and 2004, fifteen are among the two dozen most frequently discussed,[8] while a further four titles edited since 2004 are also among the titles most frequently discussed.[9] Taken together, nineteen of Haywood's twenty-four most frequently discussed works (almost eighty percent) are among those edited since 1993.[10] Of the five titles that are frequently discussed in Haywood scholarship, but which have not been edited, four are readily available: three in facsimile (*Memoirs of a Certain Island Adjacent to the Kingdom of Utopia* since 1972; *Idalia* and *The Fatal Secret* since 1986 and as e-texts since 1996) and one as an e-text only (*The Fortunate Foundlings* since 1996 and on *Google Books* since 2013). Only one title (*La Belle Assemblée*) has required scholars or students to rely on original editions, which are very widely held, or on microfilm editions, which have been generally available since 1988. Although it seems likely that convenient edited editions of *Idalia* and *The Fatal Secret*, for example, would facilitate further studies of those works, critical interest in Haywood's periodicals and longer works of original prose fiction suggests that editions of works such as *The Young Lady* and *The Fortunate Foundlings* would further expand the range of Haywood scholarship.

In 2007 Margaret Case Croskery suggested that the increasing presence of well-edited Haywood editions and "the growing number of provocative Haywood critical studies" were contributing to the "mainstreaming of Haywood texts in undergraduate and graduate surveys" ("Who's Afraid" 968). Although the rate at which Haywood's works are being newly edited has diminished somewhat since Croskery made this comment, there is a broad correlation between the still-increasing access to Haywood works and the increasing volume of scholarship on those works. While the correlation is imperfect, Croskery is undoubtedly right to suggest that both access and scholarship will continue to facilitate the "mainstreaming" of Haywood.

NOTES

[1]In the years since my *Bibliography* was published, Kathryn R. King has made one attribution on the basis of internal evidence (*Political Biography* 109, 241n72), while Leah Orr has questioned some attributions on the basis of external evidence ("Basis for Attribution" 347–49). In my *Bibliography* (16–17), I set out the principles upon which I rejected the internal evidence accepted by King, and accept the external evidence rejected by Orr.

[2]See my *Bibliography* for full details for all works published prior to 2004 and for the title codes used below.

[3]Of the seventy-two works I accept as being by Haywood, one (*Arden of Feversham*) was not published and is now lost.

[4]The eleven most frequently cited articles about Haywood on *Google Scholar* (those which mention her in the title of the article) had a total of 184 citations on 1 April 2017. On the same day, the *MLA Bibliography* recorded a total of eighty citations (forty-four percent of *Google Scholar*); *Scopus* indexed only eight of the eleven articles, with a total of forty-four citations (twenty-four percent of *Google Scholar*); *Web of Science* indexed six, with a total of eighteen citations (ten percent of *Google Scholar*).

[5]This methodology excludes books about Haywood—of which there have been few—but includes reviews of editions of individual works by Haywood.

[6]The other four are *The Virtuous Villager, The Dramatic Historiographer, The Secret History . . . of Caramania*, and *The Memoirs of an Unfortunate Young Nobleman* (see Spedding, *Bibliography* 768–69, but note that *Love in Excess* is 20.25 octavo sheets, not 15.25 as stated).

[7]The fourth being *The Young Lady*.

[8]Spedding, *Bibliography*, title codes Ab.1, Ab.4, Ab.5, Ab.7, Ab.8, Ab.22, Ab.26, Ab.31, Ab.53, Ab.54, Ab.58, Ab.60, Ab.61, Ab.64, Ab.67.

[9]Ab.9, Ab.12, Ab.68, Ab.69.

[10]Those titles that have been edited since 1993 but are more rarely discussed in Haywood scholarship include plays and theater criticism (Ab.3, Ab.49, Ab.51), three short works (Ab.28, Ab.30, Ab.32) and three long works (Ab.29, Ab.48, Ab.63 [in 2013]) of prose fiction, Haywood's final periodical (Ab.71), and two works of advice (Ab.70, Ab.72).

CULTURE AND CONTEXTS

Avoiding *Oroonoko* Syndrome: Teaching Haywood and *Fantomina* in Context

Martha F. Bowden

Despite her status as one of the most successful comic playwrights of the Restoration theater, itself one of the most vibrant periods in the history of the British stage, Aphra Behn is largely known to students as the author of a few poems, including "The Disappointment," generally linked to Rochester's "Imperfect Enjoyment," and as the writer of *Oroonoko; or, The Royal Slave.* I call this skewed version of the literary production of the first professional woman writer in England "*Oroonoko* syndrome." Not limited to Behn, this syndrome is in part the result of the uniformity of the standard anthologies used in sophomore survey courses, including *The Broadview Anthology of British Literature, The Norton Anthology of British Literature*, and *The Longman Anthology of British Literature.* These collections all include *Oroonoko* and those few poems; not one provides any of her plays, although her chief fame in her own day, and her most significant revenue, derived from her theatrical success. The same anthologies are equally uniform in their choices for Eliza Haywood: *Fantomina* and a very short excerpt from *The Female Spectator*, often only from the first issue. This choice is no more representative of Haywood's extensive and varied professional oeuvre than the Behn material is of hers and is equally likely to distort students' picture of the professional writer in the Restoration and the eighteenth century.

To enshrine *Fantomina* as *the* Haywood text—effectively her *Oroonoko*—is even more problematic. *Oroonoko* did have an extended afterlife in Thomas Southerne's adaptation, although late-eighteenth-century editions of the play omit the preface that acknowledges his indebtedness to Behn's narrative. But, as Aleksondra Hultquist demonstrates in *Equal Ardor*, *Fantomina* was by no means the work with which Haywood's contemporaries were most likely to associate her. In tables illustrating numbers of reprints for each text in the eighteenth century, *Fantomina* does not even make the top ten: *The Female Spectator*, so briefly represented in the anthologies, is in fact her most frequently reprinted work; the first novel on the list, as Hultquist points out, is *The History of Miss Betsy Thoughtless*, at number three. *Love in Excess* is seventh. *Fantomina*, in fact, never actually had a separate printing; it appeared in volume three of *Secret Histories, Novels, and Poems*. So not only is any defining connection between Haywood and *Fantomina* at odds with contemporary responses, but there is no suggestion that Haywood was thought of primarily as a novelist: as Hultquist asserts, "The bibliographic work on Haywood suggests that there is no clear sense of Haywood's work or career arc in the minds of her contemporary readership" (*Equal Ardor* 14). There is also a danger in promoting this particular work because it responds to our need to possess an eighteenth-century woman's text that fully articulates the inequities that constrain her and the artful and brilliant manner in which she subverts them. In a significant way, the desire inherent in *Fantomina* is arguably less the protagonist's and more our own: the longing to see a woman perform as we would hope to do. The unnamed heroine is not one of us, but we work hard to make her so.

The emphasis on Haywood as primarily a novelist with minor works in other genres is equally problematic. The recovery of texts that was part of feminist literary historians' most influential work in the last quarter of the twentieth century was critical in changing our ideas about the nature of eighteenth-century literature: the canon did not expand so much as explode. Haywood, having written in many different genres of fiction, was well represented in those efforts. Yet this recovery project also privileged novels to the exclusion of other genres, and that privileging still exists. Susan Staves's "Women Writers ≠ Women Novelists" calls into question the "still-present temptation to make our history of women's writing a history of women writing novels and the temptation to use novels as the primary source of our imaginative contact with the lives and minds of eighteenth-century women" (87). She points out that, when she encounters the work of scholars in fields other than literary studies, she is struck by the difference between this depiction of eighteenth-century women and their representations in the novels: "Outside of novels, eighteenth-century women often seem considerably less abject, more aware of adult sexuality, less sentimental, and more knowledgeable about money" (88). She also points out that concentrating on the novel as the primary female genre results in a misunderstanding of literature of the period more generally: "experiments with nonfiction prose produced many of the belletristic books contemporaries most celebrated as ground-breaking and characteristic of their age" (89). Staves believes that we have moved beyond this emphasis on the novel, but it is striking that at this writing it is possible to purchase a wide range of Haywood's novels in annotated editions but little of her other work. An *Amazon* search reveals that *Selections from* The Female Spectator (edited by Patricia Meyer Spacks) and *Selected Fiction and Drama of Eliza Haywood* (edited by Paula R. Backscheider), both in the Women Writers in English 1350–1850 series, are still in print, but most of the rest of the available non-novel texts are Gale reproductions of digital editions and other unedited versions that are not particularly helpful for students.

As Hultquist points out, while Haywood was "easily recognized as Mrs. Novel" in Henry Fielding's *The Author's Farce* (*Equal Ardor* 15n47) and frequently referred to as a novelist, she wrote in many different genres. Hultquist divides Haywood's top ten titles into seven different genres: amatory, conduct, translation, political, gothic, domestic, and periodical. A number of these categories are also forms of fiction, but in teaching genre it is salutary to demonstrate that many of the subgenres that we might tend to think of as later evolutions of some legendary ur-novel form in fact manifested themselves with the novel's earliest appearance in English. In discussing Haywood's specific oeuvre, it is also worth pointing out that what is striking about these categories is not that the range of genres is prodigious, but that it reflects the realities of an eighteenth-century female professional writer's life and is not substantively different from the work in which male writers engaged, as a classroom comparison with Samuel Johnson's working life quickly demonstrates.

Despite these caveats, there are sound reasons for teaching *Fantomina* to first- and second-year undergraduates. For one thing, its brevity makes it perfect for the demands of survey coverage. In just a few pages, it provides a full example of what was still being called a "novel" in 1725, thus opening the door to conversations about genre and the expectations we hold of it: for example, that a novel be an extended piece of prose fiction generally including chapter breaks. Why was this text called a novel? When did we start using the terms *short story* and *novella*? The survey course itself is uniquely placed for genre inquiry because it extends beyond the boundaries of a single period. At my institution, the second half of the British literature survey extends from the Restoration to the present. It is thus possible to move from Behn and Haywood to Alice Munro in one semester.

Another reason to teach *Fantomina*, despite its lack of representativeness, is that it is an engaging and surprising read and allows discussion of many issues raised in other essays in this volume, not least gender roles, cultural context, and what it means to be a great artist. For example, Haywood describes her protagonist as follows:

> [B]esides the Alteration which the change of dress made in her, she was so admirably skill'd in the Art of feigning, that she had the Power of putting on almost what Face she pleas'd, and knew so exactly how to form her Behaviour to the Character she represented, that all the Comedians at both Playhouses are infinitely short of her performances. (57)[1]

The heroine is presented not as a desperate woman attempting to hang on to a man but as a skilled practitioner of the "Art of feigning," an actress engaged in her craft. Thus, she fits nicely into any conversation about identity or masquerade and upends students' ideas about decorum in the period, should any illusions remain after perusing, for example, Samuel Pepys's diaries, William Wycherley's *The Country Wife*, and the poetry of Rochester, Behn, and Jonathan Swift. The character's expert manipulation convinces her beloved, Beauplaisir (with his short attention span and apparent obliviousness to details like the body of the woman he is sleeping with), that he is engaging in libertine-style romps with a long succession of variously willing and unwilling conquests. Haywood allows him a dim sense of recognition: "he did fancy he observed in the Face of the [Widow], Features which were not altogether unknown to him, yet he could not recollect when or where he had known them," but when the lady tells him, in her widow persona, that she is from Bristol—"a Place where he never was"—that is apparently enough to satisfy his incurious mind (57).

At the same time, students may note that the fiction is striking in its lack of interiority, a quality that we expect of fiction generally and of amatory fiction especially and that Haywood denies us. We know that the nameless lady is at least initially so much in love with her fickle man that she employs all her considerable talents to keep him, but we do not know any more about how she feels about him, her strategy, or the pregnancy that inevitably results from their relationship. The narrator is considerably more forthcoming in praise of the lady than she is of herself.[2] According to Marta Kvande, *Fantomina* rejects "the simple equation of female desire, self, and expression" ("Printed in a Book" 248). Even the apparently moralistic ending can be called into question; Kvande points out that it has been variously described as "a moral punishment . . . fairly neutral, or even a chance for Fantomina to continue her pleasures . . . the ambiguity of the ending supports the sense that she still has not been pinned down" (250). Though Nicholas Hudson disagrees in his essay in this volume, Tiffany Potter describes this final episode as Haywood's gift to her protagonist: "Haywood declines to betray the glory of Fantomina's autonomy and agency by having her recant, repent, or face embarrassment." Potter speculates that Haywood may be drawing on "the tradition of religiocentric French pornography and the reports of convent life . . . for a tacit implication of continuing sexual and intellectual independence in France" ("Language" 182). Thus, *Fantomina* is a perfect text for disrupting conventional ideas about gender and genre and therefore very useful in a survey course, where every text must serve a multitude of functions.

It is both possible and desirable, however, to combat *Oroonoko* syndrome in upper-level classes by choosing texts that offer a broader view of Haywood as the market-savvy, multigenre writer she was. There are many well-annotated editions of other works, sometimes with extensive appendices—a valuable resource, especially for institutions that do not have access to *Eighteenth-Century Collections Online*, the Burney collection of newspapers, and other subscription services.

Because *The Female Spectator* was reprinted the most frequently of any of her work in Haywood's own century, and because it is not a novel, it should form a more significant portion of our students' understanding of Haywood's career. There she addressed real-life concerns of the women of her period: etiquette, romance, social relations. Kirsten T. Saxton and Cassie Childs's essay in this volume describes an assignment that connects *The Female Spectator* with twenty-first-century women's digital periodicals. Haywood's periodical, available both as a paperback and on the *HathiTrust* open-access platform, would also be a valuable addition to a course that encompasses journalism, one of the period's most important contributions to professional writing. It could be supplemented with collections such as Cheryl L. Nixon's *Novel Definitions* and Paul Keen's *The Age of Authors*, which both contain reviews, periodical essays, prefaces, and conduct writing by a range of authors.

Three other texts that receive individual treatments in this volume provide different, useful insights into Haywood's career. *Love in Excess*, the seventh text on Hultquist's chart, is significant as Haywood's career-making breakthrough. Originally published without any supplementary text, Broadview's second edition of the volume includes a wealth of contextual materials in its appendixes, including poems written to Haywood and a passage from Clara Reeve's *The Progress of Romance*. Two of Haywood's other fictions, *The Adventures of Eovaai, Princess of Ijaveo* and *Anti-Pamela*, are also easily accessible in fully annotated editions from Broadview, replete with useful appendices. *Eovaai*, set in a preadamite period, is a scorching satire of Robert Walpole's government that provides a timely corrective to stereotypes of the domestic nature of eighteenth-century women's writing. *Anti-Pamela* is published with Fielding's *Shamela*, allowing for a comparison of female- and male-authored critiques of Samuel Richardson's novel. All these novels would work in a range of settings, either in period-based courses to establish the generic variety of fiction in the eighteenth century or in courses devoted to social debate or popular culture whose range extends beyond any single period. The last two texts are helpful in teaching the novel as a site of eighteenth-century political and literary satire, especially when paired with the familiar poetic satirical forms in heroic or Hudibrastic couplets.

Teaching these texts can then invite *Fantomina* back into advanced courses, where it can be taught as part of a larger body of work. Contextualized and critically powerful teaching is facilitated particularly by the volume edited by Alexander Pettit and others. The volume functions as a micro-anthology of Haywood's professional career, and its materials expand students' understanding of Haywood's work and problematize any sense of its typicality that may have resulted from *Fantomina*'s ubiquity in sophomore survey courses. In addition to *Fantomina*, the collection contains three other complete texts, none of which is a novel: *The Tea-Table; or, A Conversation between Some Polite Persons of Both Sexes*, which illustrates the private alternative to the all-male coffeehouse; *Reflections on the Various Effects of Love*, which meditates on the positive and negative results of passion; and *Love-Letters on All Occasions Lately Passed between Persons of Distinction*, which compiles snapshots of lovers' experiences. The appendices include conduct-related excerpts from two works by Haywood:

A Present for a Servant-Maid and *The Female Spectator.* The other appendices illustrate the cultural context: *Venus in the Cloister* (1724), an example of the French pornography that Potter cites ("Language"), and Nahum Tate's *A Present for the Ladies* (1692), described as a source for *Reflections on the Various Effects of Love.*

Using this edition, I taught an upper-level gender studies course that focused on the eighteenth-century female professional writer. Two of my primary goals were to break the "woman writer = novelist" equivalency and to dissuade my students from referring to all women in the period as "oppressed." The "oppressed" usage leads students to imagine that eighteenth-century women were passive chattel, forbidden to achieve anything beyond the most basic literacy and not allowed to publish or to hold down any form of employment. Instead, I wanted students to see that despite social and legal constraints, women persisted in publishing in multiple genres, including poetry, drama, fiction, conduct literature, periodical literature, and polemic and took positions that range from complicity to subversion to defiance. This edition provides a useful assortment of many of these genres, a real help in demonstrating the diverse writing opportunities available to professional writers. Supported by in-class discussion, students can draw on the primary materials when writing their research essays, as the micro-anthology provides what some libraries may lack. The text is also a helpful preparation for writers like Mary Robinson, who wrote poetry, fiction, and polemic, and Helen Maria Williams, often considered the first foreign correspondent.

Haywood was generally perceived as a disruptive force by her contemporaries, the obvious target to be skewered by Scriblerus Primus (Alexander Pope) and Scriblerus Secundus (Fielding). Thus it is appropriate that she be allowed to disrupt our students' ideas of the eighteenth century. We know that the period is not exclusively, or even primarily, marked by the reason and decorum inscribed by male writers; passion, subversion, and women's voices all exist there as well. Haywood's heroine is a good entry point into that disruption, because she is a strong example of the ways in which women, while constrained, were not silenced. But it is appropriate to give Haywood a full and nuanced treatment, especially beyond the survey level, either by teaching *Fantomina* in the rich context that the Broadview edition allows or by turning to other texts that represent the many voices in which Haywood speaks to us.

NOTES

[1]This essay quotes from the version of *Fantomina* in the collection Fantomina *and Other Works*.

[2]I am grateful to Kirsten Saxton, whose conversation with me at the 2017 American Society for Eighteenth-Century Studies meeting got me thinking about the lady's enclosed self.

Haywood and Problems of Social Class

Nicholas Hudson

The neglect of social class in scholarship on Eliza Haywood seems a particularly glaring gap since, in the words of Paula R. Backscheider, Haywood often "holds in the spotlight the differences between classes and how much class matters" ("Story" 39). This essay suggests how such problems might be effectively introduced into the classroom in a way that illuminates the special qualities of her writings. Any up-to-date discussion of Haywood's relationship to the social hierarchy must, however, tackle some difficult and subtle problems. Having outlined these problems, I propose a class-oriented approach that may be applied to some frequently taught texts: *Fantomina*, *Anti-Pamela*, and *The History of Miss Betsy Thoughtless*.

The first problem concerns our very use of the term *social class*. Although this old term will suffice as shorthand for issues of social hierarchy, historians now generally agree that *class* is an inadequate word to describe the evolving complexities of English society before the nineteenth century. Eighteenth-century culture was divided instead along lines of rank or status.[1] Despite the deceptive Marxist model of a rising bourgeoisie overtaking the aristocracy during this period, the old landed elite remained firmly in charge politically and socially until at least the second quarter of the next century (Cannon viii–ix; E. P. Thompson 33). What happened was rather the greater involvement of the landed elite, comprising both the nobility and the greater gentry, in systems of trade and finance that expanded enormously during the reign of William III between 1689 and 1702, a period marked by the creation of the Bank of England and many new avenues of investment, such as state-sponsored lotteries and annuities. For the first time, problems of trade and commerce dominated debate in Parliament, though both the House of Lords and the House of Commons remained the almost exclusive enclave of the gentry. This incursion of financial preoccupations into the old elite greatly concerned Haywood, for what she allegorized in *Memoirs of a Certain Island Adjacent to the Kingdom of Utopia* (1724–25) as "the Enchanted Well" (1: 6) of commercial self-interest had, in her view, infected the noble values and loftier sexual morals associated with the pristine nobility of a former era. There are nonetheless indications that she came increasingly to accept the commercial elite as playing a beneficial role in English society, as demonstrated by her favorable presentation of the merchant Mr. Goodman in *Betsy Thoughtless* some twenty-five years later.

A second difficult problem concerns Haywood's own status in the social hierarchy. We might expect that a woman who tended to lionize the values and manners of the old aristocracy would herself have been connected in some way to the landed elite. Scholarship, as by Christine Blouch, has nonetheless intensified the obscurity of her origins, debunking the assumption that she was once married to a clergyman ("Eliza Haywood"). Haywood may have had family in the city or in the minor West Country gentry, but all we can say for sure is that she lived as an outsider from polite society, surviving as an actress and a prolific author beginning in the 1720s. Attempts to explain her social attitudes through her Tory affiliations have also been thrown into doubt by Christine Gerrard and Kathryn R. King, who have pointed out that Haywood courted a series of Whig and government figures in 1720s, including Aaron Hill, Lady Howe, William Young, and the Earl of Suffolk (Gerrard, *Patriot* 66–71; King, *Political Biography* 25–27). She seems to have retained a nostalgia for the supposedly noble values of the expelled Stuart family late into life, when she was suspected of having written a provocatively adulatory pamphlet about Charles Edward Stuart, *A Letter from H[enry] G[oring], Esq.* (1750). But the common denominator between the younger and the older Haywood was evidently social rather than political. Haywood regarded the aristocracy and the landed gentry, which retained control under the Whigs, with the mixture of fascination, suspicion, and even at times hostility that characterized the populace at large.

These were feelings that she translated into her fiction of the 1720s, when she poured out some thirty novels and four translations. Her first novel, *Love in Excess*, which remained her signature work throughout her life (King, *Political Biography* 23), situates its characters squarely in the French aristocracy. Only Frankville, whose father came from the upper gentry, belongs to a slightly lower rank, though his jeweled sword assures D'Elmont that he is "of considerable quality" notwithstanding (Haywood, *Love* 173). There is some criticism of these elite people, as in the portrait of the vain and overbearing Alovisa, but on the whole this novel fantasizes about the consequence-free sexual libertinism of the elite in a traditionally absolutist society. Whom did Haywood intend to please? Although Blouch has rightly cast doubt on the assumption of the Victorian Edmund Gosse that Haywood was read mostly by servants and other lower-rank people, her audience does not seem to have consisted largely of the aristocracy she so fulsomely dramatized ("'What Ann Lang Read'"). The subscriber list for her second novel, *Letters from a Lady of Quality to a Chevalier*, a loose translation of Edmé Boursault's *Lettres nouvelles*, is dominated by men and women from professional and small gentry families, with only eight titled subscribers. Haywood was capitalizing on her role as a "spy" on the doings of an elite otherwise glimpsed as shining cliques in Ranelagh Gardens, creating a gossipy stir, as she observed in *The Female Spectator*, particularly "among the little Gentry" (1: 270).

At some risk of anachronism, we can compare Haywood's initial appeal with the popularity of such modern reading material as *People* or *Hello!* Yet it is clear that she wished to branch out from this formula, feeling *Love in Excess* as a kind of shadow over her literary ambitions. The fiction that followed her first novel—*The British Recluse, The Injur'd Husband, Idalia, Lasselia, The Rash Resolve*—is more varied socially as well as formally, though never dropping into the commercial ranks or further down than the middle landed gentry, the status of Belinda in *The British Recluse*. Haywood retained a mordant, and perhaps self-protective, distaste for the "mob," like the coarse and fractious workmen among whom Beauclair hides in *The Injur'd Husband* (82). Nonetheless, her view of the upper ranks became increasingly critical and even bitter as the 1720s drew on, reaching a dyspeptic mid-decade climax in *Memoirs of a Certain Island*. Here she presents a dystopian vision of an English society in which the nobility and upper ranks have been almost wholly corrupted by avarice and self-interest. Her snobbery has not disappeared: a repeated insult hurled at characters in *Memoirs*, linked to real elite figures in a key at the end of its first volume, is that they were actually basely born, having risen into the governing class through conniving and fraud. She obsessively contrasts the virtually lost ideals of true nobility, which correspond with a capacity for loyal and selfless love, with the selfish drives of modern commercial society, which she associates not only with avarice but also with the self-interested drives of lust. This hostility to financial greed and upward mobility dominated her writing of the mid- and late 1720s, including her stage comedy *A Wife to Be Lett* and her novels *The City Jilt* and *The Mercenary Lover*.

Let us turn to one of her mostly commonly taught novels from this period, *Fantomina; or, Love in a Maze*. Scholarship on this novel has duly observed that it dramatizes "dressing across and between the classes" (W. Warner, "Elevation" 587; Kramnick 468). Scholars have nevertheless seldom expanded on this issue, even explicitly subordinating issues of social hierarchy to those of sexual performance, desire, and personal identity (Comitini 73, 77–78). Yet class is central to Haywood's drama. An unnamed "Court Beauty" (50)[2] observes the attention given to prostitutes at the theater and becomes curious. There is little at stake in her decision to dress as a prostitute herself, so long as she guards her reputation, for she cares only minimally about virtue and is financially independent. When her supposed client, Beauplaisir, begins to force himself on her, she considers revealing "her Name and Quality," which would stop him, but relents because she fears becoming "a theme for publick Ridicule" (46). Having lost her virginity, she instead tells Beauplaisir that "she was the Daughter of a Country Gentleman, who was come to Town to buy Cloaths, and that she was call'd *Fantomina*" (48). She pretends, that is, to be a member of the small gentry, a role that strangely corresponds with Haywood's probable readership, who were no doubt using this novel as a vicarious fantasy of sexual adventure. Yet for "Fantomina" the stakes are much higher than for the Court Beauty. Whereas the real lady fears only that she will be "*Forsaken*," making her the object of "Mirth or Pity," the pretended Fantomina, as the rake muses sadly, is ruined and "in the End . . . would be in Reality, the Thing she had so artfully counterfeited" (48–49). Once sated, however, he goes after the lady's second persona, a servant in Bath "with a broad Country Dialect" and "a rude unpolish'd Air" (52). "Celia," as she calls herself, is just the opposite of the Court Beauty and Fantomina, caring nothing at all for her reputation and gladly surrendering herself for "a handsome Sum of Gold" (53).

Here Haywood prepares for Samuel Richardson's virtuous corrective in *Pamela* (1740), where sexual virtue is totally separated from class and where even a servant might admirably reject the lucrative advances of a handsome gentleman. Haywood does not go so far; Celia's behavior is perfectly appropriate to her low rank. Although sexual desire remains—indeed, it is the constant between the Court Beauty, Fantomina, and Celia—its fulfillment is tied absolutely to wealth and status. As Felicity Nussbaum remarks, "Gender cannot be isolated from other regnant cultural and political values" ("Speechless" 197). The lady's subsequent disguises play off the social roles that make sex more or less constrained under various social conditions. As the Widow Bloomer she again has little to lose, for she is neither a virgin nor financially dependent, and as Incognita, who is closest to the lady herself, she fears only the loss of reputation.

Not considered in recent treatments of this story is the reading by which Haywood actually meant to satirize and punish the Court Beauty, as the author harshly did other elite figures during this period in her career. This reading demonstrates how problems of social class might complicate our consideration of gender: Haywood showed a willingness to criticize the irresponsible sexual agency of upper-rank women, as in numerous cases in *Memoirs of a Certain Island* and in the character of the Baroness de Tortillée in *The Injur'd Husband*. In *Fantomina*, the wealthy, high-born lady has played carelessly with her privilege, underlining the difference between her relative freedom and the dire lot of the world's real Fantominas, for whom loss of virginity is everything. Her final pregnancy and Beauplaisir's unwillingness to marry a liar, even with all her advantages of money and rank, leaves no recourse but the convent.

If the Court Beauty retains any sympathy with the reader, it is because she pursues only sex rather than money or social advancement. For Haywood, the latter two motives were more degraded and more "vulgar," which explains why she left much less of a margin for sympathizing with Syrena Tricksy, the antiheroine of *Anti-Pamela* (1741). As Catherine Ingrassia reminds us, Syrena has something in common with Haywood herself, the disreputable outsider who had recently opened a bookshop in Covent Garden (*Authorship* 110–16). Syrena's ardent quest for advancement among the upper ranks recalls Haywood's own search for favor in the Aaron Hill circle and for patronage from the many high-ranking figures whom she flattered in her dedications. Nevertheless, Haywood's response to Richardson's *Pamela* reinforced hostility to upwardly mobile figures from "very mean Circumstances" (*Anti-Pamela* 53) who should remain where they are, as a mantua-maker in Syrena's case, and whose strategies for advancement into the higher ranks can only be deeply nefarious. In contrast with Richardson's Mr. B., a gentleman who fails to recognize the genuine virtue of his servant girl, Haywood's Lord R— rightly detects Syrena's vulgar greed and ambition and thus uses and disposes of her. By this moment in the early 1740s, however, there are signs that Haywood was beginning to adjust her view in ways more favorable to Britain's commercial expansion. Syrena's career as a jilt is brought to an end by "near Kindred in the City, who were Men of Worth and Character" and who ship her off to harmless obscurity in Wales (225). The financial lot of these city men was then much in the air. Haywood sympathized with the parliamentary opposition that blamed Robert Walpole for failing to protect British commercial interests against the Spanish. It is no surprise, therefore, that a few years later in *The Female Spectator* Haywood portrays an "English Lady" defending "*Commerce*" as "the very Life and Soul of these Islands" (1: 145). The English Lady is debating with a Hanoverian Lady, who is presented as an authoritarian snob who describes "common people" as "an animated Clod," denying their right to speak on matters of national interest (1: 150–51).

Haywood's emerging role as a populist and advocate for commerce was not inconsistent with her at least sentimental Jacobitism, another feature of her late career. Although we cannot securely claim *A Letter from H[enry] G[oring]* as Haywood's (King, *Political Biography* 181), this pamphlet sounds like her and celebrates Charles Edward Stuart as the model aristocratic gentleman of a kind that she was sometimes able to imagine in her early work. Although Charles believes that "Avarice disgrace[s] a Throne" (13), and although he is above self-interested motives, he rescues the half-naked daughter of a merchant from a fire, gallantly resisting his naturally "amorous Complexion" (19). The capacity of the old gentry to cooperate with the upper merchant ranks, each in its best form, is also imagined in *Betsy Thoughtless*. Leah Orr has cast doubt on our ability to attribute even this famous novel to Haywood with absolute confidence ("Basis for Attribution" 347–48): formally, it is certainly very different from her other novels of this late period. It is likely, however, that the restlessly experimental Haywood had found a fictional vehicle, influenced by Richardson and Fielding, for dramatizing a much broader range of English society and for mediating between the claims of the gentry and the forces of commerce.

In this new imagined society, the old elite, and particularly the best of the gentry, remain in charge, above the forces of financial greed. This is the group represented in particular by Trueworth. "Descended from the ancient Britons," Trueworth stands as the model landed gentleman: honorable, virtuous, courteous, brave, and knowledgeable from his experience on the Grand Tour (126). But he has no prejudice against commerce, defending even the absurdly ill-mannered Captain Hysom as deserving "to be held in the greatest veneration, as the strength and opulence of the nation was owing to its commerce in foreign parts" (149). More critical of Hysom is Trueworth's rival for Betsy's hand, Mr. Staple, who, though derived from a commercial family, displays the qualities and social prejudices of a gentleman. The same gentility characterizes Mr. Goodman, an honest and good-natured merchant who divides duties as Betsy's guardian with Sir Ralph Trusty and his wife, who exemplify the most responsible elements of the titled elite. On either side of these figures, representative of England's new ruling class, are examples of the aristocracy and the commercial ranks at their worst: the luxurious and plotting Lady Mellasin; the narrow and prejudiced Alderman Saving; and Betsy's first husband, Mr. Munden, a landed gentleman whose avarice denies his wife the conveniences appropriate to her genteel condition. Thoughtless Betsy must learn not only to value the character who will make the best husband but also to make a symbolic decision on who should be leading the nation.

In finally making the right choice in Trueworth, Betsy confirms the gathering consensus of British society, as reflected by its novels of the mid and late century. Contrary to the classical Marxist vision of the triumphant bourgeoisie, political and social power remained in the hands of the aristocracy and its partners in the upper gentry who filled the House of Commons. This landed elite was also the class of Fielding's Mr. Allworthy, Richardson's Sir Charles Grandison, Frances Burney's Lord Orville and Mr. Deville, and the masculine heroes of Jane Austen's novels. Britain entered the nineteenth century as a monarchy with an entrenched landed class ruling over a thriving commercial class that rarely expected increased power above the local level. What is striking about Haywood's career is her increasing movement toward this national position, her initial bitterness about the financial corruption of the inherited ruling class mellowing toward increased acceptance of England as a nation that combined traditional political structures with commercial prosperity. In teaching the evolution of her career as a novelist, we also trace the progress of English social and political society.

NOTES

[1]See Barry 1–27; Cannadine 24–56; Corfield 101–30; and Hudson, "Literature."

[2]This essay quotes from the version of *Fantomina* in the collection Fantomina *and Other Works*.

Teaching the Theatrical Thirties: Haywood, Fielding, and Stage Conversations

Sarah Creel

In 1728 John Gay's *The Beggar's Opera* kicked off an era of theatrical profusion, a rich decade of performance that included an explosion of satirical and politicized plays and the inauguration of the successful genre of ballad opera. *The Beggar's Opera* is, of course, common in eighteenth-century survey courses, but what about the texts that adapt, build upon, and transmogrify Gay's blockbuster? This essay outlines Eliza Haywood's contributions to eighteenth-century theater and demonstrates the pedagogical possibilities inherent in pairing Henry Fielding's parodic heroic tragedy *The Tragedy of Tragedies* with Haywood's musical adaptation, *The Opera of Operas*, as a case study of the theatrical culture of the 1730s.

Haywood's theatrical success goes well beyond her contributions to the genre of the ballad opera. Some of the earliest known information about Haywood relates to her theatrical career. Records for the Smock Alley Theatre in Dublin list Haywood as an actress in Thomas Shadwell's adaptation of *Timon of Athens* in 1715. By 1721 her play *The Fair Captive*, which was a revision of a play by Captain Robert Hurst (at the request of John Rich, the prominent theater manager and director), was staged, with the fourth night held as a benefit for Haywood herself. In 1723 Haywood published *A Wife to Be Lett* and acted the part of Mrs. Graspall (the virtuous lead). She also performed in William Hatchett's *The Rival Father* in 1730 and was deeply connected to both Drury Lane and Fielding's Little Theatre during the 1730s.

Her presence within the London theater scene was also profoundly political. In 1729 her play *Frederick, Duke of Brunswick-Lunenburgh* was performed at Lincoln's Inn Fields and was meant to honor Frederick Louis, Prince of Wales and center of the opposition to Robert Walpole's ministry (Backscheider, *Selected Fiction* xxv). Soon Haywood would become part of the Haymarket Theatre circle and would solidify her position as anti-Walpole. *The Opera of Operas* was arguably her largest theatrical success, running eleven nights. Her theatrical career, however, encompassed not only acting, adapting, and writing: Haywood was also a critic. Her *Companion to the Theatre* (originally titled *The Dramatic Historiographer; or, A Key to the Play*) was reissued in at least seven editions from 1735 to 1756. Only the Licensing Act of 1737 seems to have shut down Haywood's theatrical ambitions, and, as this short history of her acting and writing career attests, these ambitions—as well as her place in the theatrical scene—were strong.

In survey classrooms, we often find ourselves reaching for Haywood's early fictions, *Love in Excess* or *Fantomina*, whose amatory conventions usually make them popular with students. However, many of the conventions of amatory fiction that intrigue students can also be found in Haywood's under-studied plays, creating an exciting teaching opportunity. A teaching module that begins with *The Beggar's Opera* and Fielding's *Tom Thumb* and then pairs Fielding's *The Tragedy of Tragedies* (a rewriting of *Tom Thumb*) and Haywood's *The Opera of Operas* (a restaging of *The Tragedy of Tragedies* as a burlesque Italian opera) offers a balanced and accessible look at canonical and noncanonical eighteenth-century drama. The pairing of *Tragedy of Tragedies* and *Opera of Operas* in particular shows how Haywood's theatrical texts can offer insight into her work during the 1730s. More important, this pairing invites students to think about the ways in which Haywood takes on theatrical trends and practices and places a distinct emphasis on women's voices.

Teaching Haywood and Fielding: A Complicated History

In order to give students a historical foothold for the pairing of *Tragedy of Tragedies* and *Opera of Operas*, we must first set out their complex history, along with the history of *Opera of Operas* itself.[1] Although it is impossible to determine when Haywood and Fielding met or to understand the exact nature of their relationship, aside from what we can glean from their later barbs and nods to each other in print, their theatrical careers overlap and intertwine in obvious ways in the 1730s and end with Fielding's invitation to Haywood to join his Great Mogul's Company in 1737. Kathryn R. King notes that their relationship was once described as mutually antagonistic, "but the hostility that unmistakably surfaces in their later work is not discernible until the forties and fifties when conflicting political alliances took them on divergent paths" (*Political Biography* 65).

Haywood and Fielding appear to have been friendly by 1730, when both were involved with the Haymarket Theatre: Haywood was playing the leading role as Briseis in Hatchett's *The Rival Father* around the same time that she was amiably satirized as the character Mrs. Novel in Fielding's play *The Author's Farce*. King argues that "Fielding's good-spirited mockery of Mrs. Novel hardly amounts to an opening salvo in a 'twenty year war,' as John Elwood has argued, nor is it something for which she would later have to 'forgive him,' as Fielding's biographers would have it" (*Political Biography* 66). Fielding's jocular attitude toward the leading amatory writer of the day suggests a friendly rivalry during the 1730s. Fielding was experimenting himself with the ballad opera form: around the same time as his successful expansion of *Tom Thumb*, he extended his musical afterpiece *The Welsh Opera* (1731) into a five-act anti-Walpole ballad opera, *The Grub-Street Opera* (1731). The latter was suppressed—printed but not staged. As late as 1737, just prior to the Licensing Act's drastic changes to London's theatrical culture, Haywood played the character of "the author's Muse" in Fielding's staging of *Eurydice Hiss'd*, the last play performed at the Haymarket that season, with a benefit night for Haywood herself. The two authors' overlapping experiments, adaptations, publications, and performances invite the teaching of the dialogue among Fielding's two plays and Haywood's revisionist take.

Teaching Intertextuality: Three Plays in Conversation

Teaching Fielding's *Tom Thumb* and *The Tragedy of Tragedies* alongside Haywood's *The Opera of Operas* provides a ripe testing ground for reconceptualizing Haywood's place as a female author during the 1730s and for understanding the themes that were important to her oeuvre. My approach uses a historical contextualization of the use of the aria in eighteenth-century English and Italian opera to add a new dimension to *Tom Thumb* and *The Tragedy of Tragedies*—one whose significance students can easily see when the plays are taught in tandem. The arias open up a space for women's voices and display their feelings and concerns with a kind of emotional realism that predates this turn in eighteenth-century novels.

Because all three plays are deeply farcical and involve such characters as tiny men, giant women, sorcerers, and hungry red cows, understanding the implication of Haywood's use of the aria as a paratextual space separate from the farcical play text is significant. Within *Opera of Operas* we can read arias as revealing and strengthening women's characters, roles, and emotions. As such, they enable students to see a central thread of Haywood's writing: a preoccupation with women's spaces and their marginalized roles in her time. Allowing students to investigate Haywood's work in theatrical contexts can expand their understanding of her career and her engagement with her culture and its demands. Of course, students may not initially feel confident in their ability to analyze musical theater (and few literature professors are musicologists as well), but the brief initial framing outlined below provides concise and specific tools that students can understand and use effectively right from the start.

The success of *Opera of Operas*, it is to be surmised, is in the songs, which are an engaging paratextual accompaniment that, as Paula R. Backscheider suggests, adds to the "actions, motives, or emotions of the characters but also universalize[s] them to implicate the audience and society" (*Selected Fiction* xxxix). The songs are integral in that they break the fourth wall and provide a new universality, accessibility, and even didacticism to Fielding's original hyperbolic play text. The arias stand outside Fielding's text and can stand alone within Haywood's. The opera's musical score provides audience accessibility and most likely contributed to the popularity of the play, following as it did the footsteps of such popular plays as *The Beggar's Opera*. But it also functions as a kind of running commentary on certain aspects of the play. Where *The Tragedy of Tragedies* is a "burlesque of Restoration heroic tragedy" (Fielding, *Plays* 508–09) that includes ridiculous characters and maintains in its faux footnotes a satirical focus on drama criticism, Haywood's arias provide a sharp elucidation of women's roles within the play.

Haywood parodies arias from eighteenth-century Italian opera: long, accompanied songs sung by solo voices. By this time in musical history, arias were "the chief means of emotional and musical articulation in theatrical, sacred, and secular music in Italy" (Westrup). While most of the dialogue of operas was relayed through recitative (quick, speechlike song), arias were meant to be delivered more slowly and with dramatic effect. As such they were often considered the emotional climax to a scene, and usually the character delivering the aria exited after singing. The formal division between recitative and arias revolves around their use of poetic form: recitatives were written in fluid and variable meter, while arias were isometric, "having all the lines of the same length and maintaining a recurrent accent pattern." Due to their isometric pattern, arias are closed pieces within the opera, "totally separated from recitatives." Additionally, "while recitatives unfold the plot through action occurring in natural and realistic time, arias express affections and contemplation in a psychological, internalized tone" (Cotticelli and Maione 78).

The variable form of the recitatives within *The Opera of Operas* stands in stark relation to the arias, which typically follow an AABB or ABAB rhyme scheme. The arias are typically written in iambic tetrameter (just as ballads are), which separates them rhythmically from the blank verse of the recitative. For students, hearing the ballad performed is enormously helpful in understanding it. Excerpts from eighteenth-century operas on *YouTube* or other streaming sites provide an engaging and easily accessible accompaniment to the module.

Of course, Haywood's arias are best understood within the context of the play itself. The Fielding and Haywood versions share a highly entertaining plot that is rambunctious and rambling enough to warrant a brief plot summary here. The main male characters include Tom Thumb the Great, King Arthur, the Ghost of Gaffer Thumb, Lord Grizzle, Merlin, and the courtiers Noodle and Doodle. The main female characters are Queen Dollalolla; Huncamunca, her daughter with King Arthur; and Glumdalca, a captive giantess queen. King Arthur is immediately smitten with Glumdalca, although he declares that he cannot tell whether the pain within his breast "proceeds from love" or is only the "wind-cholick" (*Opera* 183). Potential gas pains bloom into lust, however, and he soon pursues Glumdalca. Meanwhile Queen Dollalolla falls madly in love with Tom Thumb. King Arthur plans to give their daughter to Tom Thumb, but Princess Huncamunca is concerned about whether the tiny Tom Thumb will be able to sexually satisfy her. Noodle sums up the bedlam at court quite nicely: "All Things are so confus'd! The King's in Love, / The Queen is drunk, the Princess marry'd is" (200). In the middle of this domestic drama, a battle rages onstage between King Arthur's army and rebel soldiers. Glumdalca is injured fighting on Arthur's side ("Too well you thrust, you've run me thro' the Guts. / Oh! I'm dead, but not with joy—" [211]), as is Lord Grizzle. Tom Thumb is eaten by a red cow, and the family falls to stabbing one another for grudges old and new.

In Fielding's version this burlesque bloodbath ends the play, but Haywood adds a scene with two new characters, Sir Crit-Operatical and Modely, who—in a manner similar to that of the Beggar in *The Beggar's Opera*—drastically change the ending. Sir Crit-Operatical and Modely question why everyone would die in an Italian opera and suggest that the characters are not actually dead. Merlin then enters and raises everyone with a spell, and the red cow vomits up Tom Thumb. Shortly after the mass resurrection, Lord Grizzle proposes to Glumdalca; the Queen and King are reunited; and Tom Thumb promises that he can, in fact, sexually fulfill Huncamunca. Haywood's version of this outrageous plot is substantiated by arias that reveal the feelings and psychological states of the main characters. Unsurprisingly, students enjoy it.

There are thirty-three arias within *The Opera of Operas*. Nine are sung by female characters about women's experiences. These arias give life and voice to such feminine experiences as love (with all its jealousies and frivolities) and domestic duty (for instance, motherhood and allegiance to one's spouse). Male characters sing the other arias, and seven of these are sung about issues that directly pertain to women. The remaining seventeen forward the direction of the plot or focus on the emotions of the male characters. Queen Dollalolla is portrayed as a drunk, Princess Huncamunca is an amorous character who lusts after both Grizzle and Tom Thumb, and Glumdalca is a foreign intruder into the court whose ugliness both others her and marks her as an exotic (and therefore desirable by the King). These figures are replicas of their personalities and characters in *The Tragedy of Tragedies*, but the songs offer them a chance to expound upon this experience, to put it in their own words and perform it. Women's experiences are parodied in *The Opera of Operas* just as they are in *The Tragedy of Tragedies*, but through song we are better able to understand such issues as slavery (Glumdalca), women's rights in marriage (Huncamunca), and the perils of alcohol as escape (Dollalolla).

Queen Dollalolla is on full display in the fifth aria of the play. Haywood portrays the Queen as on the verge of a diabolical, suicidal revenge plot against her husband: "Who but a dog—who but a Dog / Wou'd use me thus? / But I will be reveng'd, or hang myself" (185). The aria that follows reasserts her drunken dangerousness and also asserts her power:

> Then tremble all, who ever weddings made,
> But tremble more, who did this match perswade
> For riding on a Cat,[2] from high I'll fall,
> And squirt down royal vengeance on you all. (185)

The Queen's vitriol is surprisingly masculinized. "Then tremble all, who ever weddings made" is a direct threat to fathers, uncles, and male family members who enforce marriages, and "But tremble more, who did this match perswade" is a direct threat to her husband, who just happens to be the King of England. The reason for these threats, interestingly enough, is lust. It seems surprising that any woman, the Queen of England especially, would consider it a woman's place to "squirt down royal vengeance on you all." The sexual overtones here are not only bawdy but also inherently masculine.

This aspect of the Queen's vengeance is interwoven with conventionally feminized softness and concern for virtue: "I love Tom Thumb, but must not tell him so; / For what's a woman when her virtue's gone?" (185). Such concern coexists uneasily with her threat to "squirt down royal vengeance" over her own kingdom if she is denied her desire. Haywood subverts normalized notions of the masculine and the feminine, and we see the Queen trying on—just as she would a petticoat—both masculinity and femininity.

The three female leads in *The Opera of Operas* are given ample opportunity through song to expand on Fielding's development of them as characters. Queen Dollalolla's and Princess Huncamunca's dialogue is frequently turned into song, giving these two characters increased stage time to make their points. Even Glumdalca delivers arias that help develop her character and shed light on her situation as both a prisoner and an othered giantess. Haywood takes themes of marital strife, finding a husband, swooning, choosing servants, and other gendered problems and turns them into arias. Thus supplementing Fielding's text, Haywood's work enters into conversation with *The Tragedy of Tragedies*. And while the songs add entertainment value to the play, they also guide audiences toward a more nuanced interpretation of the text at hand by providing a peek into the psychological lives of the female characters. In a play where a giant cow swallows Tom Thumb and multiple plotlines feature illicit (and often hilarious) lust between giants, mortals, and tiny creatures, songs that call attention to the less foolish and frolicking side of women's lives provide a fairly stark contrast to the romping burlesque of the rest of the play text. Parodying what was already a parody means ramping up the original humor of the play, but this exaggeration also checks the humor and reminds us what is at stake for the female characters.

The Queen, princess, and giantess are all able to voice concerns, desires, and responses to their respective situations through the paratext of song. In doing so *The Opera of Operas* builds on the play text of both *Tom Thumb* and *The Tragedy of Tragedies* and provides students with an intertextual experience. In guiding students in a close reading of the arias, which are easily identifiable additions to Fielding's versions, my goal is to show through this set of plays the richness of Haywood's theatrical writing and the directness with which she instigates conversation with Fielding. In *The Opera of Operas*, her power is in drawing attention to moments where she is rewriting otherwise familiar dramatic conventions and in so doing is making space for conversations about gender and sexuality. These rich moments within the text remind students of

Haywood's power as an author, particularly her ability to rewrite sexual and economic scripts.

NOTES

[1] *The Opera of Operas* is often listed as a collaboration between Haywood; her oft-presumed lover, Hatchett (the two are listed as co-librettists); and Thomas Arne and J. F. Lampe, who supplied the musical score. While Milhous and Hume supply evidence to suggest that Haywood and Hatchett were collaborators (522), I argue that Haywood was ultimately the driving force behind the lyrics of the play. The self-conscious use of amatory language in the arias and the adaptation's focus on private, feminine spaces seem clearly informed by Haywood's earlier work.

[2] Both the original 1933 edition and Backscheider use the word *cat* here, but it is likely that it should be *car*, short for *chariot* or even *cart*.

Haywood and "Amatory Fiction"

Toni Bowers

This essay offers strategies for teaching Eliza Haywood's "amatory fiction" in undergraduate survey courses. This part of Haywood's oeuvre is important in such courses, arguably even indispensable, and it tends to be accessible and enjoyable for students. But teaching it presents practical challenges that have impact on students' learning, in particular problems of categorization and problems of selection. This essay focuses on the first set of challenges, problems of categorization. It aims to help facilitate incorporation of Haywood's early work on student reading lists and to encourage instructors to think about categories that limit the ways we organize and teach undergraduate courses.

The Challenge of "Amatory Fiction" as a Category

The difficulties of including Haywood's "amatory fiction" in undergraduate teaching are especially pronounced when it comes to survey courses that fulfill fixed curricular requirements. Even within the most flexible curricula, such courses tend to start from traditionalist assumptions about literary history. Virtually all college instructors reading this essay, I suspect, have been or will at some point be asked to teach versions of "the" history of "the" novel, or surveys of eighteenth-century literature in several genres, or of eighteenth-century prose fiction, or of novel theories, or of writing by women—and so on. These are curricular places where Haywood's early work is especially valuable, but the category "amatory fiction" is problematic.

Now, of course, not all survey teaching is the same. Even when rubrics sound alike, varying degrees of autonomy and creativity are granted to instructors at different schools. Institutional missions differ; student preparation to read early fiction likewise varies. Some generic subcategories, including "amatory fiction," may seem too rarefied for inclusion on some survey syllabi. And survey courses always tend to be more races than walking tours, tasting menus rather than well-savored feasts. It may seem simply impractical to parse out fine distinctions among fictional forms.

At the same time, however, even in the most constrained curricular environments, instructors aspire to give students more than a predictable checklist of texts to be read. We want to help develop in them, as far as possible, an understanding of the past as a nuanced, heterogeneous place—or, better, places—never fully displaced in the present. Past preoccupations persist, unresolved, and past voices continue to sound. Furthermore, we want to teach students to think critically, not only about obviously interested discourses like advertising, but also about the apparently objective and merely descriptive categories they encounter in academia. The category "amatory fiction" is one of these. I want to suggest that, precisely because it is problematic, the term "amatory fiction" can be useful in survey courses, particularly when students read Haywood's work. Being encouraged to question "amatory fiction" as a category of prose fiction can help students learn to think through the affordances, limitations, and ultimate contingency of what might at first look like stable literary genre divisions.

This is not to say that learning that kind of critical thinking requires Haywood in particular. But Haywood's early fiction offers a useful, concrete starting place. Undergraduates enjoy Haywood, and they enjoy recognizing that pigeonholing her work as representative of "amatory fiction" is not primarily about Haywood but about long-standing presuppositions within critical discourse. When students learn to ask why Haywood's fiction should be seen as representative of something called "amatory fiction" in the first place, they are learning to consider larger questions about the divisions and hierarchies that drive literary history, about their own educational experiences as students, and about how they will inhabit their privileges.

By now, "amatory fiction" has become a default descriptor for Haywood's work from the 1720s. But there is nothing historically authentic about the term, which gained dominance in critical discourse only toward the end of the twentieth century. Since then it has emerged as a way to corral early-eighteenth-century prose fiction thematically preoccupied (as if uniquely so) with scenes of seduction, rape, and courtship, and presumed to be precursive to the more favored subform with which prose fiction is still often equated: nineteenth-century realism (as exemplified variously, for example, in the work of George Eliot, Charles Dickens, Gustave Flaubert, Fyodor Dostoevsky, or Honoré de Balzac). The work of three towering figures in the history of English-language prose fiction—Aphra Behn, Delarivier Manley, and Haywood—has come to epitomize "amatory fiction," even though each of these writers produced many kinds of work (including many kinds of prose fiction); their work is dissimilar in important ways; and so-called realist authors continued to pursue the themes that supposedly distinguish "amatory fiction" from the novel proper. The history of "amatory fiction," in other words, is a constructed and interested tale.

That constructedness and interestedness can usefully become a focus of our teaching. Such a focus can help us avoid suggesting that prose fiction was invented in the eighteenth century, or that "amatory fiction" was only a seventeenth- and early eighteenth-century form, or that it was the only form taken by seventeenth- and early eighteenth-century fiction. Prose fiction was then what it still is—a baggy, ill-defined category that comprises many forms and addresses many audiences. To boil down that unruly cacophony to a few types and voices, each sequentially trumping the last, may seem necessary in a survey-course context, but it is also inaccurate and misleading. Drawing student attention to the problems built into the category marker "amatory fiction" can help them perceive the costs of reductive thinking, and can help us avoid insidiously reinforcing the binary fictions that we are trying to challenge in our classrooms.

Besides its constructedness and interestedness, there are further dangers involved in teaching "amatory fiction" as a simply descriptive category and using Haywood's work to exemplify it. Categorizing Haywood's early fiction as "amatory" writing can preempt the potential emergence of new ways of approaching that work (ways not already in line with traditional teleologies). It can reinforce the notion that, unlike works by Haywood that more closely approach realism, her early fictions are not novels—even when, as was often the case, "novels" is what she called them on their title pages. When we present Haywood as a writer not just of fiction but of "amatory fiction"—something more specialized, less capacious, subordinate, inchoate, transitory—we risk suggesting to students that much of the work of one of the most powerful and recognizable writers of prose fiction between 1720 and 1750 signifies only insofar as it represents a minority tradition that died out in the natural course of (a presumptively progressive) history. In the process, we make more difficult two of our own most central tasks as teachers: to restore to literary history recognition of the influence of important voices long forgotten or denied, and to distance ourselves from our sources' prejudices.

How readers use these observations will depend on where they teach. I work at an elite institution where undergraduates tend to arrive well prepared for university study. This is a luxury placement. When I teach surveys whose questionable organizing rubrics I have inherited (Eighteenth-Century British Novels; Writing by Women), I can directly address the problematic status of "amatory fiction" under those rubrics and rely on my students to quickly perceive larger issues with the way the course itself, and the curriculum, are constructed. I think that procedure is probably realistic for those working with less well-prepared students too, since there are many ways to learn critical-thinking skills besides receiving a rarefied formal education; students from all backgrounds can think for themselves. I recognize my own privileged placement, but even so I dare to make a suggestion to colleagues working at other kinds of institutions as well as to those at institutions like my own: consider organizing survey courses so as to make the label "amatory fiction" a subject for analysis rather than an untroubled, subordinated organizing category or an invisible, omitted other to the novel. Time is always short in survey courses, no matter where one teaches, and student abilities always vary. But works by Haywood that have been categorized under the "amatory fiction" rubric tend to be short and racy (or, if long, readily excerpted) and can come as a relief to students whose academic experience of prose fiction is of long tomes. It is entirely practical to incorporate Haywood titles even if you are short on time or your students struggle with eighteenth-century diction.

How, precisely, might this work—how might instructors begin to position the category marker "amatory fiction" as an object of analysis in itself? The first step is to use the label in class while explicitly defining it as a problem rather than as a transparent marker. Doing so models an approach to literary history that does not begin by assuming a *non*-subcategory—"the novel"—against which other categories may be defined as lesser, primitive, or lacking. I am suggesting that we present "the novel" as a mirage comparable to "whiteness" in social discourse: not in fact a thing in the world except insofar as it can function as an instrument of hierarchy and exclusion. When instructors refuse to assume that there really is something called "the novel"—the overarching, stabilizing, definition-driving category that makes "amatory fiction" possible—students stand a better chance of hearing a richer cacophony of prose fictional voices without prejudgment. They begin to recognize, or to perceive more clearly, the vulnerabilities of categorizing systems that seek to make from cacophony particular versions of harmony and to call them natural and inevitable. Direct attention to "amatory fiction" as a category that hides more than it illuminates can help enrich the literary histories we construct with our students, even in survey courses. The insufficiency of the category offers a rich pedagogical opportunity. (As a bonus, problematizing "amatory fiction" as a category complicates some students' traditionalist presuppositions not only about what texts count in the history of the novel but also about who counts as an author.)

There are no perfect terms, of course, no ideally capacious and just categories. And it would be foolish to pretend that we can offer students a literary road map that takes no notice at all of the usual signposts, gives no attention to received categories and the hierarchies on which they are built. The best we can do for our students, I believe, is to acknowledge the giving of attention as a choice and a political act. We can model critical thinking that takes the limitations of our own habits of thought as its object of study. By this light, what matters is not so much whether we embrace or resist "amatory fiction" as a category through which we teach Haywood, but how responsibly and transparently we position for our students the presuppositions necessarily built into the pedagogical choices we make.

A Classroom Exercise

The goal of the exercise outlined below is for students to engage critically with published scholarship on Haywood in order to think about the genre categories and literary histories they are constructing in their own minds as participants in the survey course. The exercise can be used as a stand-alone teaching tool or paired with discussions of specific Haywood fictions, such as *Love in Excess; or, the Fatal Enquiry* and *Lasselia; or, the Self-Abandoned; a Novel*, two texts considered later in this essay in a brief case study.

The exercise begins by drawing attention to one of my own published efforts to define "amatory fiction":

> "Amatory Fiction" is a term used by literary historians and critics to refer to the popular tales of sexual intrigue that appeared in considerable

> numbers between the late seventeenth and mid-eighteenth centuries in Britain. Often written in a breathless, intimate prose and authored by women, amatory fictions made female characters the center of the action and heterosexual relations the most important of all human undertakings. Themes that would come to occupy realist novels of the future—money and inheritance, travel and self-discovery, family life and manners, political struggle, the law, war, changing historical epochs, varieties of place, ethnic and racial difference—are subordinated, in amatory fiction as in the medieval and early modern romances from which it derived, to the all-important theme of sexual desire and its discontents. Other matters are present, to be sure; inheritance issues sometimes precipitate the action, for example, people move and travel constantly, babies are born, people die, duels are fought. But such matters are hurriedly recounted, not in much detail, and function mostly to set the stage for detailed, intimate, often sexually graphic accounts of beautiful people falling in and out of love, having (or, more often, almost having) sex, deceiving, betraying, degrading, and abandoning one another. The world of amatory fiction remains familiar to this day in soap operas, mass-market "romance novels," soft-core pornography, so-called "chick lit," and melodrama—all forms of entertainment that stand in a direct line of inheritance from seventeenth- and eighteenth-century amatory fiction, as its latter-day descendants. (Bowers, "Amatory Fiction" 40)

Authoritative as something called *The Encyclopedia of British Literature* may seem to students, when they close-read this entry they are likely to discern revealing problems with its attempt at definition. Guiding (and permitting) them to recognize these problems can offer students an opportunity to think creatively, from an informed position, about how critics construct literary history. I have found that leading students through a critical response to my own work is an beneficial pedagogical move in many ways. For one thing, since my work enjoys default authority among my students, in order to approach it critically in class, students have to learn to think independently and to use respectful critical language. Furthermore, in the process of thinking critically with students about my own writing, I can try to model intellectual postures that I want my students to practice: openness to revision, alertness to one's own complicities, a commitment to be always learning. And they can learn from my mistakes.

In the course of classroom discussion of this passage, students might be invited to consider some of the implications of the definition being constructed here, considering that this literary encyclopedia is designed to serve as a reference work not only for scholars and graduate students but for the general public. Reading from the top and earmarking only the most serious issues, they might first notice the almost invisible move from "amatory fiction"—an abstract category, a totalization—to "amatory fictions," a set of individual phenomena.

This quiet slippage indicates authorial discomfort (i.e., my own discomfort) with talking about "amatory fiction" as a coherent, subgeneric category in the first place. That discomfort had no place in the writing assignment I was given, at least as I understood that assignment: to define "amatory fiction" as a subset of "the novel." So my writing implies—but merely implies—that its own project might in fact start from assumptions incommensurate with specific evidence. I now recognize that too-quiet implication as a failure of imagination on my part and an act of complicity with discursive habits that I have elsewhere explicitly disclaimed.

Students might then notice the implicit displacement to somewhere else (that is, to "realism") of the whole world beyond sex, courtship, and marriage. Implicitly more widely relevant and meaningful preoccupations are recognized as "present, to be sure" but are somehow not important to the category "amatory fiction" *as* a category. In fact, though, as students who have read Haywood will know, what we might think of as "public" themes are not merely present but vital in amatory fiction, intrinsic to it, explored and even constructed within it. Virtually every work typically pigeonholed as a work of "amatory fiction" deals with both "public" and "private" matters—and indeed suggests that those supposedly separate categories of experience manifest versions of the same habitual patterns of relation (a suggestion also made in works celebrated as "realist" and routinely opposed to those designated "amatory"). When students recognize the long-policed distinction between "amatory" and "realist" for what it is—a strategy of difference-making, hierarchizing, and containment—they understand more fully the feminist axiom that "the personal is political": that making a distinction between public and private concerns in the first place, even to argue that they are imbricated, is an ideologically interested gesture that reinforces traditional assignments of power and subordination.

Why, then, students may ask, did I imply otherwise in *The Encyclopedia of British Literature*? The problem, I think, is not that I didn't understand "amatory fiction" to be a problematic category, but that I brought to my assignment limited presuppositions about the genre in which I was writing: the reference encyclopedia. I saw my job as fulfilling a fixed set of expectations rather than thinking about those expectations directly and critically, as if both functions could not be carried out at once. So I replicated the usual hierarchical division between "public sphere" themes and "heterosexual" themes, "the novel" and "amatory fiction," even though in much of my other published writing I had argued explicitly against that procedure. It is useful for students to observe this process and the unintended consequences it produced. The ongoing march of literary history remains largely untouched in this account, although it is abundantly clear even here that replicating hierarchical, teleological categories is an inaccurate and complicit gesture.

Students may notice how this definition constructs "amatory fiction" as a distinct form with its own separate lineage ("descendants")—a matriarchal lineage essentially different from, and a priori subordinate to, mainstream, linear, patriarchal novel history. Thinking together about the shape and functions of the matriarchal inheritance line imagined here can lead to another question: what does it mean to consider bestselling, most-read works to be part of a subgenre in the first place? There is no question that the supposed subset now called "amatory fiction" was in fact a hugely popular form—perhaps the dominant form—of prose fiction for many decades in the seventeenth and eighteenth centuries. Nor can it be questioned that fiction in this vein continues to be vastly powerful, whether one measures by sales, readership, influence across media, publication rates, or, indeed, anything *except* the hierarchies of academic literary history.

Students will easily notice that works not considered "amatory" on the survey syllabus or in their other courses rely fundamentally on the features that my article tries to quarantine in that category—seduction, courtship, sex, desire. They are quick to see that to proceed as if "amatory fiction" is a less evolved and now merely historic subset of "the" novel is to argue against the evidence. When students do see this, much is to be gained by encouraging them to seize the opportunity to engage critically with specific choices that their educational program is making for them. One thing they discover is that, despite ongoing expansions to traditionalist canons of literature, their teachers continue to take it for granted that genre categories represent something real, and to imagine those canons as hierarchies. When my students critically interrogate my attempt to define "amatory fiction," they see up close precisely how this happens, and some of the reasons why it continues.

Finally, someone in class might well observe that there is no mention of students or teaching in the encyclopedia entry. This absence matters. It is another manifestation of the subterranean reinforcement of persistent structures of privilege that limits how we can help our students understand Haywood's fiction. The omission of teaching might seem, once again, to be a necessity dictated by the terms of the volume. Here is scholarship, the literary encyclopedia genre silently proclaims; teaching is something distinct and implicitly subordinate, to be considered in comparative isolation (for instance, in the Modern Language Association's *Approaches to Teaching* series). But that is precisely the kind of distinction that bedevils our profession at many levels and has led to egregious inequalities and divisions within a professoriate that might more wisely and effectively imagine itself as a unified community of agents in the world. I did not set out to reinforce the already too hard-and-fast binary between teaching and research, yet that is precisely what happened when I failed to mention teaching in an encyclopedia essay defining amatory fiction. Because I was thinking as a researcher and not as a teacher when I wrote that entry—that is to say, because I failed to resist that grounding opposition—I missed an important means of defining "amatory fiction" in something more like its full complexity: through attention to the collaborative spaces in which students and teachers pay attention to texts together.

This exercise is designed to expand students' apprehensions of Haywood's work beyond the preemptively limiting category of "amatory fiction" as that category has been traditionally defined. That challenge is necessary. But it is also necessary to honor the hard-won achievement of Haywood's current place on syllabi by continuing to circulate the body of scholarship that has done so much to illuminate her work, much of which presupposes "amatory fiction" to be a distinct and stable literary category. Moreover, it is still important, at least to some of us, to retain women's writing as *women's* writing—to insist that it matters that Haywood inhabited her time and place as a woman—while at the same time resisting the automatic subordination of the category and recognizing its interested constructedness and insufficiency. "Woman," like "amatory," is an unsatisfactory label. Recognizing the interests behind the persistence of these category labels is not merely a way of complicating the existing picture: that recognition demands a new picture altogether. Yet the past (including the recent past of literary criticism) must be permitted to speak for itself, in its own languages, even if those languages have come to seem insufficient or interested. For all these reasons, I have so far found it important to retain "amatory fiction" (and, similarly, "woman") as categories when I teach Haywood, while explicitly recognizing the limitations and altering the valences of the terms. The point is to offer students different *kinds* of strategies for understanding literary history—that elusive, nonlinear not-a-thing that we are constructing again every time we teach a survey course.

Reading Haywood to Question "Amatory Fiction": Love in Excess *and* Lasselia

We can help students think differently by asking them to carry out an exercise in scholarly critique like the one I've presented. Alternatively (or in concert), we can ask them to formulate new kinds of questions in response to particular works of prose fiction by Haywood that have been seen as epitomizing the "amatory" mode. Not all of Haywood's fiction has been said to do so, and not all of her works that are routinely considered "amatory fiction" exemplify that literary-historical category in identical ways. So I suggest that students encounter more than one instance of Haywood's "amatory" fiction. Assigning varied objects of study can help students understand and respect what may indeed be characteristic of (though not exclusively particular to) the "amatory" mode in something more like its real complexity. It can be a way of countering the suggestion, implicit on so many syllabi, that "the novel" is a capacious and always-developing category of which it is necessary to encounter a number of examples in order to have even a rudimentary understanding, but "amatory fiction" may be adequately epitomized in a single example.

But how to include more works on the already crowded syllabus? Again we encounter the pressure of the semester or quarter, the contradictory (not to say ideologically problematic and perhaps impossible) demands of the survey, the varying needs of the students actually in the room. In response, I draw attention specifically to two works by Haywood that can be taught together on a survey-course syllabus without overtipping the scale: her inaugural triumph, *Love in Excess*, and *Lasselia*. Each is short. In fact, even taken together they are shorter than any novel by Daniel Defoe, Jonathan Swift, Henry Fielding (except *Shamela*), Samuel Richardson, or Jane Austen. Each is frequently taught as a representative example of "amatory fiction," but when considered together they allow students immediately to notice instructive differences and develop more sophisticated ideas.

Love in Excess is structured as a three-act drama and includes a large cast of players and interweaving plots. Though it foregrounds heterosexual intrigue, some story lines are focused on other subjects, and sexual behavior is often not a thematic end in itself. What is more, the novel argues implicit theses with impact on the most pressing ideological and political questions of its time. *Lasselia*, by contrast, can be more readily understood as a kind of primer for "amatory fiction" as stereotypically conceived: short and focused, it tells the story of a young woman's seduction, eventual desertion, and ruin at the hands of an older, more powerful man. Yet there is much more to *Lasselia*. The players exceed mere types; often, indeed, they act against type. The plot at once follows received amatory formulae and diverges in peculiar and suggestive ways, demanding creativity and self-criticism of readers; morality is complicated, responsibility fractured, meaning multiple. In other words, even *Lasselia*, which on its surface might be considered a paradigmatic amatory text, exemplifies characteristics usually attributed to novels proper and denied to "amatory fiction."

When students compare these two Haywood fictions, they find that standard definitions of "amatory fiction," like the one set forth in *The Encyclopedia of British Literature*, fall short in a number of ways. They begin to ask what it means to assign these two very different works to a single category. And as the survey course unfolds and students are able to compare Haywood's writing with works by conventionally canonical novelists, they discover that the teleology implied in positioning "amatory fiction" as a finite historical location in the history of "the novel" is also problematic. Haywood bequeathed specific, important inheritances (e.g., themes, character types, narrative pace and voice, formal experiments) not only to marginal, purportedly feminized forms such as soap operas and "romance novels," but to works long understood by literary history to exemplify "the novel." Nor, students discover, did Haywood merely imitate a small number of female authors or bequeath a limited set of short-lived narrative strategies to so-called minor (and now largely forgotten) writers. On the contrary, Haywood's influence is everywhere apparent in the history of prose fiction writ large. Part of my goal when I teach survey courses is to make that fact clear to students, along with the possibilities it opens up.

I have offered two practical teaching strategies here: an exercise in close-reading a secondary text and a comparative pairing of primary texts. Both exercises are designed to change students' perceptions of "amatory fiction," of Haywood's position in literary history, and, as far as possible, of literary history.

They ask students to think against the grain and to talk back to authoritative voices in order to reimagine the category "amatory fiction" as something more than a protoform limited to a particular historical period: as a mode indispensable to prose fiction across voices and over centuries, right up to the present.

Why do so? The goal is not to valorize "amatory fiction" per se, nor to insist that "amatory" writing (or Haywood as a writer) is just as good as other supposedly competing forms (or voices). Those purposes ultimately align with received habits of hierarchy-making and traditional assignments of privilege and subordination. Rather, the point of these classroom strategies is to raise questions about those very ways of thinking. Students learn that there are costs involved in protecting sites of privilege, that we do so at the price of our own understanding and enjoyment and of the possibility of real, rather than token or limited, inclusion. They can begin to build for themselves concrete alternatives to received literary-historical timelines that long have depicted artists and their achievements as isolated and competitive, winners and losers, influential at one moment and superseded the next. Haywood's work is an invaluable entry on survey-course syllabi, and "amatory fiction" is as good a term as any under which our students may encounter *Love in Excess* and *Lasselia*. What matters is that we help students think in new ways about hierarchies of difference and the status of literary evidence, so that they can begin to develop more nuanced and inclusive literary histories of their own.

Teasing Out Desire: Haywood, the Novel, and the Early Women Writers Course

Cynthia Richards

The current iteration of my early women writers course carries a provocative title: Bad Girls: From Eve to Mary (Wollstonecraft). My motives in giving it this title are both practical and ideological. When I created this syllabus, which includes two of Eliza Haywood's better-known works, *Fantomina* and *Anti-Pamela*, I was in part trying to figure out how to keep alive an early modern women writers course that was dwindling in student enrollment and becoming an endangered species in the academy at large. As feminists in the academy, we had done our job too well. Women writers who had once been relegated to special courses could now be folded into standard courses in Restoration and eighteenth-century literature or thematic explorations of everything from war to romance. The temptation was to abandon the course altogether, especially when students began to view its goals as more conservative than progressive, its arrival on the academic schedule every other year making it a set fixture in the curriculum and offsetting the spirit of transgression that had once occasioned its entry into the discipline.

But what would be lost by abandoning the course? I worried that my female students still needed a focus on a female tradition that had empowered my voice in the academy, and that all my students still had a lot of talking to do before they would understand what had been lost and gained—and what remained unresolved—in this battle of the literary sexes. Moreover, that body of work, despite its emerging canonicity, remained at its inception an empowering transgression. For most of the women writers included on my syllabus, the act of taking pen to paper had sufficed to label them as "bad," and if the course no longer conveyed this charged context, we could lose much of the cultural history that framed their accomplishment.

Additionally, the forces that had marginalized their work were still operative and present in the everyday language of my students, most actively in the standard antifemale slurs that continued to circulate in their vocabularies and were rampant in social media. The course's cross-listing with women's studies made this connection even more appealing, as the course also needed to speak to students who were seeking a more sociological perspective and might be less practiced in literary analysis. Focusing on the everyday language of transgression could help them understand how the gendered politics of early modern text production could relate to its contemporary incarnation and how both related to the construction of the category of "woman."

These considerations made Haywood a perfect fit. Although the broad chronological range of this fourteen-week course, covering literature from the twelfth to the early nineteenth century, meant we read her work late in the semester, and then only sparingly, it also made her the natural apex of the course. Through her long, prolific career, Haywood teased her readers with negative examples; most consistently, she used the figure of the coquette—or, as it is more provocatively labeled on my syllabus, the tease—to nominally protest the false appearance of innocence. *Anti-Pamela*, for example, carries with it the subtitles *Feign'd Innocence Detected* and the more insistent *Mock-Modesty Display'd and Punish'd*, and at the end of both this novel and *Fantomina*, the heroines are, in effect, exiled. Yet despite this apparent castigation Haywood's core novelistic focus, as many critics have noted, is the production of desire itself and the aesthetic and affective implications of choosing to craft an image that promotes desire in others but masks one's own. The coquette, by definition perceived as masking her desire while attracting others, becomes simply a convenient figure for exploring these possibilities. By focusing on the figure of the tease, Haywood could advance a sophisticated, even prescient, theory of the novel while at the same time denuding the term of its conventional meaning. The novel, as Peter Brooks argues in *Reading for the Plot: Design and Intention in Narrative*, both "delays and beckons" to its readers to sustain their interest (59), and in *Fantomina*, Haywood uses the figure of the tease to make concrete exactly how such a new narrative craft will work. In *Anti-Pamela*, by contrast, she resists staging the heroine's story as one that "beckons" and "delays" and interrogates instead the idea of female innocence. In other words, Haywood used a common eighteenth-century image of the "bad girl" to expose the ideology underlying its popularity—the purpose I set for the course.

Students encounter Haywood's rich, metafictional examples after reviewing other images of "bad girls." The course begins with the "original bad girl," Eve, and explores her representation in a series of well-known texts. We study classic Christian interpretations of the fall and the virulent pamphlet wars that emerged in the sixteenth and seventeenth centuries, which occasioned the introduction of female voices and their surrogates into the long-standing debate about Eve's culpability. We also read selections from John Milton's *Paradise Lost*, particularly the story of Eve's creation in book 4 and the story of the fall in books 9 and 10. This context helps elucidate the exile Haywood proposes as punishment for her heroines and positions her work within a long tradition of cautionary tales. It also points to significant differences in her representation of female innocence. For example, Milton's Eve, for all her remarkable complexity, never achieves the power to name that so distinguishes Haywood's coquettish heroines. Adam names the animals before Eve is created, and Milton initially frames her innocence as so complete as to deny her self-knowledge. His Eve misrecognizes herself upon her creation when she gazes into a "clear smooth lake" (4.458–59) and must be told her identity by a disembodied and reproving "voice" (4.467). Little surprise, then, that she cannot name the serpent as Satan in book 9. By contrast, in both *Fantomina* and *Anti-Pamela*, it is largely the male characters who prove unable to recognize a woman's identity and the female characters who revel in their power to name both themselves and the images they project and encounter.

Just prior to reading Haywood's treatment of the tease, students explore an even more derogatory term commonly employed in the long eighteenth century, *whore*. But like the term *coquette*, it was one employed by female writers to criticize the restraints imposed upon their aspirations for creative independence and their ability to display their work for sale. In *The Rover*, for example, Aphra Behn equates her work with that of the courtesan Angelica Bianca by giving this character her same initials and by claiming in the play's postscript that she too will "hang out the sign of Angelica" (189). Interestingly, "hang[ing] out the sign of Angelica" means here claiming the play as her own and refuting stories that she has stolen its language from another playwright.[1] Society may fear that courtesans and female playwrights are "faking it"—manufacturing private desire—for public gain, but Behn argues in the play and postscript for creative enterprise as honest work and as evidence of her natural wit.

Within this framing, students can see that the terms *whore* and *tease* work along the same continuum: both reflect societal concerns that women are not what they seem and that they may profit from these deceptions. The whore does this overtly; the tease, covertly. Haywood's *Fantomina* begins by making this connection and by squarely casting blame on a society that enforces feigned innocence, requiring that women not say or act on what they feel. Our unnamed heroine, unable to otherwise satisfy her natural "curiosity" to know more of the men she spies at the theater, must "dress herself as near as she could in the fashion of those women who make sell of their favors" (42).[2] In other words, in order to act on her desires she must first assume the mask of the whore. The heroine's later disguises will adopt a strategic "innocence," but this initial disguise makes it easy for students to see the connection between her assuming the role of the whore and her later enactments of the tease. In both, she must fake an image to tease out male desire. Importantly, Haywood's connection further frames both terms in a positive way. The lady becomes the whore and then subsequently the tease out of an authentic desire to know and experience the world. In fact, it is only by "faking it" that she can sustain a love she at least initially views as true and can empower herself to become the woman she wants to be.

This representation of female deception contrasts sharply with that found in two poems students read just prior to *Fantomina*: Alexander Pope's *The Rape of the Lock* and Jonathan Swift's "The Lady's Dressing Room." These poems focus instead on the male voyeur's curiosity and make a lack of correspondence between a woman's public image and her true desires or bodily self a source of anxiety for the male viewer and the society he represents. Both fear the female empowerment deception can represent. Yet in neither of these poems is the female coquette granted agency over her craft. Rather, the artistry used by the woman to construct a public image takes the form of supernatural machinery in *The Rape of the Lock* or prosthetic aids in "The Lady's Dressing Room." These external forces, as these poems famously foreground, can leave the woman exposed at key moments of self-representation and unable to exert control over her image.

In *Fantomina*, the woman's ability to write a script of desire—what amounts to a staging of herself as repeatedly innocent of Beauplaisir's embraces—does not leave her exposed but rather places her in control of her narrative. Even the late-discovered pregnancy speaks more to her craft than to the lack thereof; she can disguise it until the very end. Moreover, students soon recognize that the pleasure the character takes in constructing fictions becomes at least equal to the pleasure she takes in Beauplaisir himself. They also easily observe that as the novel progresses so do her narrative skills. She becomes increasingly in control. Yet, as Haywood repeatedly makes clear, in assuming these disguises she is not "faking it": her love is for the most part real, and in that regard she never actually deceives her lover. The students can readily see what Patricia Comitini points out: "*Fantomina* distances the older pleasures of the rake . . . and produces new pleasures—that is, more enduring and transcendent pleasures linked to narratives of desire" (72). In Comitini's reading, the lady's coquettish practices—repeatedly teasing out desire—can be viewed as promoting emotional depth, while Beauplaisir's acquiescence becomes deceiving. Students come to see that Haywood deliberately evokes the image of the coquette to complicate its shallow representation of desire and to criticize the limits it places on female agency and human love.

Since students readily understand Haywood's parodic treatment of the tease as a category, class time and energy can focus on the connection between the eighteenth-century preoccupation with this figure and the rise of the novel. As many critics have noted, *Fantomina* lends itself to being read allegorically,[3] and Brooks's chapter "Narrative Desire," from *Reading for the Plot*, can serve as a key to uncovering Haywood's narrative theory (37–61). I assign this reading along with the text and ask students to imagine *Fantomina's* heroine as the author of the narrative and Beauplaisir as the reader of it, and to "conceive of the reading of plot as a form of desire that carries us forward, onward, through the text," as Brooks instructs (37). Brooks argues that it is the deferral of desire that motivates reading in the novel, and that closure in fact represents a form of death—an ending we never really want to reach. My initial instructions allow students to achieve Brooks's insight for themselves. They see how desire drives the narrative but also how its "satisfaction would also mean [its] death" (58), as Beauplaisir, our reader, loses interest once each of the relationships the lady creates for him is consummated. This critical process also explains why the heroine never gives her name and—the text's greatest mystery—why Beauplaisir never recognizes her: "If narrative keeps moving us forward," Brooks asserts, "it is because narrative metonymy can never quite speak its name," or, in other words, the reader must not recognize the substitutes that keep his interest going. More broadly, Brooks's argument elucidates why the tease can serve as an allegorical figure for narrative desire itself. To maintain the reader's interest, the narrative "is condemned to *saying* other than what it *would mean*" (56). Finally, reading

Brooks allows students to understand why *Fantomina* ends with a birth. Storytelling, Brooks maintains, proves "life-giving."

> [It] takes a desire that has gone off the rails . . . and cures it by prolonging it, precisely by narrativizing it. . . . Narrating in this allegory is seen to be life-giving in that it arouses and sustains desire, ensuring that the terminus it both delays and beckons toward will offer what we call lucid repose, desire both come to rest and set in perspective. (59)

Fantomina takes these abstract concepts and makes them concrete. Students not only come to question the stereotype of the tease but also gain perspective on the role this figure played in the birth of the novel. In Brooks's argument, delaying desire equates with sustaining desire; it becomes productive of emotional depth and renders the tease no longer a "bad girl," just a good storyteller.

Understanding this connection, however, also exposes the difficulty of writing convincing virtue in narrative form—if virtue is imagined as a one-to-one correspondence between what one says and what ones does.[4] To keep the reader reading, the writer must defer and veil desire. I encourage students to explore that difficulty utilizing excerpts from Haywood's *Anti-Pamela*. I first distribute the prefatory material and many of the opening letters of Samuel Richardson's *Pamela*, concluding with the letter containing the famous country maid scene. I remind them of Richardson's avowed purpose in writing the novel—"to inculcate the principles of virtue and religion in the minds of the youth of both sexes" (3)—and ask them what makes Pamela appear virtuous in this scene. In other words, how does Richardson stage Pamela's innocence? I also provide the parallel passages from Henry Fielding's satiric *Shamela* and ask them how Fielding stages this same scene to make Shamela's innocence appear suspect. Finally, I give them a scene from John Cleland's pornographic novel *Fanny Hill; or, Memoirs of a Woman of Pleasure*, a work loosely based on *Pamela*, and ask them how Cleland stages a scene in which Fanny dresses as a country girl to arouse the desires of a paying client. By the end of this exercise, students can typically name some differences in how these scenes are represented, but the most striking lesson is just how difficult it is to do so.

In other words, the exercise exposes how hard it is to stage innocence in narrative form. Assigning Roland Barthes's essay "Striptease" in addition to Brooks helps demonstrate why. Students note that, as in Barthes's description of the workings of striptease, Richardson "establish[es] the woman *right from the start* as an object in disguise" (84)—as a country maid. Moreover, when Pamela incrementally "shed[s]" that disguise (85)—not the clothes of the maid per se but the suspicion that she has dressed that way on purpose—it does not necessarily convince the reader of her sincerity. Rather, it makes her protestations of sincerity seem like the "nakedness" of striptease: "unreal, smooth and enclosed like a beautiful slippery object" (85). Moreover, the act of ridding Pamela of any hint of artifice reframes her as an erotic object, the desire for the true or naked self incited by the presumption of an originating disguise. Hence, students conclude that it is not that women are teases, but rather that stories of women's innocence act like a tease.

Significantly, Haywood's *Anti-Pamela* refuses to play this erotic game. Syrena, the anti-Pamela of the title, assumes many disguises in the text but remains transparent to the reader throughout. In fact, because we know Syrena is feigning innocence from the beginning, the narrative can become tedious. Nor does it have, unlike these other *Pamela* adaptations, a country maid scene. Syrena routinely dresses up to attract the attention of the male onlooker, but she never dresses down. Moreover, Haywood makes clear that even if stripped Syrena would remain in disguise, her body physically capable of acting out her feigned interests by fainting.

In other words, Mrs. Tricksy—a surrogate for the text's reader, although a pointedly self-serving one—never assumes Syrena's innocence, if by that we mean an absence of desire or personal inclination. She also, however, does not assume her guilt. Rather, Mrs. Tricksy explains to her daughter that the ability to act honestly on her desires—the power she most wants for Syrena—requires that she first understand the impression she can create on others and how those impressions will impact her own choices. "The novel critiques the concept of transparency," Rivka Swenson explains, "that Richardson claimed *Pamela* promoted" (33). I point out to my students that Haywood accomplishes this critique not by making Syrena too successful a tease—in fact, she is always found out—but rather by acknowledging how much Syrena is herself driven by human emotion. This quality makes this "bad girl" more like her male onlookers as opposed to being their treacherous other. If there is any difference Haywood expects us to notice, it is that Syrena proves more physically vulnerable than the men in the story to desire's effects.

To underscore this narrative difference, I assign as a parallel scene to *Pamela*'s country maid scene the sections where Syrena is trying to hide from her mother the extent of her affection for the lieutenant Vardine. Ostensibly, these scenes are about Syrena learning to act the coquette in order to attract the male onlooker's attention and achieve her mercenary goals. In other words, she is learning to veil her true desires in false modesty and to become an erotic object to her target. However, reading like her mother, we do not read her this way. Her mother fears that Syrena is in truth attracted to Vardine and will not effectively play her teasing role. If Syrena is staging her innocence in these scenes, she is staging it for a mother who would read that innocence as successful deceit and the hidden truth as real emotion. Innocence in her mother's parlance means being immune to emotional entanglement while remaining steadfast in a quest for material enrichment. To fool her mother, then, Syrena must pretend to be a tease when in fact she truly desires. Haywood's coquette is not, as Pope proposes, "at heart a rake" ("Epistle to a Lady" 2.216) but rather at heart only human. Vardine, by contrast, plays the role of the more successful tempter whose trickery will ultimately lead to Syrena's exile to an estate in Wales. Yet, unlike the story of Eve this ending evokes, Haywood suggests that more opportunities for self-definition may arise for her heroine. At the very minimum, Haywood has complicated the idea of the coquette and created a text where feigned innocence is detected without teasing the reader with stories of woman's true self and staging her erotic dismantling.

That is also the takeaway for the course. Reading the works of these early modern "bad girls," and especially those of Haywood, helps students understand the opportunities for self-definition that exist in complicating the terms in which female transgression is defined. They leave the course, unsurprisingly, great fans of Haywood and also persuaded of the significance of the work of early women writers, of what these "bad girls" can say about their own lives, and of the vocabularies that shape gendered narratives.

NOTES

[1] For the classic discussion of the significance of this sign, see Todd 1–12.

[2] This essay quotes from the version of *Fantomina* in the collection Fantomina *and Other Works*.

[3] Among others, see Anderson, "Performing"; Craft; Comitini; and Croskery, "Masquing Desire."

[4] See Fordyce for an influential eighteenth-century discussion of the need for young women to act as transparent representatives of virtue.

Teaching Haywood to a Diverse Student Audience: Negotiating Narrative Structure and Gender, Family, and Legal Structure

Cheryl Nixon

Eliza Haywood's short fictions from the 1720s are experimental in both form and content: at the same time that she was developing new amatory plots that offered social commentary, Haywood was testing new narrative structures to find those that would best convey the importance and immediacy of her concerns. These fictions, including titles such as *Lasselia*, *The Distress'd Orphan*, and *The City Jilt*, offer students an unparalleled opportunity to work alongside Haywood to explore the connections between form and content. When presenting these early fictions, my pedagogical goal is to help students experience how the novel's structure and subject matter evolved simultaneously. This goal is accomplished by offering hands-on primary source workshops that explore the popular print contexts of Haywood's fiction. In my most creative workshops, I encourage students to take on the role of author, trying their hand at transforming nonfiction materials into fictional plots. In my research-focused workshops, I encourage students to experience the thrill of archival research, in which one primary source leads to another, allowing them to experiment with keyword mapping and to build an archive of materials that can generate classroom displays, annotated bibliographies, and research papers. Sources available on the *Internet Archive* (archive.org) and *Eighteenth Century Collections Online* (*ECCO*) can be used to guide students to popular materials that reveal Haywood's fictions' active engagement in larger cultural debates. In addition, these materials highlight Haywood's contribution to the narrative forms she uses to shape those debates.

My students find Haywood's stories of inequality, injustice, and mistreatment compelling. They also find Haywood's depiction of the ability of the individual—often the underage woman—to overcome these challenges unexpected and inspirational. I work at the University of Massachusetts, Boston, an institution that serves an undergraduate population of more than fifty-five percent minority students, more than sixty percent first-generation college students, and great socioeconomic, age, and linguistic diversity. Across these groups, students are fascinated by Haywood's dramatic portrayals of social disempowerment, which often take the form of the outcast child, duped lover, or manipulated spouse. They are surprised that an early modern woman writer could overtly criticize forces of oppression and deception; they are often even more surprised when her characters counter those forces with intelligence, wit, craftiness, or virtue. Absorbed by Haywood's dramatic depictions of inequity, my students are often initially less interested in her development of new narrative forms. However, a focus on Haywood's social commentary and its connection to cultural debates captured in popular print can make the rise of the novel more interesting and relevant: we ask not only what Haywood is criticizing and how Haywood is criticizing but also how an author can create new ways of telling new stories in order to offer new social critiques. In engaging with Haywood's commitment to narrating empowerment, my students become interested in connecting the novel's developing capacity for cultural commentary to its developing narrative form.

This essay provides brief sketches of three workshops that connect Haywood's fiction to contemporary print. The first compares *Lasselia* (or *Fantomina* or *The Injur'd Husband*) with Judith Drake's *An Essay in Defence of the Female Sex* and the anonymous *A Farther Essay Relating to the Female-Sex*, emphasizing the narrative form of the stock character and popular print's interest in dramatizing gender roles. The second compares *The Distress'd Orphan* (or *Love in Excess*) with Daniel Defoe's *The Family Instructor*, emphasizing the narrative form of dialogue and early print's interest in defining the family, specifically the authoritative parent-child relationship. And the third compares *The City Jilt* (or *The Mercenary Lover*) with the early legal treatise *Baron and Feme: A Treatise of the Common Law Concerning Husbands and Wives*, emphasizing locating and mapping conceptual keywords in order to reconstruct definitions and dramatizations of women's legal position. These workshops reveal Haywood's investment in some of the most pressing issues of the day and her contributions to the evolving form of the novel. Students enjoy making the comparisons: mimicking the interactions between Haywood and her print culture contexts, they enact her engagement.

Workshop 1: Negotiating Sexual Empowerment and Character Types

My students are fascinated by Haywood's subversive female characters, especially those who use their sexuality to manipulate and control men. They are surprised, even shocked, by the actions of characters such as the eponymous heroine of *Fantomina*. After engaging students in a conversation about the unexpectedly sexual nature of amatory fiction, I further our discussions with a workshop on contemporary popular print that addresses the unequal position of women in society. One of the most productive sets of materials for contextualizing Haywood's empowered heroines is Drake's *An Essay in Defence of the Female Sex* and the anonymous *A Farther Essay Relating to the Female-Sex*. Connecting Haywood's fiction to these two essays allows students to develop a more complex understanding of how Haywood's presentation of sexuality subverts gender expectations, including those that emphasize a woman's intellect as a route to empowerment. Both essays present comic sketches of formulaic character types, and students can analyze Haywood's narrative structuring of the female character by uncovering her reliance on and critique of those types.

Haywood's *Lasselia*, for example, features several stereotyped figures, including the passionate mistress, the jealous wife, and the vengeful scorned woman. At the opening of the narrative, the virtuous Lasselia refuses to be ruled by passion, maintaining, for her suitors, "a cold Respect, or, at most a bare liking of their Company . . . nor did she once imagine she should ever be brought to entertain any other Notions of that uneasy Passion, than what she was at present possest of—that it was all a *Chimera*" (108–09). The story then reverses this image, as Lasselia develops an uncontrollable passion for the married Monsieur de l'Amye—a passion that seems to empower her. For example, she readily voices her love, writing in a letter, "I have your Image ever in my View—your Voice always in my Ears—so strongly does Imagination bless me, that believing you indeed are present, I stretch out my Arms to clasp the dear Illusion. . . . O! to what an elevated Height does Love, like mine, transport the Soul!" (120). She also takes her fate into her own hands, leaving the home of her friend and agreeing to be de l'Amye's mistress. However, Lasselia is ultimately discovered and betrayed by the schemes of two other characters: the jealous spouse Madame de l'Amye and the vengeful Mademoiselle Douxmourie, who earlier had been promised in marriage to and rejected by de l'Amye. Lasselia retires to a convent and replaces her passion with "Piety" (149). Students can readily analyze these depictions of the three women and discuss whether the characters are typecast and whether they are empowered or ruled by their passion for de l'Amye.

In our class workshops, students dissect our comparison texts. Drake's *Essay* provides rational arguments that women's intellects, souls, and bodies are equal to men's, but that men have the advantages of "Education, Freedom of Converse, and variety of Business and Company" (6). Due to the fear that women might prove superior, Drake says, men "began in good time to make use of Force (the Origin of Power) to compell us to a Subjection, Nature never meant . . . to train us up altogether to Ease and Ignorance" (21). The essay supports these arguments with unexpected evidence: it depicts foolish male character types that demonstrate that men are just as flawed as women. Character sketches of the Country Squire, Bully, Beau, and Coffeehouse Politician, among others, inject an element of fiction into the work's serious philosophical arguments. For example, Drake's lengthy comic description of the Beau explains, "His looks and gestures are his constant Lesson, and his Glass is the Oracle that resolves all his mighty doubts and scruples. He examines and refreshes his Complexion by it, and is more dejected at a Pimple, than if it were a Cancer" (69).

A Farther Essay emphasizes this narrative element, containing only character sketches and dispensing with an overarching philosophical argument. And, most interestingly, it re-genders the sketches, criticizing female types, such as the Coquette, Hypocrite, Opinionate, and Gamester. Like Drake's work, the sketches are satirical; for example, Opinionates

> pass from the *Topick* of *Instruction* to customs, from custom to opinion, from what is grave and serious to what is frolicksom and wanton, from

> solid matters to trifles, and in two hours space they will run over the Interest of all the *European* Princes without being privy to the affairs of one of them; exhaust an argument, without touching upon it; shock reason, by pretending to understand the Precepts of *Logick*. (31)

Each sketch is followed by a didactic essay; for example, the chapter "The Coquette" is followed by one entitled "Modesty." Students immediately see that *A Farther Essay* uses the narrative forms of Drake's *Essay* in order to radically undermine its argument for female equality; a structure used in one context to advance empowerment can be used in another to encourage subservience.

Connecting Haywood's fiction to Drake's *Essay* and *A Farther Essay* allows students to engage in a complex assessment of how Haywood both employs and criticizes stereotypes. Students could certainly write analytical papers that encourage these comparisons, but I've found that providing creative opportunities to explore these connections results in a more engaged understanding of narrative form. I ask students to take on the role of the early-eighteenth-century author and to write one text in the form of another: for example, Haywood's passionate Lasselia, jealous Madam de l'Amye, or vengeful Douxmourie could be rendered in a character sketch in the style of *A Farther Essay*; similarly, any of the sketches presented in the essays could be rewritten, as if by Haywood, into a short dramatic scene. In this workshop, students not only consider but also enact Haywood's construction of character: is she supporting or challenging character stereotypes as a narrative strategy? Is her sexually empowered woman a character type? Students also question how Haywood's use of stereotypes connects to social criticism: are her female character types advancing an argument for gender equality, as seen in Drake's *Essay*, or are they advancing an argument for women to assume virtuous social roles, as seen in *A Farther Essay*? After trying their hand at authorship, students understand more fully how Haywood is working within an early-eighteenth-century understanding of character, both relying on and complicating stereotypical characters.

Workshop 2: Negotiating Family Authority and Dialogue

When turning to Haywood's novels that feature an underage, unmarried daughter, students often remark on the extreme subservience the young woman must show to her parents and are gratified when she rebels and achieves some measure of liberty from the family. One of Haywood's most popular works, *The Distress'd Orphan*, dramatizes the rebellious daughter figure's escape from an abusive family. The wealthy Annilia is under the care of her guardian, Giraldo, who plans to marry her to his son, Horatio. She refuses, explaining, "The Love of Liberty is natural to all, and I should have more reason to regret, than be pleas'd with the large Fortune left me by my Father, if it must subject me to eternal Slavery" (45). Her guardian attempts to force her into the marriage by declaring that she is mad, locking her up in her bedroom ("to her great amazement she saw the windows with Iron-Bars grated like a Prison" [47]), and then moving her to a madhouse, where she is "disturb'd with Sounds, which struck so great a Dread into her, that nothing is more strange, than that she did not die of the Fright. . . . The rattling of Chains, the Shrieks" (50). She is ultimately triumphant, making a dramatic escape from the madhouse and marrying her beloved, Marathon.

In order to encourage students to think more clearly about structures of subservience and authority that define the family, I ask them to read Defoe's *Family Instructor*, one of the eighteenth century's most popular conduct books. Its success rested, at least in part, on its ability to convey moral lessons through short, lively dialogues in which parents and children, masters and servants, and husbands and wives discuss religion, child-rearing, and household authority. The "fathers and children" dialogues focus on parents who, after indulging their vain and superficial children's every wish, determine that they must enforce a religious household. *The Family Instructor*'s parents espouse religious virtue, while the children are immoral and insubordinate. When comparing Defoe and Haywood, students must connect opposing depictions of familial authority: when is subservience warranted? What is the correct expression of authority? Can a parent confine a child at home? When should a child rebel? Students conclude that *The Distress'd Orphan* reverses the conduct book's moral structuring of the family to imply that the disempowered child is the source of morality and the empowered parent must be reformed.

The Family Instructor has the added benefit of highlighting fiction's still-developing use of dialogue to convey emotion, advance action, and explain conceptual ideas. My students delight in comparing Haywood's melodramatic language to that of *The Family Instructor*, and I often open our workshop sessions with dramatic readings of Defoe's and Haywood's dialogue. For example, in Defoe's text, the mother exclaims, "O I have ruin'd all my Children!" to which the father replies, "*No no*, you have not ruin'd them, *it is I* have ruin'd them; for it was my Duty to have exercis'd the Authority *of a Father* . . ." (70). The mother then worries, "I do not think I shall ever be able to break my Daughter from her foolish Habits, such as . . . reading foolish Romances, singing idle Songs . . ." (71).

The dialogues capture the parents' attempt to exert authority. The mother refuses to allow her elder daughter to visit friends on the Sabbath, criticizing her "undutiful Language," to which the daughter responds, "I don't trouble my self about it," and starts to hum the "Tune of a new Playhouse Song." The mother proclaims, "Unsufferable insolence!" boxes her on the ear, and then gathers up her "Books, PLAYS, SONGS, &c" and burns them (116). The father similarly tries to keep the eldest son at home by not allowing him to use the family's coach. The son argues, "[Y]our Children will not fail to think it hard to be confin'd so . . ." (148). The father explains that he "will not bear the Title [of father] without the Authority," to which the son replies, "Liberty is a Native Right, the Brutes seek it; not a Bird will be in a Cage, if it can be free" (149). In response, the father tells him he must "submit to the Regulations and Orders which *I shall give*" (151). This causes the son to storm out, exclaiming, "*This is intollerable!* . . . I'll be content to go to the West Indies, or be a Foot Soldier, or any thing, rather than be made such a Recluse . . ." (157).

This workshop then guides students in locating additional texts that address parent-child relationships. Searching *ECCO* turns up numerous contemporary titles, including religious guides such as Robert Warren's *Practical Discourses on Various Subjects: Proper for All Families*, educational guides such as *The Common Errors in the Education of Children and Their Consequences*, and popular pamphlets documenting family disputes, such as that of the Oade family: *The Unnatural Parent*; *The Indulgent Parents, and Rebellious Children*; and *A Full Reply to a Late Pamphlet*. Although I typically assign a research paper using these materials, the class also shares its findings in more inventive ways. For example, we've created a family conduct archive in which each student locates, analyzes, and displays a self-selected conduct book as part of an in-class event. Together, a class can collect and display numerous titles in an informal collaborative exhibit. Suddenly, Haywood is embedded within a rich, multifaceted popular print context, and her presentation of family power dynamics is more compelling and complex.

Workshop 3: Negotiating Legal Disempowerment and Keywords

Haywood repeatedly examines women's disempowered legal position and dramatizes overcoming that disempowerment by outthinking the law. In order to help students contextualize Haywood's critique of women's unequal position in marriage and inheritance law, I direct them to the anonymous legal treatise *Baron and Feme*, which offers substantive explanations of the legal issues defining women and has the added benefit of showing students the often difficult writing style that characterizes early-eighteenth-century nonfiction. This dense style throws into relief the ways in which fiction makes ideas accessible to early modern readers.

In this workshop, students trace popular print's circulation of key terms, demonstrating how fiction and nonfiction create a culture of ideas. *Baron and Feme* uses vivid vocabulary to define a woman's legal position and to prescribe what a husband can and cannot do to his wife. Students select words that resonate with Haywood and, after examining the definition of those terms in the *Oxford English Dictionary*, perform searches using those words in *ECCO*. They enter the words as title, keyword, and subject terms and experiment with limiting the results by subject area and date range. In addition to selecting texts for further analysis, students keep track of their searches and create maps that present their results. Mapping the keywords employed, number of results returned, and choices made while searching reveals how students narrow broad terms or how they follow the trail of an unexpected term. For example, an early chapter in *Baron and Feme* is called "The Nature of a Feme covert." It defines "coverture" by explaining that "Law of Nature hath put [the wife] under the Obedience of her Husband, and hath submitted her Will to his," and has given her less "free-Will" and power than an underage minor or infant because he can "act for his own Advantage" and she cannot (7–8). Because they are considered "one Person in Law," the husband "cannot grant Lands and Tenements to his Wife" (8). Students are often unfamiliar with these legal ideas, and searches for "coverture" and "feme covert" produce a new understanding of the woman's legal erasure in marriage. Productive searches can also be performed using the phrases "law and nature," "free will," and "baron and feme" itself.

As a result of these searches, students quickly see that *The City Jilt* evidences Haywood's detailed understanding of the legal position of women—and her interest in depicting women who use the law in unexpected ways to exert unexpected power. The story features two women who, mistreated by the same man, seek revenge and use legal means to do so. The story opens with the lovers Glicera and Melladore about to marry. However, when it is revealed that Glicera has no fortune, Melladore seduces, impregnates, and abandons her and marries the supposedly wealthy Helena instead. Helena also proves to be without a fortune, because her mother and father were not married correctly. Melladore undertakes an expensive lawsuit to prove the mother's marriage and Helena's legitimacy. When the lawsuit fails, love turns to hate; Melladore's treatment of Helena arouses "all that was vindictive in her Nature," and she determines to run up huge debts in his name before eloping with a lover, "[taking] up, on the Credit of her Husband, not only all manner of Apparel, Jewels, Plate, rich Furniture, but also several large sums of Money" (90). Helena uses the position of the feme covert to her advantage. Glicera similarly uses her disempowered position to enact revenge. To pay off Helena's expenses, Melladore mortgages his lands to the alderman Grubgard. A vain, elderly beau, the married Grubgard aims to seduce Glicera and is completely under her power. In expectation of sexual favors, Grubgard loses the mortgage to Glicera in a game of cards. Glicera immediately calls a lawyer to make sure the mortgage is properly reassigned and witnessed. When Grubgard makes sexual advances, she mocks his age and proclaims, "[Y]ou are Betrayers all;—vile hypocrites! Who feign a Tenderness only to undo us,—the Man who truly Loves would Marry me; that is not in thy power, already art thou wedded, then what pretence hast thou to a noble Passion" (99–100). Grubgard soon dies of shame, Melladore dies while serving in the army, and Glicera is able to live a happy, independent life. After examining both the legal text and the fictional narrative, my students are asked to outline the women's revenge and explain how they use the law to their advantage.

Once students understand the concepts defined in the range of comparison texts discussed here, they have a new appreciation of Haywood's clear presentation of legal conflicts and dramatization of legal inequities, as well as the ways in which her characters turn legal concepts and social convention on their heads. Through these workshops, students come to appreciate the narrative impulses in much of Haywood's early fiction and to comprehend the way she tackles meaningful social conflicts by presenting disempowered individuals who are able to overcome forces of injustice.

Haywood and the Rise of Modern Popular Culture

Paula R. Backscheider

Eliza Haywood was one of the first major producers of modern popular culture, and she modeled and even publicized the practices and awarenesses these writers must have. By modern popular culture, I mean art that is easily available, affordable, associated with a profitable endeavor, and calculated to succeed because composed with high awareness of audience-pleasing elements. In a variety of ways, from direct to hearsay, people of every social class become familiar with it (Paulson x). In Haywood's work, both constitutive "practices and products" are obvious (Leavy and Trier-Bieniek 12). Whenever I teach a Haywood text, I always highlight the popular culture dimensions. Not only does this characteristic feel relevant to students, but it also helps raise respect for Haywood's contributions to the development of the novel and to print culture.

Most people teach one Haywood text, not Eliza Haywood, and the course itself and the specific form and content needed to complete the syllabus dictate the text. Haywood's diversity provides a delightful opportunity to teach a lot of Haywood in a lot of different ways. Her work exemplifies most of the major forms of writing and the details of the print culture of the century in the liveliest, broadest, most accessible way. I teach Haywood in courses on the eighteenth-century novel, early women writers surveys, and our major authors course, usually with some attention to another contemporary author, often Defoe or Pope. I also teach Haywood texts in various feminist theory and cultural studies courses such as The Rise of Mass Popular Culture. This essay highlights texts useful in these courses and relates Haywood's career to some of the most important practices of popular culture production.

In 1719 Haywood published the first full-length, French-style romance written in English. Rife with the French genre's characteristic violence, sex, and unrestrained human passions, and punctuated with sensational life stories of multiple characters, *Love in Excess* joined Defoe's *Robinson Crusoe* in unequivocally demonstrating the market for prose fiction. Simultaneously, romance and travel-adventure became the first categories of popular fiction. Here are some of the popular culture practices that Haywood developed.

First, Haywood recognized the kinds of prose fiction rapidly gaining popularity. She identified her second fiction, *The British Recluse*, as a secret history, a form almost as popular as the French romances. In reality, it was an isomorphic text—half French romance and half English rape-seduction courtship novel, a rapidly growing form. *The British Recluse* also demonstrates Haywood's mastery of the developing genre of the novelistic courtship story (a third contemporaneous form that developed female protagonists like Jane Barker's Galesia). In

Haywood's narrative, Cleomira and Belinda meet and, feeling a kinship, share their stories of being seduced, unbeknownst to them by the same man, Bellamy. Furthermore, Belinda has lost Worthly, her faithful fiancé who did not abandon her when she lost her fortune. Swept away by "Courtal," as Cleomira was by "Lysander," who "melted every Thought to soft Compliance" (178), Belinda confesses that "my Ingratitude for the *one* and Weakness for the *other* shocked all that was noble and generous in me" (208). In this early fiction, Haywood set the plotline of the dashing rake triumphing over the solid gentleman and provided the harsh didactic elements that would allow readers to claim novel reading as an acceptable, even instructive, activity. For example, after Cleomira becomes pregnant, "Lysander" writes her that women's "foolish Fondness" is "*before Enjoyment* charming" but afterward is "tiresome, and in time grows odious" (192), and Belinda sees "Courtal" at the theater sitting between his wife and a mistress.

Modeling and Branding: Problems and Coping Strategies

Over the next eight years, Haywood published dozens of variations on her first two prose fictions. As with successful modern popular writers like Nora Roberts or Dan Brown, stories propagated stories, continuations, and serialization. The creation of popular, perhaps even faddish, configurations of plots, characters, and style by a single author or a group of authors gave rise to accusations of redundant "formula fiction." For teachers and students, however, Haywood's texts are entrée into understanding the ways popular culture works. Theorists now recognize that small variants within apparently formulaic, repetitive texts reveal attempts to expose current problems and to model situations, outcomes, and potential remedies (Backscheider, "Story" 23–25, 31–36). Haywood modeled ways to actualize the desire to expose "what is really happening" and to influence consumers. In fiction after fiction, she replicated the courtship plotline and a repertory of situations that show the mores that prevent a woman from knowing a man and the conditions that transform a fiancée into a target of seduction or rape.

Light as Haywood's texts seem, throughout her life they offered her a way to comment on private and public matters. In lively, sometimes lurid stories, she depicted the unequal powers of the sexes and pointed to specific needs for reform within societal and legal practices and to ways individual women could avoid or recover from apparent ruin. The entire sequence of modeling shows how women might cope with the consequences of mores. Several of the women who triumph or extort revenge possess legal documents, written testimonies, or careful notes that give them power over evil men. That is as true of Althea in *The Mercenary Lover* as it is of Alinda in *The Invisible Spy*,[1] both of whom are prey but leave damning letters as evidence. Those who know, learn to navigate, and take advantage of the economic and legal terrains survive and thrive; those who do not know are doomed. In *The Invisible Spy*'s shocking rewriting of Alexander Pope's *Eloisa to Abelard*, Haywood makes Alinda a ghastly victim of her tutor, but in *The City Jilt*, Glicera, who is knowledgeable about law and the new credit economy, becomes wealthy by preying on foolish men; she bankrupts her seducer and happily moves into his mansion. In all her writing Haywood highlights the situation of women and offers dramatizations that remedy, requite, or revenge. Without having to undertake the damaging experimentation of a "Fantomina," women who read Haywood's novels will learn about seduction and to guard against trickery, desire, and gullibility.

Writers of popular culture today also understand Haywood's second innovation: she built a brand. The complimentary prefatory poems in *Secret Histories, Novels, and Poems* identify it. James Sterling writes in "To Mrs. Eliza Haywood on Her Writings": "You sit like Heav'n's bright Minister on High, / Command the throbbing Breast, and watry Eye, / . . . / Born to delight as to reform the Age." *Fantomina* is often perceived as paradigmatic. The protagonist goes to the theater curious about the discourse of liaison in the pit, a victim of the courtship ritual that restricts knowledge of a possible suitor who she wishes "wou'd abate some Part of his Reserve" (42).[2] She is trapped into the part she is playing—sex worker—and her disguises expose the situations of women that the culture perceives as sexually available or "wanting it." In truth, I shudder when the only Haywood text taught is *Fantomina*, for it is often taught badly or in a way that is not true to Haywood's commitments. In fact, *The British Recluse* is more paradigmatic, as it develops every aspect of the characters (including Bellamy) in more detail. It includes the entire popular culture modeling sequence, as the two women illustrate two responses to the seducer. Sterling identifies Haywood as "Great Arbitress of Passion," and *arbitress* is exactly the position from which she wrote throughout her career.

Once established, the brand leads to the commodification of the author, a sure means of increased commercial value. The title page of *The British Recluse* reads, "[B]y Mrs. Eliza Haywood, Author of *Love in Excess*," and after this her name appears on twenty-five out of forty-seven publications in the 1720s (Orr, "Basis for Attribution" 342). Her name now sold books and was a guide to their content, and by 1726 her work was identified by reference to *Mercenary Lover.* "The Female Spectator" became her sobriquet in the last decade of her life. The lessons and practices in her periodical of that name replicated the satisfactions readers found in the originals and spawned variants that commodified her name as well as those of the fictional members of the Female Spectator Club. "Mira," the married member, became the fictional author of the letters in *Epistles for the Ladies*, *The Wife*, and, by implication, *The Husband* (Powell, "Eliza Haywood" 167). Students enjoy Haywood's satiric city-life essays, such as the one in which a woman in a hoop skirt meets a flock of sheep on a narrow street.

Manushag N. Powell argues that Haywood composed within a culture of periodicals, but it would be equally accurate to say she did so in a culture of conduct books, another popular, vigorously selling genre. Her identity as the "Arbitress of Passion" grew in range, and many readers, upon seeing these covers displayed on booksellers' racks, would have immediately recognized the author and her combination of entertaining stories and admonitory observations.

Commodifying Celebrity

The most prestigious and profitable venue in the eighteenth century was the theater, and Haywood as actress-playwright-critic belongs in drama and major author classes. Her *Dramatic Historiographer* is the first book of dramatic criticism in English, and from beginning to end her fiction shows her comprehensive knowledge of plays. The narrator of *The Invisible Spy* is offered two magic gimmicks that were familiar devices. One is a girdle that makes the wearer invisible, such as the article Colonel Fainwell offers Periwinkle in Susanna Centlivre's lasting hit *A Bold Stroke for a Wife*. The other is an equally trendy magic tablet, the material embodiment of "pure recording" (Benedict 145). Haywood's second play, *A Wife to Be Lett*, replicated the brand of her fiction and had her name on the title page. Newspapers noted that it was by the author of *Love in Excess*. Apparently because of the illness of an actress, Haywood played the part of Mrs. Graspall, whose husband wishes to "lett" (rent) his wife to Sir Harry Beaumont, a plot echoed later in *The History of Miss Betsy Thoughtless*. Again, Haywood displays the ability to recognize and combine fashionable elements, including forced marriages, a deserted beauty in a breeches part, a May–December marriage, and servants tricking a widow eager to marry. Haywood spoke the epilogue, which claimed "the newest things best please ye" and called attention to the originality of her cuckold (80). In March 1729 at Lincoln's Inn Fields, in a blatantly political move, her play *Frederick, Duke of Brunswick-Lunenburgh* welcomed Frederick, Prince of Wales (a political faux pas, as Frederick was already seriously out of favor with his father).

Haywood's work at the Haymarket Theatre deserves a full chapter in the history of popular culture. The Haymarket was London's thriving, even mature popular culture locale, with notable "practices and products." The rowdiness and collaboration of those associated with it were multidimensional, and Haywood was highly visible among a group of notorious playwrights who knew how to use her fame. Notably, Henry Fielding cast her as the Muse and Mrs. Novel in two of his plays. In 1732 Haywood played Lady Flame, "a mad lady," alongside the playwright Samuel Johnson of Cheshire as the "mad lord" Wildfire in *The Blazing Comet*, Johnson's follow-up to his ridiculous but spectacular hit *Hurlothrumbo* (which ran thirty-two nights in its first season in 1729). Haywood was listed on the playbill as Madame deGomez, the author of the scandalous *La Belle Assemblée*. Sally O'Driscoll describes Haywood's bestselling translation as a "dizzying sequence of terrible possibilities [that] makes it clear that all kinds of sexual behaviors are thinkable" (39).

Haywood, like some popular culture writers with a sizable, established audience today, used her fame as a political activist.[3] Her career was punctuated by her ability to grasp events and genres around her: to recognize a popular genre, adapt it for new purposes and audiences, and make it more sensational and popular. Increasingly, she actuated the potential of popular culture to be a complex cultural phenomenon. In the second great burst of print propaganda during the controversies over Robert Walpole, one of the most powerful, controversial, and scheming politicians of the century, Haywood wrote *The Adventures of Eovaai, Princess of Ijaveo*, which transforms the education of a prince into an education of a princess and brings together oriental tale, romance, social satire, magic, allegory, ideological debate, and political propaganda. It is a dazzling display of orchestrated genres and serious staged debates among characters about the relations between the state and the people and the efficacy of various forms of government (Backscheider, "Shadow" 12–17). Scenes of nudity, rape, and women whipped with nettles punctuate the story of Eovaai, who is finally married to her prince within an embrace of Lockean theories of government.

Interpreting Popular Culture

Teaching Haywood as a popular culture writer often moves her work into students' comfort zone and leads to emphasizing things that are already standard parts of our teaching—for example, recognizing fashionable, appealing elements and related texts by others. In fact, it should be remembered that consumers, not authors, make a text mass art. Students in my classes like doing close readings and identifying episodes that continue to resonate today. Without prompting, they point out the degree to which the texts are enmeshed in many domains of the eighteenth century. To facilitate such discussions and trace Haywood's development of these popular culture strategies increases respect for popular culture and fosters understanding of some of the ways that work in popular culture requires recognition and analysis of complex connections among events and texts.

The practices of popular culture are visible in *Betsy Thoughtless*, which rewrites *The British Recluse* and includes isomorphic forms. In the courtship half, Betsy enters into a hilarious, but mercenary and dangerous, flirtation with a parade of satiric suitors, all highly familiar in the most popular plays on the British stage. Each parodies the stage discourse associated with his character, and Fineer and Captain Hysom are classics. Betsy herself is a Lady Betty Modish type, and when I pause after this half of the novel to teach Colley Cibber's *The Careless Husband*, students can judge Betsy through another contemporary lens and see how Haywood is contesting Cibber. Popular culture attracts large readerships when it incorporates or even gestures toward fashionable genres, characters, and plots, thereby creating devastating effects. *Betsy Thoughtless* self-consciously and wryly absorbs classics, Richardson, Fielding, and more.

Lady Trusty's patriarchal advice is drawn explicitly from Lord Halifax's *The Lady's New-Year's Gift*, a conduct book devoted to telling women how to get along with every manner of bad husband (Stuart 560). Haywood confronts head-on the idiocies and injustices of the last steps of the coercive courtship ritual. Betsy is only fifteen with no desire to marry, and yet she is pressured on all sides to choose a husband. Haywood parodies the lesson of her society, thereby exposing it.

The second half of the novel offers a major change in the subject of the novel form, which concentrated on courtship, not the experience of married women. Young Betsy is already able to parody society's lesson: "it seemed strange to her, that a young woman who had her fortune to make might not be allowed to hear all the different proposals" (127). Haywood now develops a picture of the miserable wife who tries to endure with grace and some shreds of autonomy, a major focus of novels for the last forty years of the century. Haywood's depiction of conflict over contracted economic securities and Munden's attempt to rent Betsy to a superior to advance his career victimize a new kind of character for Haywood, as Betsy's aspirations, joie de vivre, and caring personality have been carefully and winningly developed. A brilliant moment is one of the first episodes of domestic violence. When Munden hurls Betsy's pet squirrel against the chimney, he obviously would have preferred to dash his wife to pieces. Haywood exposes another loophole in the laws, as Munden is very careful not to cross the line of domestic violence that would allow Betsy to sue and receive a separate maintenance. Here Haywood invents the midlevel, market-segment "woman's novel,"[4] taken up by socially acceptable writers like Sarah Fielding and Charlotte Smith but most without her wit and parodic flair. At this point, I ask students to identify modern novels or movies in which a woman attempts to preserve some autonomy and identity in a terrible relationship. They recognize the modern ones as popular art and then can compare what they have in common.

Popular culture works are subject to a special kind of reaccentuation, and that is an important part of my teaching. Students gain new understandings of how changes in interpretations come about. For instance, nineteenth-century "lessons" are now frequently read back on the conclusion to *Fantomina*, making it a punishment. However, Haywood's contemporaries knew that young women went to nunneries to learn modern languages, dancing, and singing. Rather than seclude herself as a ruined woman, the protagonist will likely return to London metamorphosed and ready for new adventures. Haywood included another happy ending. Beauplaisir offers to support the baby, for at that time children belonged to the father; instead, the protagonist and her mother are allowed to keep the infant girl.

In response to another lucrative genre context, *Eovaai* had a second, reaccentuated life, reissued as *The Unfortunate Princess*. In this genre placement, the reissue brings to mind another of the most popular fictional forms in England, the feminist fairy tales of the Countess d'Aulnoy, who could have invented the evil magician who turns women into pigeons and monkeys. Srinivas Aravamudan emphasizes that when *Eovaai* was published, "popular fiction was still in tremendous flux" and "the so-called 'rise' of the English novel was still to occur" ("Wake" 16, 24). At least thirty-six editions of d'Aulnoy's fairy tales were published in England between 1691 and 1740, and they were an important mass culture river flowing into novels (Backscheider, *Elizabeth*).

Displaying Haywood as a Popular Culture Writer

Betsy Thoughtless and *The British Recluse* display the dazzling range of Haywood's literary skill and her part in the genesis of modern popular culture, as they incorporate the tactics, style, and plotlines of some of her plays and early fiction while integrating stunning examples of the novel to come. A variety of Haywood's texts anchor several of my regular and cultural studies courses.[5] Topics in Gender and Literature: Romance mixes canonical and popular literature. It begins with paradigms of modern mass romances in Haywood's fictions and John Dryden's *All for Love,* then takes up bestsellers from the twentieth century, such as Erich Segal's *Love Story* and the Elizabeth Taylor–Richard Burton film *Cleopatra.* Haywood is especially useful here, for her fictions illustrate the characteristics that have stigmatized the genre, which has been called "addictive opium" and "fantasy machines" and described as badly written and giving women unrealistic dreams of ideal marriages (Richetti 263). Her texts also include aspects that readers recognize as empowering, such as strong single or unmarried women and models of relationships in which the balance of power between the sexes is negotiated.

My Age of Revolution course uses Virginia Woolf's famous quotation, "Of greater importance than the Crusades . . ." (*Room* 65), to pose this question: what revolutions followed when women published? In all of these courses, Haywood amazes students with the range of subject positions she imagined for women. *The Life of Madame de Villesache*'s heroine chooses to be a bigamist, and *The Rash Resolve* offers perhaps Haywood's most moving depiction of maternal love on the birth of a child. Throughout her career, Haywood developed the narrator as witness, as in *The Injur'd Husband* with Du Lache and Mademoiselle La Motte. Somehow Haywood's tale-tellers ground themselves and readers in normalized mores but also make readers strangely sympathetic to the unsettling possibilities rolled out before them.

Many students and even teachers are trained to denigrate popular culture writers, and yet its creators must have a sophisticated, even nuanced understanding of high culture, fashionable tastes, and a moment's important events. They understand what established canonical writers don't need to: how successful techniques and stories propagate more stories, how to get readers to continue consuming related books, and how to commodify themselves. Many of them are deeply committed not only to weighing in on social and political issues but also to influencing them. Haywood is exemplary and a delight to teach from this perspective.

NOTES

[1]Alinda's story is one of the many told in *The Invisible Spy* (Kathryn R. King discusses another in her essay in this volume). Haywood's Alinda story is an adaptation of Alexander Pope's heroic epistle *Eloisa to Abelard* (1717). Haywood exposes the older tutor as a sexual predator whose young pupil leaves a manuscript that is quite different from Eloisa's abject letters. The full text of Alinda's tale is reprinted in Backscheider, *Selected Fiction* 257–85.

[2]This essay quotes from the version of *Fantomina* in the collection Fantomina *and Other Works*.

[3]King's chapter "'Her Approach to Fame': 1714–29" gives a parallel telling of Haywood's print journey to mine and includes in-depth contextualizing information (*Political Biography* 17–34).

[4]These are still contemporary categories; on the rise of the "women's novel," see Spencer, *Rise* 21–22.

[5]The syllabi for these courses—Eighteenth-Century Literature (2015), Topics in Gender and Literature: Romance (2013), and Age of Revolution (2017)—are on my Web site (www.auburn.edu/pkrb).

Professing the Ineffable: *Love in Excess*, Affect Theory, and the Matter of Romance

Stephen Ahern

The hothouse world of amatory fiction can seem an alien place to the new visitor. Students coming to *Love in Excess* for the first time find the writing oddly stylized and the narrative populated with characters who do not act in everyday ways. Haywood's best-selling first novel is a gripping read, chock-full of charged emotion, hyperbolic rhetoric, twists of plot, and a feeling of high stakes in play. Yet these qualities can seem not just alien but all a bit too much: students may find characters' thoughts, motives, and actions unrealistic, certainly compared to what they encounter in a nineteenth-century novel course. My goal is to offer some ways into Haywood's work, to help students come to understand the contexts in which this and other amatory fictions are embedded—in literary history, as inheritors of the generic conventions of romance narrative; and in the history of emotions, as texts governed by an early modern psychology that differs markedly from the picture of the self-determining individual that emerged decades later. I hope in so doing to answer a question posed by a colleague some twenty years ago, when the canon of early fiction was making room for women writers such as Haywood, Delarivier Manley, and Aphra Behn: "But what can you *do* with these texts in a course?" Repetition, recursiveness, lack of differentiation of character and even of plot—these are the very qualities that have interested me as a scholar and teacher because they are key to grasping what is at the heart (so to speak) of these tales of conflicted passion preoccupied with intense states of being that are at once profound and ineffable.

The Persistence of Romance

One of the first comments made in class when students have read *Love in Excess* often regards the female characters: that it's hard to keep them straight ("Amena, Alovisa, Anaret; Camilla, Charlotta, Ciamara: why do they all have names that start with the same letter?"). I've found this a good jumping-off point for considering the unfamiliar model of character in play, as implications ensue for gender politics, for genre, and for theory of character. Considering naming practice in this novel is a neat opportunity to model feminist analysis for undergraduate students. I ask the class what we should make of the fact that almost all female characters seem fundamentally indistinguishable or at least to represent a single pole in a good girl / bad girl binary. We track what happens to these figures, asking, Who dies; who survives? Who is banished; who thrives? Asking students to track such results helps train them to be attentive to the moral ground of the narrative—an especially complex task when we're faced with an intrusive narrator who points up the double standard to which young women are held and celebrates unbridled passion, yet asserts in the end a fairly conservative, heteronormative ideal of virtuous companionate marriage.

Attending to the generic resonances of Haywood's naming convention is something students can't do on their own, unless perhaps they have studied medieval verse or early modern prose romance in another course. Considering in class the emblematic, even allegorical, function of character in earlier iterations of romance such as *The Faerie Queene* sheds light on Haywood's deployment of character. The naming of female characters signifies the one-dimensional nature of their function in a narrative system that is more symbolic than aimed at verisimilitude. So we have Amena, born to please, and Melliora, marked out as superior to her peers—as David Oakleaf notes in his edition, the Latin root of Amena means "charming," and that of Melliora, "better" (Haywood, *Love* 41n2, 85n3). These characters inhabit a moral universe in which a woman's success, and often mere survival, depends on the strategic regulation of desire.

The predominance in *Love in Excess* of a flatness of character speaks to a model of agency radically different from post-Romantic notions of a self characterized by psychological depth. This model is remarkably in line with more recent accounts of being human that emphasize our embeddedness in networks of bodies subject to fields of force outside our psychic control. Haywood depicts bodies in the grip of intensities that run through them but are not their own. They are not self-possessed, but, rather, in the explicit terms of the text, these forces are something by which *they* are possessed. Getting a handle on what is in play here is a first step to helping students grasp bigger implications for how we should approach the literature of the eighteenth century, a time when celebration of intense feeling came to be a cultural good in most European societies and their colonies. Attunement to the insights of recent affect theory can shed light on the preoccupations of Haywood and her contemporaries, and can be an important addition to a student's literary-critical toolbox for approaching other literary texts in other courses and in other periods (for more on the broad relevance of an affect theory approach, see Ahern, *Affect Theory*).

Historicizing Haywood's Character Psychology

By reading Haywood's fiction on its own terms, students may recover the mindset of an earlier culture and thereby learn to avoid anachronistic assumptions about the contours of human agency depicted through character. A problem I've faced in teaching such texts is that there's little to draw on in the published criticism, as readings of early fiction tend to impose a model of psychology that was not available to writers at the time. Representations of the workings of the passions in amatory fictions of the 1710s and 1720s are read by critics as assembling a picture of the individuated self, as building an account of interiority that comes to full expression in the realist tradition that begins, say, with *Robinson Crusoe* in 1719, the same year *Love in Excess* appeared, or perhaps with *Pamela* in 1740, and reaches fruition with the nineteenth-century novel. It may be difficult to articulate in words the felt qualities of a grand passion—a difficulty thematized in the narratives themselves. Even so, critics have suggested, there's little doubt as to the authentic foundation of such experience and to a fullness of comprehension that exceeds discourse but is grasped by an inner self, even one "ravished"—in the terms of Haywood's amatory idiom—by the annihilation of consciousness in moments of impassioned excess. The protagonists of Haywood's novels are viewed by modern readers as possessed of the kind of stable psychic identity that is the hallmark of selfhood. So in a recent study one critic writes of the attempt by Haywood and her circle "to develop a language for the passions that clearly conveys the deepest felt emotions," those "innermost feelings" (Wilputte, *Passion* 2).

I myself have argued for this kind of reading, but now want to change tack in order to guide students to investigate such naturalized understandings of emotions from a stance of healthy skepticism. A more historically accurate way to proceed, I would argue, is to interpret the model of affective agency at work here as one not of interiority but of subjectivity, in the true sense of the word: the state of being subject to forces outside one's control. Here the most fundamental insight of recent affect theory comes in: that no embodied being is independent, but rather affects and—most significantly—is affected by other bodies, profoundly and perpetually, as a condition of being in the world. The move from self to subject here is not that of the New Historicist, not a rehearsal of Michel Foucault's determinism, but rather an attempt to escape the prison house of discourse. Affect theory offers the literary critic rich accounts of the phenomenology of felt experience that might help us better grasp what's at stake in early modern depictions of human agents under pressure from passions that rule more often than does reason.

I read Haywood's work as emphasizing what recent affect theorists posit to be the precognitive, even prepersonal, quality of affective experience, such that there is no room to assume a stable foundation for identity that precedes the buffetings of the passions. As in many amatory fictions, in *Love in Excess* a lover's charged subjectivity is irreducible to verbal characterization or rational analysis, and is as a result opaque to others and even to herself. True lovers are, however, able to communicate with each other using a vocabulary of looks, gestures, and sighs that cuts through the barriers that separate individuals from one another. This is the dream of romance, in the eighteenth century given voice by a sentimental idealism that seeks to overcome class, gender, race, even species difference. Affect theory and its fellow traveler the "new materialism" offer a powerful paradigm with which to better understand the import of scenes of affective excess in early fiction (see Ahern, "Nothing more?").

But how to introduce these admittedly complex questions and nuanced distinctions to undergraduate students in an early fiction course? It may be useful to describe my frame of reference. Like many students of eighteenth-century culture, I have long been fascinated by the preoccupation throughout the period with the psychophysiology of response, especially with how sensitive souls housed in particularly refined bodies react when subject to extreme emotional states. Many years ago now the literary theorist Northrop Frye acknowledged the centrality of this preoccupation by placing the culture of the latter half of the eighteenth century under the sign "the age of sensibility." I have argued for a broader chronological sweep for the culture of sensibility, seeing it emerge much earlier in the amatory fiction of women writers like Haywood (Ahern, *Affected Sensibilities*). My approach has been a version of what is increasingly called a "history of emotions" approach, focused on developing an understanding of how human affective agency was understood at the time. A guiding influence has been the work of cultural historians such as Thomas Dixon, who show that our modern conception of the emotions emerged much later, in the nineteenth century.

In some ways parallel to the recent emergence of approaches to the history of emotions has been the development of affect theory, less close relative than in some ways alien cousin. I've found this work compelling in its challenges to many basic assumptions, even if the theoretical complexity and entanglements of its many strains can seem at times a bewildering thicket in which to lose one's way. As a literary critic I've found to my surprise that much of what affect theorists are describing is *already there* in portrayals of character and action in early English fiction. The editors of the influential collection *The Affect Theory Reader* identify as a shared feature among theorists a drive to recognize the constant modulations of affective states and, in the process of trying to capture what cannot be captured in words, to produce "an inventory of shimmers," a more complete picture of life lived moment by moment (Gregg and Seigworth 1). Texts such as Haywood's act collectively as register of the ineffable shimmerings of embodied being, interested in representing especially those moments charged with a surplus or surfeit of affect, in which transmissions of intensities create new communities of feeling agents. Familiarizing students with recent accounts of affect equips them to approach amatory fictions open to the emancipatory possibilities implicit in the texts as well as the theory—and in the process introduces them to exciting ideas currently reshaping scholarship in the humanities and social sciences.

Feeling Is All That Matter(s)

As the title promises, feeling is everything in *Love in Excess*. There is a hierarchy of character subjectivity at work here; at the low end of the scale are those who cannot feel enough—such as the libertine Baron D'Espernay, who feigns a grand passion for his selfish ends—and those who feel too much, without any attempt at self-control—such as Alovisa, whom we regularly find "abandoned to the whirlwinds of her passion" (43). Those like Melliora and D'Elmont, who are able to feel intensely and yet try to discipline their desire, rank highly in the hierarchy, one established by a narrator who comments on the feelings and actions of those affected by the amorous intrigues that are always afoot. There may be added complexity to these subjectivities, but every character is little more than an amalgam of volatile, fleeting feelings. They are susceptible to those outside influences that enter through the inlets of the senses, especially the eyes and the ears. I ask students to consider key scenes in which characters respond impulsively to environmental stimuli and lose control in the throes of joy or distress, to note how often they are struck by a combination of cognitive confusion and physiological paralysis. When we track the terms used to characterize their response, we find a clear constellation: they are "disordered," "astonished," "amazed," "stupefied." All these words denote a loss of self-possession. This is a world in which seduction begins with a process of unconscious influence that bypasses rational reflection and is therefore not easily controlled by the will.

Even characters like Melliora and D'Elmont, who are intent on remaining true to their sense of self, have little defense against the onslaught of a passion that operates according to a self-annihilating metaphysics of "transport." Haywood's narrator explains the mechanical basis of the forces that impinge on the desiring subject: "Honour, and virtue may distance bodies, but there is no power in either of those names, to stop the spring that with a rapid whirl transports us from our selves, and darts our souls into the bosom of the darling object" (122). Melliora and D'Elmont are able to reassert some control, to govern errant affect through sheer force of will. (Though more often fate intervenes to prevent them from giving in to desire, as when a well-timed knock at Melliora's bedroom door prevents them from consummating their lust.) The picture presented here is of intensities coursing through bodies, of contagious affect generating "dis-ease" as often as pleasure, with finally little room for lasting self-governance, even if the narrative trajectory is marked by a certain conservative moral drift, as unthinking libertine turns domesticated man of feeling.

To make sense for students of this picture of what we might call *un*-agency, I suggest it's important to realize that this psychology derives from a romance convention whereby terms of magic are invoked to portray the workings of love. The presence of the beloved is figured as a threat to the integrity of the self; lovers are bewitched, possessed by the other, lose all agency in the moment of erotic connection. So, for example, struggling to discipline her desire for D'Elmont, Melliora exclaims, "I can no longer withstand the too powerful Magick of your Eyes, nor deny any Thing that charming Tongue can ask" (123). More broadly, it is crucial to realize that Haywood wrote at a time when a notion of "the passions," rather than of "emotions," was still dominant in the understanding of what it means to be human (see Dixon). This understanding entailed in the first instance a conception of being acted upon, rather than operating actively, when it comes to the drivers of motive and behavior. In amatory fictions as well as in the sentimental novels that follow, much attention is focused on the suffering of virtuous bodies—suffering not as a primarily solitary experience but as an intersubjective one founded in an interplay of forces acting on ungoverned bodies. A key scene to consider in class comes early on, after Melliora's father has died. As she tries to speak while racked by grief, Melliora's power to charm exerts a physical influence: "a flood of tears, here interposed, and hindred her from proceeding, which falling from such lovely eyes, had a magnetick influence to draw the same from every beholder" (88). The world of Haywood's fiction is ruled not by self-determining individuals but by a model of attraction and repulsion derived from Lucretius and Thomas Hobbes. We might call this the "old materialism," a worldview that arguably undergirds the "new materialism" that has recently emerged to counter dualistic thinking in a postmodern, even posthuman, dispensation.

In Haywood's fiction, scenes of impassioned ardor spur circulations of energies across and through bodies. The transmission of affect—to invoke Teresa Brennan's influential formulation—happens without warning or intent, as characters are drawn involuntarily to one another. This is the model of "unfelt affect" that James Noggle has shown pervades all forms of writing in the eighteenth century, a model revealed in the prevalence throughout the period of adverbs such as "insensibly" and "imperceptibly" (125). The challenge for the teacher comes in trying to articulate the contours of a phenomenon that is—because rooted in the body—by definition prelinguistic and whose intensities exceed attempts to capture them in words. I've found it effective in class to point out that it's not that I am reading too much into the text, but that Haywood's narrator herself repeatedly highlights this difficulty of expression. We look at examples in key scenes, as when we are told that "[i]t is impossible to represent the agony's which filled the heart of D'Elmont," or that "[i]t would be endless for me to endeavour to represent poor Charlotta's affliction" (87, 252).

Such moments of narratorial intrusion are wonderful for throwing into relief the process of composition and, in so doing, shaking up the naturalized experience of narrative consumption common to many undergraduate readers. The result is a healthy, if bracing, distancing, a making-strange for the reader pulled into the subjective disorientation of the world of Haywood's characters.

Professing the ineffable effects of affect is challenging, doubly so for readers of literary texts when all we have to go on are representations of bodies in motion. Yet asking students to think in these ways is productive because it gives them tools for formulating a more accurate account of what's on the page, and because attending to affected bodies through the lens of recent theory offers a strange yet compelling model, one that can seem overdone but that just may be closer to the truth of being in the world. Affect theory offers hope that we might move beyond a history of possessive individualism to acknowledge the contingency of identity and so be open to assembling new communities. Early fiction, with its insistence that we are permeable and interconnected and forget this at our peril, still has lessons to teach about the importance of respect for the other as well as for the self.

Teaching beyond the Heteronormative: *Fantomina* and Queering Haywood

Catherine Ingrassia

As Patrick Spedding's essay in this volume documents, for previous generations of teachers, Eliza Haywood's prose fiction could be accessed only through microfilm, a Garland facsimile edition, or a visit to an archive. Teaching *Fantomina* was not really an option, except for those creating photocopied course packets, a gesture that materially underscored the still-provisional place of Haywood in the canon. *Fantomina*'s current presence in commercial anthologies, however, marks the discipline's recognition of Haywood's significance within eighteenth-century literature and culture.[1] Yet such volumes, by the very nature of their genre, situate *Fantomina* within a predetermined context and inevitably assign potentially ossifying descriptors with an often-familiar critical shorthand. Like much scholarship on Haywood, most anthologies locate *Fantomina* within a tradition of amatory fiction, describing Haywood as a commercially successful writer who, while challenging the cultural limitations women endure, ultimately does not stray from the heteronormative assumptions of her historical moment. That is, they assume heterosexuality, normalize a strict gender binary, and affirm patriarchal cultural structures. *Fantomina*'s presence and placement within these anthologies obscures the queer elements of the text: those moments that destabilize gender performance, undermine male dominance, and allude to nonnormative intimacies. In *The Norton Anthology of English Literature*, for example, nestled between Alexander Pope's *The Rape of the Lock* and Lady Mary Wortley Montagu's "Epistle from Mrs. Yonge to Her Husband"—poems that each in their own way testify to the power of heteronormativity—*Fantomina* is necessarily infected by those contemporaneous texts. How can instructors help students who have read Pope's question in the opening lines of *The Rape of the Lock*—"Oh say what stranger Cause, yet unexplor'd, / Cou'd make a gentle Belle reject a Lord?" (2513)—avoid reading *Fantomina* only as a text compliant with those dominant cultural norms?

The deeply ingrained habits of thought and the familiar modes of reading that have shaped Haywood criticism include reading with a culturally defined, heteronormative lens. As scholars like Susan Lanser remind us, readers "immured in heteronormative paradigms" (e.g., many students) can find it challenging to "identify queer eighteenth-century formations," especially when they have "little or nothing . . . to do with queer sex." This situation provides a rich opportunity, then, to urge students to scrutinize "seemingly normative" and familiar "systems and spaces" in order to uncover "subtler formations" that have previously remained hidden (277). What happens when we ask students to read a text that apparently conforms to the conventional patterns as though it instead defies the heteronormative cultural narrative? Can a gesture of reading that asks students to "scrutinize what passes for the heteronormative" reveal moments in a text like *Fantomina* that show how the work "already carr[ies] the seeds of its own resistance or critique" (283)? *Fantomina* offers particularly rich possibilities for exploring how a modified reading practice might reveal the degree to which the nonnormative "operates in the very midst of ordinary heteronormative systems, 'queering' aspects or pockets of the mainstream" (277). Urging students to resist the traditional, perhaps more immediately accessible, reading of Haywood's text not only provides them with the opportunity to expand their understanding of eighteenth-century forms of intimacy and gender formation but—equally important—teaches them to resist a text's dominant reading in order to extract more nuanced interpretations. Facilitating such a reading enables students to recognize the experimental nature of Haywood's early writing and, arguably, instills a practice of resistant reading that will serve them well regardless of the text. At first glance such an approach might seem most appropriate for English majors or advanced students. However, reading against the dominant (and familiar) interpretation of a text, interrogating the assumptions of that interpretation, and realizing that one text can yield multiple, complex readings remind students at every level of the rich play of language, the ambiguity of literary texts, and the need to be mindful of the preconceptions with which they may read.

Teaching *Fantomina* this way does not suggest teaching a "queer" Haywood who explores same-sex physical intimacy. Rather, it suggests that pursuing the disruptive, nonnormative moments in *Fantomina*, and in turn shedding the heteronormative lens with which most students read, allows the text to emerge anew: it invites students to consider the complexities of Haywood's writings. Ultimately, to read *Fantomina* as a text that exists solely within and ultimately conforms to a heteronormative context limits the opportunities for understanding Haywood's complicated work, diminishing the skill and insights accorded to her as an author.

What strategies can instructors use to help students arrive at a resistant or at least more challenging reading of *Fantomina*? When teaching Haywood from a commercial anthology, particularly in an introductory course, it can be useful to spend some time unpacking the assumptions brought to (or perpetuated by) the headnote and editorial framing of the text in a shorter version of the sort of exercise proposed by Toni Bowers in this volume. Instructors may find it productive both to analyze the headnote from the volume used in class and to bring in examples of headnotes from other anthologies. For example, the *Norton Anthology* uses language that hews to the stereotypical reading of Haywood: it characterizes her first novel as "racy," perpetuates the unsubstantiated story of her "two illegitimate children," and describes the character of Betsy Thoughtless as "an indiscreet charmer" (Greenblatt et al., "Eliza Haywood" 2739). Further situating *Fantomina* within a heteronormative world, the headnote describes the title character as a "player" and love as "an irresistible impulse" and "a risky exciting game." In stark contrast, Blackwell's anthology *British Literature* offers a far more sophisticated setup, observing that "in some of these works Haywood explores the possibility of more lasting relations between women" (DeMaria 786). By considering the implications and connotations of the ostensibly objective editorial commentary, students learn that editing is a form of interpretation: a useful consideration in any discipline. This comparative exercise also reminds students of the constructed nature of literary history and the degree to which that history is shaped by gender. The ambitious instructor can also ask students to read the entry on Haywood from the 1885–90 *Dictionary of National Biography* (see Lee), which will provide an opportunity for meaningful comparison.

At this point, students tempted to take advantage of the abundant online commercial resources related to *Fantomina* might be reminded that such sites perpetuate a similarly heteronormative reading (at a particularly superficial level). For example, *GradeSaver*'s extensive material on *Fantomina* unreflectively reads the characters and plot solely within the prescriptive gender norms of the period, suggesting that the female subject's actions spring from a "love" that is "both constant and sincere" ("*Fantomina* Themes"), effectively providing the same kind of unsupported moralistic justification one might expect from an uncritical reader. At this point, regardless of the level of the class, instructors can usefully share the eighteenth-century title page to *Fantomina* for a discussion of how that too positions the eighteenth- or twenty-first-century reader.

After considering how the text is editorially situated, students might be divided into two groups: one that is instructed to read the text as unquestionably heteronormative and one instructed to read it as resistant, subversive, or disruptive. (Simply urging students to read from both perspectives simultaneously can have the same effect, although prompting students to have an intellectual investment in the perspective assigned by the instructor can facilitate more engaged classroom discussion.) This essay will not rehearse the numerous heteronormative readings of the narrative in which the unnamed fictional female subject we call "Fantomina"[2] seeks to seduce the same man, Beauplaisir, on different occasions and under different aliases. The rich body of scholarship on *Fantomina* cited elsewhere in this volume offers ample resources for that familiar and important line of thinking. The novel remains a narrative cipher onto which scholars project interpretations in which the plot serves as a metaphor for Haywood's navigation of the literary marketplace, an exploration of disguise, or a critique of contemporary models of sexuality. These readings exist within (and perhaps because of) a hyper-heteronormative paradigm, and the students reading within the traditional structure will have little difficulty locating supporting material at the text's pivotal moments.

But what will the students reading against the heteronormative find, and how does an instructor help them locate those moments within the text? Looking closely at the first sentences of *Fantomina*, students will see that it begins with the heroine's focus on the women around her: the "great Number of celebrated Toasts" and the "Woman who sat in a Corner of the Pit, and by her Air and Manner . . . might easily be known to be one of those who come there for no other Purpose, than to create Acquaintance with as many as seem desirous of it" (41).[3] Fantomina reacts quite negatively to the "several Gentlemen" who "extremely pleased themselves with entertaining" that woman: she "could not help testifying her Contempt of the Men, who, regardless of either the Play, or Circle, threw away their Time in such a Manner." Her contempt is matched by her own preoccupation with the woman, and her wonder "excited a Curiosity in her to know in what Manner these Creatures were addressed." Her imitative behavior—dressing herself "as near as she cou'd in the Fashion of those Women who make sale of their Favours" and "practising as much as she had observ'd . . . the Behaviour of that Woman" (42)—is driven by her desire to align herself with this observed female community. She seeks "the Gratification of an innocent Curiosity." While certainly her attraction to the "accomplish'd Beauplaisir" fuels Fantomina's actions, that fascination does not mitigate or diminish her abiding focus upon and identification with the woman she initially spies in the theater.

At this point, students' attention should be directed to the initial sexual encounter with Beauplaisir, considering both the pressing question of Fantomina's agency and the moments of divergence from a heteronormative pattern. Their "unrestrain'd" verbal exchange leads to a "Difficulty, which before never enter'd" her head—his desire to consummate the relationship (43). Certainly that failure of imagination stems in part from her own naïveté and sexual inexperience; she has not fully considered the expectations her actions demand within an oppressively patriarchal culture. Yet the "Difficulty" also bespeaks the degree to which her motivations do not lie along a heteronormative paradigm. The varied emotions she experiences do not fit within any recognized or established cultural narrative: her whimsies are "Strange and unaccountable," her desires "wild and incoherent," her resolutions "unfix'd and undetermin'd" (44). At this point instructors should have students look up these key terms in the *Oxford English Dictionary*, if available, or in an online edition of Samuel Johnson's *A Dictionary of the English Language* (available on open-source sites such as the *Internet Archive* [archive.org] or *HathiTrust* [hathitrust.org]). Beyond the obvious benefit of introducing students to a useful research tool and reminding them of the historically contingent meaning of language, asking them to delve into words such as *strange* (*OED*: "Abnormal; unfamiliar; queer") or *unaccountable* (Johnson: "not explicable," "not controlled"; *OED*: "of a strange or puzzling disposition") establishes the fundamentally unstable, unnarratable quality of Fantomina's emotions and underscores their stark departure from the established cultural norms.

After the sexual act is completed (an act fraught with a complex dynamic of power, resistance, and vulnerability), Beauplaisir is "both surpris'd and troubled at the Mystery" of Fantomina's response. Her reaction—"Her Tears . . . and the Distraction she appeared in" (46)—confounds his expectations: "He could not imagine for what Reason a Woman . . . had counterfeited the Part . . . and taken so much Pains to engage him," only to now "lament a Consequence which she could not but expect" (46–47). Fantomina's fundamental illegibility goes a long way toward highlighting her subversive, disruptive quality. She defies the cultural narrative and remains inscrutable. Beauplaisir's immediate response to her postcoital distress falls within patriarchally normed behavior: offering her financial compensation. That gesture "made her quite forget the Part she had assum'd" (47), and she lashes out verbally. "The amazed Beauplaisir heard without being able to reply" his expectations defied at every turn. Her capacity to render him speechless, to silence him, goes to the heart of her strategy to "queer" his world. Her defiant behavior even diminishes the sexual pleasure that initially motivates him: as it "heighten'd his Wonder, so it abated his Satisfaction" (46). She recognizes "the Consternation he was in" (47). Students might profitably explore *consternation* in the *OED* ("Amazement and terror such as to prostrate one's faculties") or Johnson's *Dictionary* ("Astonishment; alienation of mind by a surprise") to understand the degree to which Fantomina's strategy includes disordering Beauplaisir's mind. The personas of Celia and Widow Bloomer similarly destabilize the signifiers of class and gender performance, further obscuring Beauplaisir's interpretative capacity. By the time Fantomina assumes her fourth and final iteration as Incognita, she exists completely outside the realm of Beauplaisir's comprehension. "Not imagining this *Incognita* varied so much from the Generality of her Sex" (64), Beauplaisir is confounded by her hidden identity. He expresses "all Perplexity imaginable" (66), and ultimately resentment, at her refusal to reveal "her Face and Circumstances" (67). His "Perplexity" (*OED*: "mental perturbation or anxiety"; Johnson: "Distraction of mind") again reminds students of the psychological manipulation in which Fantomina engages.

Because she "had the Power of putting on almost what Face she pleas'd" (57), Fantomina deviates from the normative performance of gender (varies from "the Generality of her Sex" [64]); challenging the structural hierarchies and destabilizing the sexual and cultural practices foundational to heteronormativity are themselves forms of queerness. She knew "exactly how to form her Behaviour to the Character she represented. . . . She could vary her Glances, tune her Voice to Accents the most different imaginable from those in which she spoke when she appear'd herself" (57). She is physically unreadable. More important, she is culturally unreadable, in part because she resists any real emotional investment in Beauplaisir: "Knowledge of his Inconstancy and Levity of Nature kept her from having that real Tenderness for him she would have else have had" (59). Rather, "She made herself, most certainly, extremely happy in the Reflection on the Success of her Stratagems" (57); her satisfaction exists in the intellectual, not the physical, realm. This reaction is, perhaps, the logical extension of the "Contempt" she expresses in the first lines of the novel. Operating largely as an unattached woman outside the moral and economic confines of eighteenth-century patriarchal culture, Fantomina not only transgresses but actively disrupts the status quo.

Although Fantomina's body ultimately betrays her when she can no longer conceal her pregnancy, the real subversion of Haywood's text lies in the fate of

Beauplaisir and the epistemological distress in which Fantomina strategically leaves him. When in the throes of labor she names Beauplaisir as the father of her child, her mother summons him, and he is "prodigiously surpris'd" to learn her identity: "All the Idea one can form of wild Astonishment, was mean to what he felt" (69). He is thrown into a "profound Resvery [Reverie]" (70). Again, the language describing Beauplaisir's psychological state merits student use of the *OED* or Johnson's *Dictionary*. Words such as *perplexity*, *astonishment*, and *reverie* warrant discussion.

Most profound, however, is the final description of Beauplaisir: "he took his Leave, full of Cogitations, more confus'd than ever he had known in his whole Life" (71). Students will learn that the word *confused*, with its specific associations with disorder, reveals Fantomina's successful disruption of Beauplaisir's worldview. That confusion, more "than ever he had known in his whole Life," potentially compromises his ability to reintegrate into the heteronormative culture in which he previously circulated. Beauplaisir's experience with Fantomina explodes his naturalized attitude about male dominance within a patriarchal culture, his assumptions about stable markers of gender performance, and his confidence in the masculinity foundational to heteronormativity. Fantomina, by introducing a new uncertainty, undermines Beauplaisir's ability to have any subsequent stable relationships with women. In this way, Beauplaisir anticipates Strephon of Jonathan Swift's "The Lady's Dressing Room," another epistemologically altered male, who, shaken by his experience with Celia, "conceives a lady standing by" every time he encounters an "unsavory odor." Similarly, Beauplaisir emerges damaged by his experience with Fantomina, unable, one presumes, to ever believe that any woman with whom he interacts is not perhaps again Fantomina, one whom he has already known sexually. He must now circulate essentially outside the heteronormative framework, stripped of the confidence with which he previously acted. The word *cogitation* pointedly suggests that complicated situation. While *cogitation* describes the process of consideration, reflection, or meditation after an event or action, significantly it also speaks to "reflection *previous* to action" (*OED*, emphasis mine). Considering the term in a global sense, Beauplaisir's "cogitations," his reflections previous to subsequent sexual action, must inevitably shape any encounter he has with another woman. He can no longer trust his perceptions or understanding of his own experiences.

Fantomina herself retires to "a Monastery in France," the abbess of which was once a "particular Friend" of her mother's (71). That relocation codes Fantomina's complete removal from a heteronormative space that she has, in some small measure, made potentially uninhabitable for at least one man. It is a strategic move to a feminocentric community, which, Valerie Traub reminds us, may be one of "independence and intimacy" as well as potentially "a site for erotic contact" (62). Although some students may want to suggest that Fantomina's destination summons the slang associations of *nunnery* with *brothel* found in Shakespeare, Haywood's use of the term "monastery" seems designed to forestall that association. Indeed, as Margaret Case Croskery reminds us, such "banishment to convent or monastery" neither guarantees "moral transformation" nor ends the opportunities for "erotic pleasure." Thus, "the story's ending suggests not a conclusion, but a sequel" ("Masquing Desire" 92). Despite its seemingly excessive heteronormative perspective, the text in fact disrupts those expectations, rendering them so strange as to seem unfamiliar (queering them, if you will).

Throughout her oeuvre, Haywood's texts expose and resist heteronormative structures. Fictional female subjects find escape routes or alternative endings that enable them to exist (if sometimes only temporarily) outside the cultural consolidation of gender. Multiple texts tease out the limitations of the heteronormative world as Haywood imagines alternative emotional intimacies. Haywood's texts of the 1720s offer particularly rich territory for such an examination, for they present a diverse, experimental, and prolific range of publications (see Ingrassia, "'Queering'"), but students need not be aware of this pattern throughout Haywood's work to see how it might function in this particular text. At any level and at any institution, offering students the intellectual and research tools to challenge the dominant, widely accepted reading of *Fantomina* helps them question the assumptions with which they read any text (and perhaps the unexamined editorial premises of the volumes from which they read). That kind of reflective reading not only enriches their reading of *Fantomina* but also positions them to be more insightful readers of eighteenth-century women's writing overall.

NOTES

[1] Norton introduced *Fantomina* in its eighth edition in 2006, Longman in its fourth in 2009, Broadview in its first in 2006, and Blackwell in its first in 1996.

[2] For ease of reading, *Fantomina*'s unnamed protagonist will be referred to as "Fantomina" throughout.

[3] This essay quotes from the version of *Fantomina* in the collection Fantomina *and Other Works*.

Performativity and the Rack of Nature: Identity in *Fantomina* and *The Masqueraders*

Kim Simpson

In *Against Transgression*, Ashley Tauchert suggests that the search for transgression in eighteenth-century women's writing has become a mainstream critical move that "poisons our critical sensibilities" (2). Students encountering Eliza Haywood's *Fantomina* for the first time are invariably drawn to discussions about the unnamed heroine's gender transgression and the extent to which she possesses agency through masquerade. This approach can open up a space in which to explore Haywood's treatment of desire, power, and sexuality. But discussion of transgression in *Fantomina* can also get mired in polarized readings that are overly celebratory or pessimistic or that generalize about gender prescriptions in the period. I would argue that some of the most interesting insights that students might glean from *Fantomina* fall outside the radical or reactionary framework through which the text is often read and concern the text's treatment of identity. These insights can be augmented by reading *Fantomina* (published in August 1725) alongside another of her less studied and only slightly longer masquerade texts, written during the same period: *The Masqueraders* (published in two parts, in April 1724 and January 1725).

The classroom approach I propose here is attentive to what Catherine Craft-Fairchild has called the "unrelenting circularity" of Haywood's early fiction (59); it interrogates the repetitions integral to the plots of both texts and the ways in which they are interrupted or punctuated by pregnant bodies. My approach brings awareness to the ways in which these two texts use masquerade and pregnancy to engage with different modes of identity formation—what we now think of as discursive-performative and materialist modes. In this context, students are able to examine the ways in which text, clothing, disguise, and the body come into conflict in Haywood's works, which also become training texts in which students can test out new theoretical tools and approaches from queer and feminist theories.

Course and Unit Design

In its current iteration, this unit is designed to be taught to upper-level undergraduates as part of a twelve-week course called The Enlightenment Body, which aims to introduce students to intellectual, cultural, and literary debates relating to the body in the long eighteenth century. Students read novels, poetry, medical treatises, periodicals, and pornography and are introduced to concepts including dualist and monist theories of mind and matter, atomism, empiricism, sensibility, and the humoral system. They are encouraged to consider how these concepts have translated into modern understandings of bodies and identities, and this is often a fruitful means of allowing students to engage with texts that are historically situated as they work through ideas that continue to interest theorists today. Reading Haywood's masquerade fiction enables students to consider the gaps and tensions between performance, performativity, and materiality, and the aim of the unit is to establish a more critically informed distinction between the discursive body and the material body in eighteenth-century culture and the narratives that represent it.

This unit, which I suggest running over two weeks (six hours), begins with a lecture to introduce students to amatory fiction as a genre and to demonstrate how, in its concerns with surface appearances and bodily readability, amatory fiction draws on both the stylized artifice of the Restoration court and emerging discourses of sensibility. The lecture also introduces quotations and ideas that form the basis for seminar activities from the theorists Judith Butler, Elizabeth Grosz, and Vicki Kirby. These three theorists provide tools for thinking through amatory fiction's treatment of the mind-body question and allow a naturally scaffolded approach to Haywood's masquerade fiction. Butler's notion of performativity forms the first stage, enabling students to read identity as constructed through discourse in the texts. Grosz's attention to the corporeal then allows students to locate potential limitations in Butler's argument. Kirby's more challenging ideas about the relation between nature and culture push advanced or specialist students further still. Quotations introduced and unpacked in the lecture are repeated on the worksheets (see appendix) that students use as a resource in a debate at the end of the unit.

Unit Content

Fantomina and *The Masqueraders* work well together because they function as mirrors of each other; in both texts, the male character is unable to distinguish his female lovers from one another. *The Masqueraders* sees Dorimenus seduce four interchangeable women, while *Fantomina* sees Beauplaisir unable to recognize the same woman in four different disguises. In both texts, the female characters deal in archetypal femininities, covering the female "progress of life" but also drawing on a coded world in which masquerade costumes—the shepherdess, the Gypsy, the nun—carry recognizable associations and implied power positions (see Castle 56–71). The heroine of *Fantomina* becomes a prostitute, a maid, a widow, and a mysterious masked aristocrat. *The Masqueraders* makes use of patterned oppositions between characters, contrasting characters who are easily seduced (widow Dalinda and wife Lysimena) with more knowing doubles who avoid seduction temporarily (Philecta and Briscilla).

Just as in *Fantomina* four disguises lead back to one woman, apparent distinctions between the characters in *The Masqueraders* are highly unstable, because both letters and sartorial disguise allow women to become, in a sense, one another. In volume 1, Philecta pretends to be her friend Dalinda, replicating

Dalinda's masquerade costume and forging letters from her, thereby subsuming her identity and her place in Dorimenus's affections. In volume 2, Lysimena's nun costume enables her to temporarily take Briscilla's place, at least in Dorimenus's eyes. Characters, therefore, both in terms of costume and in terms of written letters or handwriting, are easily exchangeable and create constantly shifting and tangled layers of referentiality in the novel.

The women in *The Masqueraders* are also linked by circularities in their fates, in that they suffer at the hands of neglectful male lovers: Dalinda's abandonment toward the end of volume 1 leaves her in a position similar to that of Philecta, who at the novel's outset had "suffered much by Love, and the Ingratitude of a Man who had deceiv'd her with Professions of much the same nature" as those made by Dorimenus to Dalinda (73). The instability of the novel's resolution rests on the fact that Briscilla, although successful at keeping Dorimenus's affections, is at risk of being abandoned by him—a potential mirroring of Philecta's fate. Moreover, when, in her shepherdess outfit, she finally chooses to consent, Briscilla gestures back to Dalinda dressed as a shepherdess and fainting at the masquerade in the opening scene. *The Masqueraders* is a text that is compelled to repeat the seduction narrative over and over, just as the heroine of *Fantomina* is compelled to repeat her seduction of Beauplaisir. Both texts refuse closure, straining against the narrative conventions that seek to confine them. The protagonist's banishment to a monastery after the birth of an illegitimate daughter does not, to readers familiar with amatory fiction, signal the definitive ending of *Fantomina* any more than Briscilla's happiness with Dorimenus at the end of *The Masqueraders* is suggestive of permanence.

My course uses Butler's theory of gender performativity as a way to read the formal patterns deployed by Haywood in these two texts. In *Bodies That Matter*, Butler argues that "[p]erformativity must be understood not as a singular or deliberate 'act,' but, rather, as the reiterative and citational practice by which discourse produces the effects that it names" (xii). In other words, rather than having a preexisting gender, we are compelled to perform gender, and in the repeated performance it becomes real. With this formulation in mind, students can be guided to read the structural repetitions, the lack of closure, and the circularities in Haywood's narratives as examples of a process of performative identity construction, with neither origin nor end. Our discussion is framed by a quotation crucial in enabling students to distinguish between performances that allow for agency and choice and enforced performativity within a closed system. Butler writes,

> To enter into the repetitive practices of this terrain of signification is not a choice, for the "I" that might enter is always already inside: there is no possibility of agency or reality outside of the discursive practices that give those terms the intelligibility that they have. The task is not whether to repeat, but how to repeat or, indeed, to repeat and, through a radical

> proliferation of gender, *to displace* the very gender norms that enable the repetition itself. (*Gender Trouble* 202–03)

For Butler, performativity takes place within an inescapable linguistic system in which one can only repeat. As a way of conceptualizing this, I ask students to imagine experiencing the world without language. The exercise demonstrates how integral language is to our understanding of matter but also prompts students to consider how language might limit the scope of what we are able to comprehend. The aim is to lead them to an understanding of the aliases in *Fantomina* as legible or recognizable versions that the heroine is compelled to create in order to continue her existence.

Haywood parodies essentialist and prescriptive female identities, drawing attention to their constructedness but also experimenting with iterations of femininity. Despite parallels and replications, students recognize that there are subtle differences between the women in *The Masqueraders*, just as there are differing degrees of knowledge and manipulation in each of the personae in *Fantomina*. *The Masqueraders* provides examples of a woman abandoned, a pregnant woman abandoned, a woman abandoned in marriage, and a woman not abandoned. This is repetition with slight differences each time, and the differences allow Haywood to make room for a certain elasticity within the boundaries of feminine identity construction—"not whether to repeat, but how to repeat," as Butler puts it. While identity is mapped as performative and repetition-based in Haywood's masquerade fictions, these texts also test out and stretch the discursive identities available in a bid to reshape them.

In an essay on Haywood's first novel, *Love in Excess*, that also applies to her masquerade texts, Elizabeth Gargano differentiates between verbal speech and bodily speech, the letter and the gaze, as "two forms of language that will exist in a problematic and dialectical relation throughout [Haywood's tale]" (523). The clash between the word and the body is a useful starting point for introducing students to materialist feminism. Butler's theory of performativity can be situated within a wider intellectual movement now known as the linguistic turn, which suggests that we can comprehend experience only through language. Language thus becomes crucial not only in shaping but also in producing experience and identity. Some materialist feminists are critical of this focus, however, which they claim ignores material realities. "What lies outside language? What about the body?" they ask. Their questions can usefully be brought to bear on *Fantomina* and *The Masqueraders*. These texts might be recognizing and charting identity as a series of repetitions, but how then are we to account for the compulsive returns to the body in these texts, which often put a stop to performances? While the body acts as a site for dissimulation and disguise in both narratives, pregnant bodies disrupt disguises, and exploring the different moments of embodiment in these texts enables students to see that the body is not simply a passive tool available to amatory actors to manipulate at will. The heroine of *Fantomina* might appear to have no identity beyond her performances, but in giving birth, her body, and all the possibilities engendered by it, is duplicated. Likewise, Philecta's pregnancy closes her action and the first volume of *The Masqueraders*, but it also enables the next narrative repetition that begins volume 2; Philecta is duplicated beyond the confines of the text, while Lysimena takes her place in Dorimenus's affections.

Kirby notes, "There is little risk in most contemporary criticism . . . of attributing agency and intelligent inventiveness (culture) to the capacities of flesh and matter" (216–17). Her essay "Natural Convers(at)ions" reflects on the relation between culture and nature, suggesting ways around a view of nature as essentially textual or discursive. It can be set as reading for advanced students looking for a challenge and wanting to develop a more nuanced understanding of ways that intersections between the material and the discursive might be theorized. But even for students who do not read the whole essay, Kirby's suggestion that "perhaps the meat of the body *is* thinking material . . . intelligent, capable of interpreting, analysing, reflecting and creatively reinventing" (221), can be thought through in terms of involuntary bodily acts in Haywood's texts (e.g., fainting or pregnancy). I ask students to consider the extent to which the body acts independently of the mind, drawing them beyond an understanding of a passive body awaiting inscription toward an understanding of bodies as both communicative and in a constant state of flux. Materialist feminist theory can provide potential ways of understanding the complex connections that Haywood charts between text, mind, and body, in which the bodies and their involuntary acts appear unstable, changeable, and creative rather than passive.

Teaching Method

In order to unpack these ideas with students, I open discussion with questions designed to get them thinking about basic questions of personal identity, with a view to eliciting responses that see identity both as performed and as constituted by material realities. Questions might include the following:

> What is the difference between you and your online self?
> How does being masked or disguised change what we are able to do?
> Are there certain things that we do automatically or that we are forced to do in order to signal aspects of our identity?
> Are we the same alone as we are with other people?
> What, if any, limitations do our bodies place on our identities?

This opening discussion is then followed by a short exercise that asks students to consider the difference between performance and performativity: they should grasp that, whereas performance enables an actor to choose a role and play it, performativity actually makes something real as it is being done. Performance states something and implies an element of choice, whereas performativity produces something and, for Butler at least, does not involve choice.

During the remainder of the session, I divide the students into two groups, and each is given an approach to apply to the materials: one group works on applying theories of gender performativity from Butler, and the other works on applying materialist feminist theories from Grosz and Kirby. The groups are given time and support in establishing readings informed by a series of quotations and questions and augmented by their personal research. In the next class they present their arguments to each other, engaging in a debate over which approach is more compelling. The worksheets in the appendix frame the assignment for students, providing both questions for reflection and quotations aimed to aid student recall of the critical material they have read in preparation.

The aim is for each group to present a careful close reading of its text based on one strand of theory. Groups are normally seven to ten students but often divide into subgroups, with each focusing on a different question. The activity could therefore be adapted to suit larger groups. Students are encouraged to meet outside of class before the final session to decide how best to present their reading. After the in-class presentations, with a question-and-answer session for each, students have a more general discussion about their experience of working with these theories, sharing some of the ideas that the questions generated. These discussions have yielded fascinating insights in past versions of the unit: some students read Haywood's highly stylized writing as an indicator of her investment in discursive identity construction, or have drawn from other theorists, such as Luce Irigaray, and focused on the violence associated with Haywood's portrayal of bodies; others read the discursive world as a female fantasy interrupted by a masculinist fixation with punished bodies. These varied readings have helped guide students in articulating specific and concentrated critical positions for the written assignments that form the last phase of this unit.

The literary and critical reading, small-group discussions, and collaborative debates lead into the written assignment, equipping students with areas of focus as well as theoretical tools they can apply to other texts on the module. The essay assignment paired with this unit is a two-thousand-word research paper on a question such as, What is the relation between gender performance and the sexed body in any two texts? As a whole, this session is focused on allowing students to explore the clashes between differing identity theories by considering their own experience and by reading queer and materialist feminist works. It then encourages students to apply these theories in their readings of Haywood's masquerade fiction in order to illuminate the ways that Haywood is working through tensions between appearance and reality, performance and matter.

APPENDIX

The version of *Fantomina* quoted in these worksheets is published in the collection Fantomina *and Other Works*.

Worksheet for Group 1: Questions on Performativity

The protagonist of *Fantomina* "was so admirably skill'd in the Art of feigning, that she had the Power of putting on almost what Face she pleas'd, and knew so exactly how to form her Behaviour to the Character she represented, that all the Comedians at both Playhouses are infinitely short of her Performances. She could vary her very Glances, tune her Voice to Accents the most different imaginable from those in which she spoke when she appear'd herself" (57). What tools do the characters have at their disposal to shape their own identities? What sort of femininities or personae do the women in *Fantomina* and *The Masqueraders* take on, and how do you account for these options being the available ones?

Gender identity is "performatively constituted by the very 'expressions' that are said to be its results" (Butler, *Gender Trouble* 34). From the evidence provided in the text, who is the real woman behind Fantomina, Celia, the Widow Bloomer, and Incognita? Is her identity performative?

"Performativity must be understood not as a singular or deliberate 'act,' but, rather, as the reiterative and citational practice by which discourse produces the effects that it names" (Butler, *Bodies* xii). What is the significance or function of Haywood's repetition of the seduction narrative in these texts? How can we use Butler's formulation of performativity to read Haywood's repetitions?

Butler writes: "To enter into the repetitive practices of this terrain of signification is not a choice, for the 'I' that might enter is always already inside: there is no possibility of agency or reality outside of the discursive practices that give those terms the intelligibility that they have. The task is not whether to repeat, but how to repeat or, indeed, to repeat and, through a radical proliferation of gender, *to displace* the very gender norms that enable the repetition itself" (*Gender Trouble* 202–03). Is there any scope for change or subversion of norms in Haywood's repeated plots, or are the women here doomed to repeat the same limited versions of femininity?

Worksheet for Group 2: Questions on Materialism and the Rack of Nature

Why doesn't Beauplaisir recognize his lover's body throughout *Fantomina*? Why does Dorimenus have such difficulty distinguishing between women? What does this suggest about bodies?

What do the appearances of pregnant bodies in the texts excerpted below tell us? What effect do they have on the narratives? What is the relation between performance, disguise, and the body?

> "[N]ature may be understood not as an origin or as an invariable template but as materiality in its most general sense, as destination." (Grosz 21)

> "She could not conceal the sudden Rack which all at once invaded her; or had her Tongue been mute, her wildly rolling Eyes, the distortion of her Features, and the Convulsions which shook her whole Frame, in spite of her, would have reveal'd she labour'd under some terrible Shock of Nature." (Haywood, *Fantomina* 68–69)

> At the end of volume 1 of *The Masqueraders*, Philecta is abandoned by Dorimenus, exposed to gossip, and also pregnant. Haywood tells us that Philecta "is sufficiently convinc'd how infinitely to blame she was, in indulging a Curiosity which proved so fatal to her Virtue, her Reputation, and her Peace of Mind; and which, 'tis highly probable, will in a short time be found so to her Life." (99)

Can the body in the texts excerpted below be thought of as in the realm of nature or culture? Is the body in these texts a blank canvas, or does it have agency? In what ways does the body speak?

> "[H]e was almost at a loss how to proceed with a Lady who he found so well furnish'd with the Weapons of Defence; and if he had not been inform'd by some tell-tale *Cupids* in her Eyes, which now and then flew out with tender Messages, that he had a Friend within, might probably have given over both the Hope and the Attempt of Vanquishing." (Haywood, *Masqueraders* 82)

> "There is little risk in most contemporary criticism . . . of attributing agency and intelligent inventiveness (culture) to the capacities of flesh and matter (nature). In sum, nature is deemed to be thoughtless." (Kirby 217)

Tiffany Potter has suggested that Haywood employs "a feminised structure of multiple climaxes" in the form of her novels and, in doing so, aligns the texts themselves with the female body ("Language" 175). How would you characterize the relation between the body, language, and the written word in these texts? Which triumphs in the end?

Fantomina and *Betsy Thoughtless*: Repetition with Difference

Catherine Craft-Fairchild

Eliza Haywood's extensive, multigenre body of writing is highly self-reflective about what it means to live as a woman under patriarchal constraints. At both undergraduate and graduate levels, I draw on Haywood's work to engage students in conversations about gender. *Fantomina; or, Love in a Maze* is a core text in my undergraduate women's studies course, where the central question is the degree to which women can achieve agency within the performance of femininity, especially when that performance is further inflected by race and class. At the master's level, Haywood appears in context with other eighteenth-century writers, and the core discussion centers on the pairing of *Fantomina* with *The History of Miss Betsy Thoughtless* to investigate continuity and divergence between Haywood's early and late career. The approach in both courses focuses on repetition with difference, putting texts into conversation with each other, connecting women's texts across time and space, and allowing the voices of early women writers like Haywood to lay the groundwork and speak to the concerns of current feminists.

U.S. News and World Report lists my institution in the "National Universities" category among the "A-Plus Schools for B Students," noting that this "Catholic university . . . emphasizes values-based education and career preparation" ("University"). Instructors find classrooms filled with earnest, hard-working undergraduates, many majoring in business, some pursuing careers in teaching, and most with little exposure to literature. My pedagogy takes into account bell hooks's warning against "assaults [on] the fragile psyches of women struggling to throw off patriarchy's oppressive yoke" that occur "when students, most of whom are female, come to Women's Studies classes and read what they are told is feminist theory only to feel that what they are reading has no meaning, cannot be understood, or when understood in no way connects to 'lived' realities beyond the classroom" (10). This danger is particularly acute with my undergraduates, so we proceed gradually and interactively, beginning with John Berger's eminently readable *Ways of Seeing*, accompanied by its BBC television corollary. Berger explores the subject of spectatorship by interspersing text with images; although students are amused by the dated clothing styles and advertisements, they readily embrace Berger's analysis of the ways women are read as objects of sight, which launches our discussion of the male gaze, an important concept for later close reading of *Fantomina*. In the classroom, we update Berger's second-wave text by applying his ideas to media images from the present that students gather and discuss. With *Ways of Seeing* as our foundation, we go on to read excerpts from Susan Sontag's *On Photography*, Judith Butler's *Gender Trouble* and *Bodies That Matter*, and Roxane Gay's *Bad Feminist*.

Iris Marion Young notes that "part of the situation of being a woman is that of living the ever present possibility that one will be gazed upon as a mere body, as shape and flesh that presents itself as the potential object of another subject's intentions and manipulations, rather than as a living manifestation of action and intention" (198). Berger offers a partial, imperfect answer to this dilemma by posing the possibility of a divided consciousness: "A woman must continually watch herself. . . . From earliest childhood she has been taught and persuaded to survey herself continually. And so she comes to consider the *surveyor* and the *surveyed* within her as the two constituent yet always distinct elements of her identity as a woman" (46). This passage suggests the potential for performance: the self who is surveying does not necessarily need to be identical to the enacted self who is being surveyed by others. Women, insists Berger, cannot wholly escape from the system of spectatorship in which they are enmeshed, but they can exert some control over it by anticipating how their acting selves will be viewed, perceived, and responded to:

> Men survey women before treating them. Consequently how a woman appears to a man can determine how she will be treated. To acquire some control over this process, women must contain it and interiorize it. That part of a woman's self which is the surveyor treats the part which is the surveyed so as to demonstrate to others how her whole self would like to be treated. (46)

In order to assert agency, women must consciously reflect on and interiorize the process, performing femininity intentionally and shaping the ways they appear so as to determine the range of responses they will receive. Postmodernists like Butler would deny the possibility of intentionality with regard to gender performance:

> [C]oherent gender, achieved through an apparent repetition of the same, produces as its *effect* the illusion of a prior and volitional subject. In this sense, gender is not a performance that a prior subject elects to do, but gender is *performative* in the sense that it constitutes as an effect the very subject it appears to express. . . . [T]here is no performer prior to the performed. ("Imitation" 319)

Yet within this same discussion Butler admits that "acting out of line with heterosexual norms brings with it ostracism, punishment, and violence" (319). In *Fantomina* and *Betsy Thoughtless*, the female characters act, literally, as a way to avoid those negative consequences; Haywood, like Berger, seems to posit a possibility of a consciously constructed performance.

Berger indicates that when a woman's visual performance is unreflective and unintentional, she quickly becomes a spectacle for a man's pleasure, which does not alter women's status as an object of male vision and masculine desire.

Berger's argument leads naturally to Laura Mulvey's work on the male gaze and the idea that a woman's presence constitutes "to-be-looked-at-ness." I excerpt portions of "Visual Pleasure and Narrative Cinema" for the class to read and illustrate Mulvey's concepts by showing clips of midcentury films, such as Charles Vidor's *Gilda* and Alfred Hitchcock's *Vertigo*. In these cinematic works, the female protagonist performs femininity impulsively, acting in ways that cede agency to men.

Other classic films, such as Billy Wilder's *Double Indemnity* and Hitchcock's *Marnie*, can be used to illustrate a performance of femininity that intentionally confounds the male gaze. Tippi Hedren's title character in *Marnie*, for example, uses ultrafeminine disguise to play male desire against itself, robbing male employers who are so busy looking at, as Mark Rutland (Sean Connery) describes her, "the brunette with the legs" that they don't bother to check her references. Marnie anticipates the ways in which various male bosses will respond and consciously constructs the visual cues of her female personae to redirect male attention away from her controlling self (who is stealing their money) toward her performing self (whose sexual desirability distracts them). In this case, performance becomes a disruptive resistance to patriarchal control. Mary Ann Doane writes, "To masquerade is to manufacture a lack in the form of a certain distance between oneself and one's image. . . . By destabilising the image, the masquerade confounds this masculine structure of the look" (139). Doane's work provides the class with another way to consider the gap that exists between a woman's controlling, surveying self and the self who acts and performs—and the potential agency this gap allows. With these theories in hand, students write about different facets of women performing femininity in relation to the photographic or cinematic images that they selected earlier for class discussion.

These readings, discussions, and writing assignments set the stage for reading Haywood's *Fantomina*; in this short narrative, the concepts of performance, identity, and agency raised by feminist theorists can readily be examined. Emily Hodgson Anderson, for example, writes about Haywood's heroine in ways that echo Berger: "In *Fantomina*, the heroine understands and implements strategies of self-conscious performance. . . . [She] manipulates the male tendency to read a woman by her context, shaping her context to create her own roles" ("Performing the Passions" 2, 6). The Lady of Haywood's narrative performs femininity for her own ends: she destabilizes the gaze of her lover, Beauplaisir, by refocusing his look upon her four consciously constructed images of womanhood. The distance she maintains between her disguised self and her controlling self, surveyed and surveyor, brings the heroine many forms of enjoyment: when she masquerades as a prostitute, her vanity is flattered, as the crowding males and Beauplaisir remark that "she very much resembled that Lady whom she really was," and she "receiv'd no small Pleasure in hearing herself prais'd, tho' in the Person of another" (42).[1] The Lady rejoices that she need not suffer "a cold, insipid, husband-like Lover," for her "Arts of passing on him as a new Mistress whenever the Ardour . . . begins to diminish" has Beauplaisir "always raving, wild, impatient, longing, dying" (65). During their various sexual encounters, "Possession" does not abate "the Vigour of Desire" (65), because the Lady uses her theatrical abilities to stage sex scenes for herself and Beauplaisir in which he believes he is making new conquests over several different women.

Along with relishing the intensity of their lovemaking, the Lady delights in her own theatrical abilities: "she was so admirably skill'd in the Art of feigning, that she had the Power of putting on almost what Face she pleas'd, and knew so exactly how to form her Behaviour to the Character she represented, that all the Comedians at both Playhouses are infinitely short of her Performances" (57). As Juliette Merritt insists, the Lady's "sexuality is expressed through charade itself . . . . [T]he brilliance of her performances is also fundamental to her pleasure" (*Beyond Spectacle* 55, 60). Finally, the heroine relishes the very act of fooling Beauplaisir, congratulating herself that she has "outwitted even the most Subtle of the deceiving Kind, and while he thinks to fool me, is himself the only beguiled Person" (59); Haywood's heroine laughs "heartily to think of the Tricks she had play'd him" (64). If sex in *Fantomina* is theater, the Lady is the person with agency because she creates the stagings, while Beauplaisir remains an unwitting performer.

This aspect of the text bothers many students, who ask, What are Beauplaisir's rights to know the realities of the sexual liaisons he is engaged in? Does he forfeit his claim to truth by practicing sexual deception himself? Is Beauplaisir objectified in the story? Students point to role reversal in the Lady's plots. With each new persona, the heroine moves up in rank; in the masquerade that comes closest to her affluent, aristocratic, everyday self—the masked Incognita—she puts Beauplaisir "much out of Humour" by disappointing "his Curiosity" and keeping her face hidden (67). Discussing Merritt's work, students focus on her assertion that in this disguise the Lady "evades the dominating male gaze entirely, while subjecting Beauplaisir to the discomforts of being the object of someone's unhindered and unobstructed looking" (62). Students often express concern that role reversal risks reversion back to the same dynamics; it doesn't destabilize patriarchal structures. If this is what is happening in *Fantomina*, then Toni Bowers's critique of women's amatory fiction generally—that these works "show women exercising sexual desire, and at the same time bolster phallocentric patterns of sexual dominance" ("Sex" 57)—applies to Haywood's writing. Our interpretive work with *Fantomina* raises a core question that preoccupies us for the remainder of the semester: Is there a difference between the male gaze and the female gaze, and if so, in what does the difference consist?

To provide fuller historical and critical context in my classes, I compile a packet of material for each course text that includes biography—for Haywood, drawing on the important investigative work of Christine Blouch and Kathryn R. King—and selections from articles and book chapters by Anderson, Merritt, Patricia Comitini, Margaret Case Croskery, Stephanie Harzewski, Jonathan Brody Kramnick, and Tiffany Potter. Study questions for small-group discussion are linked to these scholarly sources. In each unit, one class day is led by a student team that must engage in more extensive research to prepare a lesson plan. I also ask the class to undertake micro–research projects. The assignment is a sort of historical scavenger hunt: students in pairs must use *PowerPoint* or *Prezi* to produce ten slides—half images, half text—on a particular period topic and spend five to ten minutes presenting them to the class. We spread these brief introductions of historical material over several class periods, then move to discussion of the relevant text enriched by the content of the presentations. The activity encourages student investment and nudges quieter students toward low-stakes public speaking in a way that may make future participation more comfortable.

After analyzing the scholarly literature, some students agree with the many critics who argue that *Fantomina* "offers a surprisingly contemporary model of female agency" (Merritt 45), allowing its protagonist a measure of freedom and control unusual in early literature. Yet, as twenty-first-century readers, many students worry that the text reproduces rape culture when, during his second meeting with Fantomina, Beauplaisir insists on having sexual intercourse despite her protests. The packet of readings for students engages with a range of viewpoints on this important issue. Croskery insists that this scene is "powerfully disturbing" and "raises the deepest questions surrounding the definition of consensual sex" ("Masquing Desire" 73), while Potter states directly that Fantomina "is raped" ("Language" 178). Kramnick complicates the issue:

> The episode . . . is among the trickier accounts of volition in the Haywood canon. . . . Haywood's understanding of these questions may not be ours. . . . Either the young lady's behavior has been misunderstood by Beauplaisir and she was never consenting at all, or she had consented up to a point in time and now attempts to draw back, or she is unable to separate her internal volition from the external world it inhabits and wants what she doesn't want. (462–63)

Like Kramnick, students believe that Haywood does not settle the question of consent (464); discussing date rape on college campuses, students note that even today we cannot always agree about what consent means.

Students pursue this line of thought: Why would the Lady continue to desire a man who has raped her? What *is* her desire? Does she love Beauplaisir? The narrator says sometimes that she does but at another point insists, "Knowledge of his Inconstancy and Levity of Nature kept her from having that real Tenderness for him she would else have had" (59). Since readers see little of Beauplaisir apart from his sexual faithlessness, students label him an undesirable "player." Usually, several align with Harzewski, reading *Fantomina* as a trauma narrative in which the heroine, as a victim of rape, attempts to reintegrate the event and reassert control by "repeatedly reenact[ing] some aspect of the trauma scene in disguised form without real understanding" of what she is doing (189–90). Students see unconscious reenactment as a possible explanation for why the heroine becomes so obsessed with Beauplaisir that she will not let go of him when he tires of her first persona.

Students revisit *Fantomina* and approach it from different angles as we go on to compare Haywood's work with that of other women writers. Course texts include Jane Austen's *Sense and Sensibility*; Nella Larsen's *Quicksand* and *Passing*; Patricia Highsmith's *The Price of Salt* and its film adaptation, *Carol*, directed by Todd Haynes; *La double vie de Véronique* (*The Double Life of Veronique*), a film directed by Krzysztof Kieślowski; and Natasha Trethewey's *Bellocq's Ophelia*. Reading Austen's novel, for example, students note the importance of Haywood's heroine's seemingly limitless wealth. Elinor Dashwood's immense self-restraint, her emotional masquerade intended to keep up appearances, seems the antithesis of the Lady's self-indulgent forms of disguise; yet students can see how, in a world where Elinor and her mother and sisters are economically and socially dependent on the goodwill of wealthy men, Elinor's efforts are necessary.

Similarly, Helga Crane of Larsen's *Quicksand* mirrors Haywood's heroine with differences that highlight the Lady's immense privilege and Helga's disempowerment. Helen Thompson takes issue with my and other critics' reading of *Fantomina*'s protagonist as having "some species of interiority preserved behind her mask" and insists that "she consists only in the wholesale substitution of herself for herself" ("Plotting Materialism" 207). Haywood's "heroine . . . resolves patriarchal contradiction not because she has been freed from patriarchy's laws, but because she repeatedly manifests her observance of them" by "serially reinsert[ing] herself into the . . . position of objecthood" (196, 205). In *Fantomina*, though, there seems an intentionality in the heroine's performance of personae, an intentionality absent from Helga Crane's total immersion in her various roles. What Thompson claims for Haywood's Lady, my class insisted upon for Helga: "the absence of any subjectivizing residue that would linger outside the rigorous discontinuity of her performances" (204). Helga cannot maintain any gap between the surveyor and surveyed within herself. One student writer, Meghan Heitkamp, summed up our class's interpretation of Haywood's and Larsen's works:

> Unlike the Lady in *Fantomina*, however, Helga seems completely to throw herself into each new construction of self, rather than maintaining an independent self-concept at a distance from these masquerades. Helga does not have the same resources that seem to be endlessly available to the Lady. . . . While the Lady can freely choose to create a new identity or retreat back to her (relatively) comfortable upper-class life, Helga has no other option, no safety net. The desperation inherent in Helga's identity-creation is a key difference between her and the Lady: while the Lady pursues power for her own fulfillment and actualization, Helga pursues it simply to live, and each failure affects her life more and more permanently.

Reading *Quicksand* next to *Fantomina* spurred a discussion of intersectionality regarding questions of gender, race, and class. W. E. B. Du Bois's idea of "double-consciousness," for example, dovetails with Berger's sense of women's self-surveillance:

> It is a peculiar sensation, this double-consciousness, this sense of always looking at one's self through the eyes of others, of measuring one's soul by the tape of a world that looks on in amused contempt and pity. One ever feels his twoness;—an American, a Negro; two souls, two thoughts, two unreconciled strivings; two warring ideals in one dark body, whose dogged strength alone keeps it from being torn asunder. (3)

At the advanced level, where I focus exclusively on the eighteenth century, Anderson's article serves as a core critical text. Anderson pairs *Fantomina* with *Betsy Thoughtless* to argue that, in the latter work, "Haywood recasts scenes from her earlier novella, placing characters who do not have Fantomina's foresight in situations that bear striking parallels to scenes in *Fantomina*" ("Performing the Passions" 2). Exploring these "recast scenes," which emphasize the thematic continuity of earlier and later Haywood novels, is ideal for my students pursuing a master of arts in English or a teaching certificate. A large number of these are high school teachers bolstering their credentials or teachers pursuing a master's degree in order to work in the community college system. For these students, materials that can be shaped into future lesson plans prove most valuable; *Fantomina* and *Betsy Thoughtless*—fictions that bracket Haywood's writing career—together form an eminently teachable unit.

Paula Backscheider first called into question the long accepted "Story" that "for purely commercial reasons, Eliza Haywood 'reformed' and became a moral novelist" ("Story" 19). Backscheider writes, "Rather than a marked break in Haywood's fiction, I find a remarkable consistency in her stated 'morals' and the plots and themes that dramatize them" (31). Aleksondra Hultquist adds, "If we agree that Haywood never converted from her amatory aesthetic to a didactic one, then we need to reevaluate the way we read her 'moralistic' domestic fiction of the 1750s" ("Marriage" 31). Anderson enacts these views by exploring Haywood's career as "repetition with difference" ("Performing the Passions" 11), as does Potter, who refers to Haywood's "practice of 're-telling'" as a method whereby readers who "know how the story is supposed to go . . . can be conscious of the significance of the variants" ("Life" 43).

My class examines these variants in detail. Following Anderson, we pair scenes from *Fantomina* with those in *Betsy Thoughtless*, contrasting, for instance, Fantomina's knowing choice to sit in the pit at the theater and Betsy's reckless choice to place herself in that spot. My students do their own close reading of theater and masquerade scenes in the two books, matched episodes that suggest Haywood deliberately rewrote portions of *Fantomina* in *Betsy Thoughtless*. When the Lady of *Fantomina* pursues Beauplaisir in her guise as the mysterious masked Incognita, she insists upon concealing from him the knowledge of who she is by repeatedly denying Beauplaisir "the Sight of her Face," a phrase repeated during the scene (65–66). What is being contested is control: Beauplaisir wishes to gain access to the Lady's social identity, which would allow him power over it, while she is determined to protect her everyday persona by keeping it hidden. The heroine maintains agency by refusing Beauplaisir's demands.

Haywood's rescripting of this scene in *Betsy Thoughtless* affirms the necessity of the Lady's choice. Betsy's frenemy, Flora Mellasin, approaches the controversially named hero Trueworth in exactly the same way, as a masked Incognita, and achieves a sexual liaison with the man she has long desired by appearing to him as an alluring stranger. Like Beauplaisir, Trueworth is impatient for the discovery of his lover's face; Flora, unlike Incognita, complies with Trueworth's demands, saying, "[Y]ou are not to be resisted, and I will venture" (312). By this sudden collapse of the distinction between her performing self and the self orchestrating the performance, Flora places herself in Trueworth's power.

Trueworth, the novel's best young man, maintains an illicit relationship with Flora while he courts Harriot Loveit; upon his engagement to the latter, he brutally discards the former. Reading backward from this scene in *Betsy Thoughtless* to *Fantomina*, my students wonder whether the emphasis in *Fantomina* on the heroine's dashing disguises and knowing manipulations obscures the selfish male behavior that establishes the need for the ruses in the first place. Students tend to think that the earlier novella let Beauplaisir off too easily; they feel that in *Betsy Thoughtless*, Haywood much more fully interrogates male behavior. If Haywood is, as Shea Stuart asserts, questioning conduct-book values for women in *Betsy Thoughtless*, she is doing so mainly in order to show that the need for female reform exists only because of male aggression. Over and over, Haywood emphasizes that male violence is used to restrain female behavior; the final volume of *Betsy Thoughtless* goes beyond interrogating the male gaze into examining abusive relationships, a realm where no female intentionality or performance can offer protection. Betsy, although desiring only innocent amusements, cannot take a tour of a university or go on a walk through a church cemetery without finding herself in danger of being raped. Pattern women who mirror conduct literature, like Miss Harriot and Miss Mabel, remain safer than Betsy because they willingly give up their autonomy and mobility to stay at home.

My class reads excerpts from the Marquess of Halifax's *The Lady's New-Year's Gift: or, Advice to a Daughter* in order to examine firsthand the injunctions to silent suffering and patient virtue typical of conduct advice for women. We then perform scenes from Colley Cibber's *The Careless Husband*, a play referred to directly in *Betsy Thoughtless*. Haywood, through Lady Trusty, explicitly mentions conduct literature only to illustrate the inefficacy of its teaching in dealing with abuse. Both Halifax's advice and Cibber's drama urge female forbearance in the face of adultery or other mistreatment, urging the power of tears to soften the hearts of husbands. In *The Careless Husband*, Sir Charles Easy commits adultery, cheating on his ideally virtuous wife, Lady Easy, with several women, including her own maid in her own house; similarly, Betsy's husband, Munden, sleeps with her brother's mistress under her own roof. The parallels, however, end there, for Haywood rescripts Cibber's ending to emphasize that performance cannot avail against violence. In *The Careless Husband*, Lady Easy's steady good humor, her refusal to upbraid him or complain, finally causes Sir Charles's reform. Sir Charles tells her, "[S]ince I see you are so generously tender of reproaching me, 'tis fit I should be easy in my gratitude, and make what ought to be my shame, my joy. Let me be therefore pleased to tell you now, your wondrous conduct has waked me to a sense of your disquiet past, and resolution never to disturb it more" (103). In Haywood's novel, Betsy behaves with the same moderation and forbearance as Lady Easy, although inwardly Betsy is seething with anger. Yet Betsy's efforts at restraint only render Munden more outrageous until his violence culminates in his killing of her pet squirrel, an act of domestic violence with an additional implied threat toward Betsy. Munden, writes Haywood, "took pleasure in giving pain to [Betsy]" (509). No performance, however well enacted, can deliver Betsy from this.

Whether placing Haywood's *Fantomina* into conversation with women authors across time and space or examining it with *Betsy Thoughtless* in the context of Haywood's long and significant writing career, exploring repetition with difference helps students recognize Haywood's nuanced treatments of women's desires and agency and their immersion in, or resistance to, dominant social codes.

NOTE

[1]This essay quotes from the version of *Fantomina* in the collection Fantomina *and Other Works*.

Limits of the Letter in Haywood, Richardson, and Fielding: Teaching *Anti-Pamela* with *Pamela* and *Shamela*

Robin Runia

Jane Austen's narrator in *Northanger Abbey* defends the novel as a "work in which the greatest powers of the mind are displayed, in which the most thorough knowledge of human nature, the happiest delineation of its varieties, the liveliest effusions of wit and humor are conveyed to the world in the best chosen language" (24). She also defends these superlatives—explicitly exemplified in the works of Frances Burney and Maria Edgeworth—against the poetry and prose of John Milton, Alexander Pope, Joseph Addison and Richard Steele, and Laurence Sterne. In so doing, Austen's narrator insists on a gendering of the novel in a gesture that, while perhaps true to her early-nineteenth-century moment, does not accurately reflect the form or content of the novel as it developed throughout the eighteenth century. Teaching Samuel Richardson's *Pamela*, Henry Fielding's *Shamela*, and Eliza Haywood's *Anti-Pamela* alongside one another shows students a more complex history of the novel. Eschewing simplistic labels of realist or sentimentalist, didactic or satiric, male or female, this approach reveals how the eighteenth-century novel's formal elements and critical focus reflected the practices and values of its reading and writing community, specifically communities of letter readers and writers.

Richardson's *Familiar Letters on Important Occasions* provides valuable context when introducing students to the relation between epistolarity and the novel. *Familiar Letters* takes the form of a letter-writing manual. A popular genre since the seventeenth century and with examples dating back to the classical period, the letter-writing manual commonly provided samples that readers might use as models in their own correspondence. Specifically, the manual presents sample letters from apprentices, shopkeepers, merchants, servants, and employers, as well as fathers, mothers, sons, daughters, aunts, uncles, cousins, and friends from all walks of life. It instructs correspondents from these various social strata to use the letter form to secure their own personal, political, and economic interests, accordingly rendering Richardson's text a political statement. Janet Altman has argued, "The proliferation of such letter manuals in England . . . made letter writing a possibility for the working classes. More importantly, the ideology of the manuals shows workers using the post office to emancipate themselves. It can thus be argued that the letter manual contributed to the democratization of writing in eighteenth-century England" (154).

In order to help students recognize the emancipatory and democratic potential of letter writing, it is useful first to compare excerpts from *Familiar Letters* with *Pamela*. Specifically, by examining letters 138 and 139 in *Familiar Letters*,

"A Father to a Daughter in Service, on hearing of her Master's attempting her Virtue," students are able to see the letter as a tool by which individuals negotiate competing moral and economic demands. Richardson's manual instructs:

> *My dear Daughter,* I understand, with great grief of heart, that your master has made some attempts on your virtue, and yet that you stay with him. God grant that you have not already yielded to his base desires! For when once a person has so far forgotten what belongs to himself, or his character, as to make such an attempt, the very continuance with him, and in his power, and under the same roof, is an encouragement to him to prosecute his designs. And if he carries it better, and more civil, at present, it is only more certainly to undo you when he attacks you next. Consider, my dear child, your reputation is all you have to trust to. (165)

Through Richardson's instructional letter, students clearly see the vulnerability of servingwomen to sexual assault and the sexual double standard applied to them as victims. In the manual's following letter, the daughter's response also displays the potential of the epistolary form to give voice to women's desire for economic and sexual independence: "*Honoured Sir,* I received your letter yesterday, and am sorry I stay'd a moment in my master's house after his vile attempt. But he was so full of his promises of never offering the like again, that I hoped I might believe him; nor have I yet seen any thing to the contrary" (165). In this instance, the daughter is able to attempt justifying her behavior according to her own capacity to read the situation.

As many scholars have recognized, *Pamela* begins upon this same model. And whether one teaches the entirety of Richardson's novel or not, close examination of a few select letters exposes the implications of the letter for the development of the novel form. Letter 18 in particular provides Pamela's response to her parents' previous letter expressing concern over her relationship with her employer. In many ways similar to the example from Richardson's manual, its differences are particularly instructive. Students immediately recognize the shift from the dialogic epistolary structure used in the manual, in which the young servingwoman and her father are each allowed a voice, to a monological record of Pamela's plight. Accordingly, they perceive how this clearly reorients the reader's attention away from the father's warnings and censure, toward the young woman's attempts to navigate her precarious situation as well as justify it to herself and others. In particular, students recognize how Pamela's claims in this letter to embrace poverty in a return home to her poor parents and their "New-Old Lot," with its "Rags" and "Rye-bread," function as a strategic attempt to placate her parents' concern (38).

Further, juxtaposing this with letter 19 helps students recognize the considerable power of monologic epistolarity to privilege one character or individual's perspective over another. In the following description of one of Pamela's conversations with Mrs. Jervis, Pamela is able to provide yet another example of her intelligence and experience: her reading of the situation and its potential implications as further justification of her decision not to return home:

> Well, but, Mrs. Jervis, said I, let me ask you, if he can stoop to like such a poor Girl as I, as may be he may, for I have read of Things almost as strange, from great Men to poor Damsels; What can it be for?—He may condescend, may-hap, to think I may be good enough for his Harlot; and those Things don't disgrace Men, that ruin poor Women, as the World goes. And so, if I was wicked enough, he would keep me till I was undone, and 'till his Mind changed; for even wicked Men, I have read, soon grow weary of Wickedness of one Sort, and love Variety. (41)

In comparing these *Pamela* letters with those of Richardson's manual, students recognize how the control of narrative perspective authorized by the act of letter writing can allow a heroine to carefully negotiate the relation between gendered, sexual, and economic demands and expectations.

Examining eighteenth-century perceptions of Richardson's success in this endeavor is a valuable next step for students exploring the impact of epistolarity upon the novel genre at that time. Students firmly grasp the power of the letter when introduced to only a couple of examples of contemporary readers' responses. In *Pamela Censured*, for instance, the anonymous author reveals his anxiety about the ability of letters to present women's desire:

> SHEWING That under the Specious Pretence of Cultivating the Principles of Virtue in the Minds of the Youth of both Sexes, the MOST ARTFUL and ALLURING AMOROUS IDEAS are convey'd. And that, instead of being divested of all Images that tend to *inflame*; Her Letters abound with Incidents, which must necessarily raise in the unwary Youth that read them, EMOTIONS *far distant* from the PRINCIPLES of VIRTUE.

In contrast, Belinda, in "To the Author of Pamela," writes:

> To thee, kind author, what unusual praise
> Shall we instructed damsels raise?
> Who fir'd, by thy Pamela's merit, scorn
> The servile deeds to which our rank is born;
> With virtuous dignity our minds improve,
> And teach e'en lawless lords connubial love.

Juxtaposing these responses helps students further grasp the stakes of the letter's potential, in general, to give voice to women through a monologic epistolary perspective within the novel and, in particular, to challenge norms for women's behavior.

Following these introductory examinations and discussions, close readings of Fielding's *Shamela* and Haywood's *Anti-Pamela* provide students further insight into the complex relationship of letter-writing to women's agency and its role in the novel. Catherine Ingrassia's introduction to the Broadview edition of these adaptations provides students with an excellent grounding in the historical contexts and social implications of the ideological contests among Richardson, Fielding, and Haywood around *Pamela*. I outline here several valuable points of intersection among the three texts, and classroom discussion can begin, perhaps, with the fruitful comparative site of the title page and front matter of each text.

Shamela, of course, registers Fielding's moral disgust as well as his intellectual critique of Richardson's form and content. The title page, even while acknowledging its debt to its supposedly inappropriate forbear, links women's epistolary activity with deception. *Shamela* asserts that *Pamela* is a morally corrupt sham, an untruth that should be repented of. No longer *Virtue Rewarded*, the subtitle becomes *An Apology for the Life of Mrs. Shamela Andrews*, with the added description, "In which the many notorious Falsehoods and Misrepresentation of a Book called PAMELA are exposed and refuted." By transforming Pamela into Shamela, Fielding signals that his text is a parody; his reliance upon his audience's ability to recognize the original upon which his text is based signals ambivalence about the ability of the letter to empower women and of epistolary novels to provide readers with examples of moral behavior.

This ambivalence is seconded by the dedication to "Miss Fanny." Once informed that *fanny* functioned as a slang term for female genitalia, students may consider how Fielding's text conveys the author's grudging acknowledgment of women's sexual power even in an attempt to diminish it. Most important, however, to grasping Fielding's ambivalent commentary on the potential of the letter form to provide women with agency is analysis of his introduction of a polyvocal epistolarity. After comparing the perspectives of the characters through their own letters, students often begin to look for an objective truth beyond the limits or interests of any one character. And Fielding provides a convenient model: while Parson Tickletext's recommendation of *Pamela* as representative of "an epidemical Phrenzy now raging in Town" is suspicious, as his very name belies his susceptibility to narrative manipulation, Parson Oliver's denial of Tickletext and insistence on his own "authentick" version proves grounded in reason and fact, suggesting the importance of monovocal narrative control (238).

More particular comparison of Shamela and Pamela further complicates students' understanding of the relation between letter writing and women's agency. Shamela's first letter, for example, not only counters Richardson's character's claim to willing poverty but also celebrates a sexual economy in which women's economic opportunities are limited to prostitution. Shamela describes her imminent arrival in London accordingly: "I beleve Mrs. Jervis will come along with me, for she says she would like to keep a House somewhere about *Short's-Gardens*, or towards *Queen-Street*; and if there was convenience for a *Bannio*, she should like it the better; but that she will settle herself when she comes to Town" (242). Unlike Richardson's virtuous model, Shamela's literacy and chastity are explicitly questionable. Rather than inquiring about men's motives and struggling to anticipate their compatibility with moral value, Shamela cares only to appear to her best advantage in the hierarchy of London prostitution.

In addition to complicating the relationship between women's agency and letter writing, Fielding's text also questions any essential association between the letter and verisimilitude. Students immediately reject Shamela's claim to "write to the moment," as in this passage: "Thursday Night, Twelve o'Clock, Mrs. Jervis and I are just in Bed, and the Door unlocked; if my Master should come—Odsbobs! I hear him just coming in at the Door. You see I write in the present Tense" (247). They readily recognize that only a "sham," desperate to convince her audience of her clearly questionable veracity, would feel the need to insist on her use of tense, especially when it's clear that Shamela has purposely left the door unlocked in order to allow her Master to "steal his Hand into [her] Bosom" while she fakes sleep and "counterfeit[s] a Swoon" (247).

Further evidence of Fielding's undermining of laboring-class women's claims to truth and virtue can be found in Shamela's mother's letter to Mrs. Jervis. In particular, Shamela's mother's misspellings assert an essential relationship between education and virtue, truth and right: "I Received the Favour of your Letter, and I find you have not forgot your usual Poluteness, which you learned when you was in keeping with a Lord" (250). By debating the orthographic relationship between *pollution* and *politeness*, students come to recognize the irony that Mrs. Jervis's proximity to the fashionable manners so often equated with politeness has only polluted her. Similar attention to orthographic parody reveals that by transforming Richardson's Mr. B. into the utterly ridiculous Squire Booby, Fielding demands his readers agree that *Pamela* is "by no means innocent" because, in it, "Young Gentlemen are here taught, that to marry their Mother's Chambermaids, and to indulge the Passion of Lust, at the Expence of Reason and Common Sense, is an Act of Religion, Virtue, and Honour; and, indeed the surest Road to Happiness" (274–75). Blame and credit are redistributed according to gender and class in completely opposite ways by the two male authors, and in Fielding's version, epistolarity is equated with debauched femininity and wronged masculinity that must be corrected and contained by additional male authority and reason.

Students can at this point turn to Haywood's volley in this debate around gender, rank, and morality. Her *Anti-Pamela* appeared some three months after *Shamela* and shifts the attack strategy from garish parody to critical revisionism. In contrast to Richardson's *Pamela* and Fielding's *Shamela*, Haywood's *Anti-Pamela* reveals the lack of any essential relation connecting or opposing epistolarity and narrative truth or gendered virtue. First, the two titles of Haywood's novel speak explicitly to the role reader response played in audiences' rejection of Richardson's narrative. *Anti-Pamela; or, Feign'd Innocence Detected* is described on the title page as "A Narrative which has really its Foundation in

Truth and Nature; and at the same time that it entertains, by a vast variety of surprising Incidents, arms against a partial Credulity, by shewing the Mischiefs that frequently arise from a too sudden Admiration" (51). Following the best of classical models set forth in Horace's *Ars Poetica*, Haywood's novel claims to instruct while it entertains, even though it also proclaims itself "Publish'd as a necessary Caution to all Young Gentlemen." In contrast, the second title, provided on the first page of the novel—*Anti-Pamela; or, Mock-Modesty Display'd and Punish'd*—draws students' attention to the double bind of epistolarity and the novel form by simultaneously warning men and illuminating the social mechanisms that drive women to desperation.

Significantly, the essential unreliability of letter writing itself becomes crucial to successful detection and punishment of sexual impropriety in Haywood's narrative. Unlike Richardson's and Fielding's texts, *Anti-Pamela* features a third-person narrator who provides crucial background information about the main character, Syrena Tricksy. The fact that letters are included in the narrative but are not the dominant form provides students with the first clue about Haywood's stance on the insufficiency of the letter form to provide any kind of truth. An exemplar of neither virtue nor vice, Syrena (whose name connotes both the deadly sirens of the *Odyssey* and the more mundane threat of Georgian London's vibrant criminal culture) is the product of her environment, the precocious daughter of a successful "Woman of Intrigue," "one of the most subtil Mistresses in the Art of Decoying that ever was" (53). Because we are immediately informed of this part of Mrs. Tricksy's past, students are not surprised when Syrena's first letter of the novel begs her mother not for advice about how to preserve her virtue or how to gain most from its absence but instead how to escape boredom and servitude in "an old-fashion'd sanctified Family" (59). Accordingly, students are prepared to discuss how Syrena's letters, unlike those of Pamela and Shamela, show neither a supposedly authentic and blameless virtue nor the utter corruption of an ignorant virago. Instead, Haywood's letters reveal the potential for rational reflection to serve either virtue or vice. For example, when Syrena writes to her mother of a potential suitor's advances, she exposes not only her knowledge of good and bad behavior but also her ability to reflect:

> When I began to consider on what had pass'd; I thought I had been a little too rough in the latter part of my Behaviour; for tho' I did not repent my having refused the Stockings (tho' indeed they were very pretty) yet I did that I had not done it with more Complaisance.—I verily believed he loved me; . . . and so have drawn him in by Degrees, till it was not in his power to go back. These Reflections kept me awake all Night. . . . (62)

Repentance vies with necessity in negotiations of power between lovers as a tool independent of virtuous action. But most important to this portion of the narrative is Syrena's own "too sudden admiration" of the handsome gentleman she sees out her window. We later learn from the narrator that Syrena has fallen for

Vardine's appearance as a gentleman, mistaking his "Pinchbeck's Metal [snuff-box] for Gold" and thus selling herself cheap (78).

As part of a larger discussion recognizing Haywood's qualifying of the criminal-victim, reason-passion, man-woman dichotomies presented in Richardson and Fielding, reflection on epistolarity and audience can help students see how Haywood further complicates the letter's relationship to authenticity. A useful example is the incident in which Syrena's mother's letters are found, specifically Mrs. Tricksy's computations of the value corresponding to her daughter's attempt to force herself, as mistress, upon Sir Thomas or, as wife, upon his son, Mr. L. In this incident, we are told by the narrator that Syrena's letters are taken out of the post bag and thrown into a ditch by thieves. When they are "afterwards found by a Country-Fellow, who seeing what they were, carry'd them as directed," Sir Thomas reads Syrena's mother's letter and is persuaded only to avoid a "public Trial," concerned about laying the family "so open to Ridicule" (121). In this case, the physical misdirection of the letter reveals its imbrication in communicative practices simultaneously authentic and deceptive. In the end, Haywood's characters use letters, more or less successfully, to facilitate their desires for economic mobility and stability, but, in contrast to their counterparts in Richardson and Fielding, their limited successes are not essentially tied to the letter's ability to authentically reveal a woman's sexual virtue or vice but instead to the very real ways in which letters circulated in the world, deliberately or inadvertently revealing individual insecurities and vulnerabilities, truths and lies.

While authors, critics, and readers alike have tended to dichotomize the relations between genre and gender in the novel, it is important to note that the reality is much more intriguingly complex. By teaching *Pamela*, *Shamela*, and *Anti-Pamela* together, we can provide students with a first-row seat to the eighteenth-century novel, in which members of the novel-reading and -writing communities directly negotiated the genre's form and content. By reading *Anti-Pamela* alongside *Pamela* and *Shamela*, students are able to grapple with the centrality of concerns about female virtue and authenticity in the eighteenth-century novel and the ultimate limits of the letter's reliability as form in determining either.

"Syrena Was a Girl": Teaching *Anti-Pamela* as Protest Literature through Role-Playing

Laura Alexander

Eliza Haywood's satirical novel *Anti-Pamela; or, Mock-Modesty Display'd and Punish'd* was written at the height of the controversy surrounding the publication of Samuel Richardson's popular novel of sensibility, *Pamela*. *Anti-Pamela* appeared shortly after Henry Fielding's *An Apology for the Life of Mrs. Shamela Andrews*, but Haywood provides a darker, more complex female heroine in Syrena Tricksy than either Richardson's original Pamela or Fielding's parodic Shamela. Haywood satirizes the social world that presents Syrena with a series of impossible choices and ultimately asks the reader to sympathize with Syrena's initial victimization as a child prostitute. This essay outlines a teaching strategy that engages students by asking them to think carefully about the novel, the characters' choices, and the time period as they role-play characters from the novel. The in-class game lends itself to critical engagement, research, writing, and oral argumentation skills. It also is a hands-on activity for teaching the novel and its sociohistorical context.

The approach I have taken with students modifies the award-winning Reacting to the Past (RTTP) interactive game format. There are ten published games in the series, which began at Barnard College in the 1990s and had gained broader recognition by 2001. The games are now widely popular and published as a Norton series. Instructor resources and more information about the history of the games can be accessed on the RTTP Web site (reacting.barnard.edu). As the game editors explain,

> Reacting to the Past (RTTP) consists of elaborate games, set in the past, in which students are assigned roles informed by classic texts in the history of ideas. Class sessions are run entirely by students; instructors advise and guide students and grade their oral and written work. It seeks to draw students into the past, promote engagement with big ideas, and improve intellectual and academic skills.

The game format is ideally suited to a literature course and, as April Lidinsky argues, can be used to introduce students to feminist history, literature, and ideas (208). Further, Lidinsky argues,

> From the perspective of feminist standpoint theory, students often have found it quite transformational, as well as enjoyable and shocking, to write, speak, and debate from a complex standpoint (race, class, ethnicity, gender, sexuality) that is unlike their usual one. Thus, role-playing can

> unsettle the usual power dynamics of a classroom and offer opportunities for empathy, a hallmark of feminist pedagogy. (210)

I have also found this to be true in my use of the role-playing game format to teach Haywood's novel. No such RTTP game about Haywood's novel or time period is currently published for use in the classroom, but an instructor can adapt the game format and design a game pack for students using the novel and primary source texts from the eighteenth century—or have students select sources if the course is an upper-level course for literature majors. I have adapted the game for a general education literature course on British women writers that I teach at High Point University, a small liberal arts university. While this adaptation of the game format is not meant to be as extensive as any of the published games in the series, which may take a month or longer to finish, the arc of the assignment will span approximately two weeks.

Framing Anti-Pamela

Prior to playing the game, I introduce the novel as a work of protest literature. My course focuses on women's resistance to patriarchy, commodification, and objectification in literature written prior to 1900. As a class, we first consider Haywood's text in its literary, cultural, and historical contexts, and I ask students to compare passages from the novel with primary texts from *The Ladies Dictionary* (N. H.) and records from Bridewell Prison and Hospital and the Magdalen Hospital for Penitent Prostitutes. I create a series of handouts to supplement the primary source materials that are included with Catherine Ingrassia's edition of *Anti-Pamela*. During the debate segment of the role-playing game, students draw on these materials and other resources they find through their own research.

We hold class discussions prior to the game that consider Syrena's social world. Forced by her mother to participate in an exploitative system, Syrena enters prostitution and blends characteristics of pathos with cunning; she is at some times predatory and at others clearly victimized, her virginity lost early in the novel to an older, more experienced man. Though "our little *Syrena*" (53), as her mother frequently calls her, often directly borrows phrases from Richardson's heroine, as a child prostitute she is ultimately in very different circumstances from Richardson's Pamela or Fielding's Shamela.

Alongside the novel, students read selections on eighteenth-century prostitution from Tony Henderson's comprehensive *Disorderly Women in Eighteenth-Century London*. Together, we also discuss the underground guidebook *Harris's List of Covent-Garden Ladies*. In addition to this sociocultural framing material, I introduce students to philosophical ideas informing the novel and Haywood's writing more generally. Particularly useful in my most recent version of the assignment was Rivka Swenson's article "Optics, Gender, and the

Eighteenth-Century Gaze," which argues that Haywood's novel focuses on seeing the body of the young girl, an assertion that becomes important to arguments students make during the game debates around women's bodies and identities and the systems of commodification the novel interrogates. Swenson traces the optical theories of Isaac Newton, among others, that may have influenced Haywood's adaptation of the body in her text:

> Richardson's *Pamela* constructed a heroine whose apparently virtuous bodily and textual spectacle seemed calculated to reform her spectators and readers both within and without the novel. Nevertheless, *Anti-Pamela*, Haywood's complicated response, exploits the narrative possibilities attached not to just female spectacle in *Pamela* but to a larger body of visual-process metaphors. (31)

The novel depends on the male gaze: Syrena is a sexual object, her body a constant site of negotiation. Haywood extends the traumatic sexual encounters Syrena has with men and the gritty reality of her being forced into prostitution by her mother. Syrena's survival instincts are combined with the practical knowledge of men that she gains over time, and Haywood suggests that to be "anti-Pamela" is to be a woman who wants to control her life in a system that forces her to commit sex acts for profit. Haywood asks the reader not to judge Syrena, however, but to understand her circumstances, which are out of her control, and her life choices, which help her secure her future against destitution. Syrena acquires "A Share of Understanding uncommon for her Years" (77), and the novel concentrates on the system that exploits her youth.

Like many heroines in Haywood's earlier novels, Syrena is thrust into a patriarchal world of predatory males, and she takes action to protect herself from sexual assault and rape. Lacking money, Syrena allows herself to be guided by her mother, Ann Tricksy, a bawd figure. Given her upbringing and her economic circumstances, Syrena sees no option for herself but prostitution. Through letters, her mother mentors her, teaches her to flirt and to trap men, and helps her terminate an unwanted pregnancy. Haywood draws attention to an important concern that appears in earlier works, like her novel *Fantomina*, in which the heroine is banished for her pregnancy while her lover, Beauplaisir, returns to his daily life unperturbed. The protagonist's mother has no compassion for her, but we feel for her plight by the end of the story, though her own mother cannot. As a class, we read and discuss *Fantomina* before reading *Anti-Pamela* to engage with the attitudes of mothers and daughters, sexuality, pregnancy, and marriage in both works.

Syrena's mother is self-serving, and she exerts tremendous power over her young daughter, who sometimes tricks her mother as well, for example in order to meet her first lover. After the relationship is over, Syrena listens to her mother's general counsel about men, but she must contrive her own plots when she finds herself caught between men. Regardless of Syrena's capacity for honesty or deception, she exists in circumstances where she finds agency to be impossible. She has two choices: to be a victim or to manipulate the men who want to take advantage of her. This circumstance is illuminated in Ingrassia's introduction to the novel, which helpfully points out how little agency poor women and female servants had in the 1740s, an important point I also make to students to help them overcome preconceived ideas and judgments about the women in the text.

Syrena learns to navigate the dangerous public and private spaces of the town and the country estate. The novel ultimately concentrates attention upon the skills Syrena must acquire in order to cope with life. After her first seducer, the soldier Vardine, abandons her, Syrena is left a victim. Her first relationship with a man is one that leaves her alone and pregnant. Without her mother's help, she could starve. Most students do express some compassion for the young Syrena, seduced after the soldier encourages her to drink. Students often discuss the meanings of sexual assault and rape, including contexts for consent, as we consider Syrena's circumstances and choices.

Syrena believes Vardine loves her and repeatedly shows through her actions that she feels love even when she says she does not. While she knows Vardine has no money and little prospect for supporting her, she still waits for him with hope. Her unintended pregnancy by him leaves her ill, but her symptoms are remarkably like those of heartbreak. As a class, we compare Syrena's story with the accounts in the anonymously penned *Drury-Lane in Tears; or, The Ladies of Pleasure in Mourning* and the Bridewell Royal Hospital Minutes of the Court of Governors, which can be found online at www.londonlives.org. Students are struck by how seemingly authentic Syrena's story is.

Role-Playing

The discussion of the novel and its time period helps frame the role-playing game in which students put to active use the primary source documents discussed above. I also give students, working in groups, character descriptions adapted from Haywood's novel. To begin the game, I assign each group a character from the novel. The groups consider the historical sources that inform the social class position of their assigned character and think through the choices that character makes in Haywood's text as a way to examine the social and moral consideration that the novel gives to the characters. Students also research their character and the time period, then role-play their character in a debate. Informed by research, their arguments consider different outcomes and directions the novel could have taken had a character had different opportunities or made different choices. They think through the way Haywood situates characters in the novel based on their social class position, economic considerations, and circumstances. Our goal is to see if by the end of the game the students would have made the same choices for their characters that the characters made for themselves or if there are viable alternatives. Those who win have made the best arguments grounded in research.

The game can be adapted for large or small class sizes. I typically teach fewer than twenty-five students. As part of the framing work described above, over the first week of the project students read the supplemental primary texts included in the appendixes to Ingrassia's edition of *Anti-Pamela*. At the end of the discussion portion, the students are divided into groups and assigned a character in a random draw. I typically create six groups, each speaking for Syrena, Ann Tricksy, Vardine, Mr. D——, Harriet Manley, or one created character. This last group (or potentially groups) must create a character that could have appeared in the novel but does not; the invention can be modeled on a minor character in the novel or can be an entirely newly designed character that could plausibly fit into Syrena's social world. The purpose of the game is not a faithful recounting of the novel so much as a debate about how to approach characters, both the actual ones Haywood created in *Anti-Pamela* and the ones she could have created.

Groups then collaborate to study their character and to align the character's values with the primary texts in the appendixes to make their arguments. I structure the game by having the role-played characters debate on panels, mirroring some of the dialogue in Haywood's novel first. Students can be assigned any question, but one that works particularly well is whether one's birth predetermines one's life, a topic that allows discussion of gender, economy, and family to overlap. Each team is given a total of ten minutes to present arguments and to rebut or engage with one another, and all arguments must be made in character. As always in student debates, it is important to ensure that more talkative students do not overwhelm the dialogue. Instructors can use a structured format and a timer to organize the debate itself. Though each group member contributes equally to the preparation and arguments, only one member of the group will speak; to ensure equitable division of academic work, at the end of the project students submit a reflection detailing their individual contribution to the character and outlining the contributions of each group member.

The debate is scored by the instructor: points are won and lost on how persuasive the argument is and how effectively the teams use evidence from Haywood's novel and other resources. The more evidence they integrate into their arguments for the classroom debate, the more points they receive. The length of the debate can vary widely, depending on how well students have prepared. If the game goes very well and students have completed a lot of outside research, I change the schedule to allow us extra time. The character with the most points at the end of the game wins.

The strength of the RTTP interactive game is that it opens students' minds to ethical debates and choices, in some ways mimicking the kind of casuist training eighteenth-century writers like Daniel Defoe experienced.[1] The game promotes an active-learning approach to research, writing, speaking, and argumentation. Because the students' actions in the game are research-based rather than personal responses, students can confidently enter the perspective of the character, even if they do not necessarily endorse that character's values or perspective. Students do not have to agree with the character, but they do have to argue for the character using the research they prepare.

I emphasize to students that the purpose of the game is not to recap and explain the choices Haywood's characters make—that is a point for class discussion prior to the game—but to consider the implications of potential alternatives. One question all students must address in their approach to the game is this: how does and how would a particular character make decisions? The research and historical readings prior to the game allow students a perspective on this question as they navigate choices—social, economic, and ethical—that their assigned character makes. Students are often surprised at how little power many of the main female characters really have, including Syrena's mother, Ann Tricksy, and how much power and decision-making influence the seemingly minor characters—like the upper-class men Syrena meets and "tricks"—actually wield. Students react negatively to the prostitute figures, but this typically changes during the course of the game as they develop more empathy for the difficult choices Syrena faces.

In scoring the game, I award extra points for demonstrating research in character, but because this is a general education class, I do not assign lengthy research papers. Instead, students compile and submit an annotated bibliography and the project reflection, and the final assessment is based on the presentation. Students in an English or literary studies program could be assigned a formal essay as a capstone assessment for this project, putting into a more traditional scholarly form the research material and critical processes behind the role-played debate. Because I teach at a small liberal arts university, we do not have ready access to *Eighteenth Century Collections Online*; this archive of primary resources could expand assignment options further.

After we finish the game, we have a final class discussion about how *Anti-Pamela* confronts patriarchy, child prostitution, and the unnatural system forced on Syrena. Readers of eighteenth-century texts about women will recognize the familiar pattern of violence and systematic prostitution in the novel. It is a cycle of economic, social, and educational deprivation still faced by many girls. As a class, we consider parallels in the novel with later fiction and contemporary debates, which we discuss in the latter third of the course, drawing connections between women writers from the past and current works and debates by and about women. We revisit Haywood, among other women writers, as we study documentaries examining modern iterations of forced prostitution, arranged marriage, and bonding. Many of my students have seen accounts of gendered violence from all over the world in such documentaries as *He Named Me Malala*, and as a class we connect discussions about violence and sexual trauma to our reading of texts like *Anti-Pamela* and Defoe's *Roxana*.

Students have responded with high levels of engagement to this researched role-play approach to *Anti-Pamela*, particularly as it resonates with current social and cultural debates. They have especially gained more empathy for characters like Syrena and have drawn parallels with contemporary issues such as women's health and bodily autonomy. We discuss sex trafficking, especially of young women, and think through national and international responses to child prostitution and child marriage. The game ultimately fosters in students the tools to connect this eighteenth-century debate—and literature generally—to their world, choices, ethics, and responses.

NOTES

The title of this essay refers to the opening line of Haywood's *Anti-Pamela* (53).

[1]See Starr's *Defoe and Casuistry*, which examines Defoe's casuist training and its influence on his fictional worlds.

Reforming the Reformation Narrative: Demythologizing Haywood and the Rise of the Novel through *Betsy Thoughtless*

Aleksondra Hultquist

The History of Miss Betsy Thoughtless is a central part of a tenacious but incorrect narrative of Eliza Haywood's long career. The novel is traditionally read as a narrative of reformation both of Betsy as a character and of Haywood as an author, in terms of moralist tenor and writing style. However, the novel can be read more effectively, in a way that addresses both parts of this doubled narrative of reform, as a tale of experience than as a tale of ethical development. The reform narratives privilege the view of the mid-1700s as a period of moral improvement—both of the author and of fiction writing itself—in which the novel form gained respectability to the extent that fictions guided female characters from vice (amatory fiction / early Haywood) to virtue (domestic novel / late Haywood), thus elevating fiction from cheap entertainment to moral modeling (W. Warner, *Licensing Entertainment*). The reform narrative in terms of Haywood herself appeared as early as Clara Reeve's *The Progress of Romance*, which claimed that, Haywood's earlier work notwithstanding, *Betsy Thoughtless* was "in the service of virtue" (1: 121). Like the larger narrative of the rise of the novel, this account of Haywood's life, character, and career has proved hard to displace despite repeated arguments to the contrary.[1] When students conduct their own research, they unearth the old Haywood myths, whose tidiness makes them tempting.

This essay demonstrates a successful approach to teaching *Betsy Thoughtless* as a novel of experience rather than a novel of reformation. I first contextualize the problems of thinking of *Betsy Thoughtless* as a reformation narrative: making the novel emblematic of both authorial and character improvement devalues Haywood's earlier works and enforces an implicitly essential preeminence of the moral heroine in mid-eighteenth-century British fiction. Second, I offer an account of my experiment in leaving the reformation narrative out of the conversation in my class Amatory Fiction and the Rise of the Novel. When I presented *Betsy Thoughtless* to students as part of a continuum of the amatory genre, they saw little evidence of two Haywoods. Such a reaction allows room for instructors to reconceive the inception of the novel as a genre and to offer alternative narratives of the rise of the novel in the undergraduate classroom, as well as to reimagine the arc of Haywood's career. This approach makes clear that, far from reforming her style and content, Haywood extends her amatory work to challenge the effectiveness of virtue as passivity.

Much work on *Betsy Thoughtless* reads it as the narrative of a reformed coquette who moves "from indiscriminate desire into discriminate choice"

(Braunschneider 112). Published ten years after the first edition of Samuel Richardson's *Pamela*, *Betsy Thoughtless* has been widely understood to be part of the domestic theme of the reformation of character (lively coquette to sedate wife)—and thus also the reformation of the author (amatory fiction scribbler to domestic novelist). Such a reformation narrative matches well with Haywood's other projects contemporary with *Betsy Thoughtless*, especially *The Female Spectator*, in which an exemplary story—often a less dynamic version of an amatory fiction—is followed by explicit authorial advice. However, since Haywood had already staked her claim in the 1741 *Pamela*/*Shamela* debates with *Anti-Pamela*, it isn't off the mark to consider *Betsy Thoughtless* as another salvo on the trope of virtue as reward as the core of a young lady's education.

A domestic narrative, such as *Pamela*, champions innate virtue and patience as the hallmarks of the heroine's character. When *Betsy Thoughtless* is read as an inheritor of domestic fiction, the novel falls short: it becomes another coquette narrative about learning how best to regulate the self to fall into social order. The problem with this reading is that Betsy's lessons in domestic reform do not work in the novel. Her reform—of accepting marriage over flirtation and trying to be a good wife to the self-serving Mr. Munden—brings only the hardship and fear that Betsy expects from matrimony. When the novel is read as an extension of Haywood's early amatory narratives, rather than as a text preaching inviolate virtue or reformed behavior, both Betsy's and Haywood's narratives privilege learning, experience, and self-discovery.

Teaching *Betsy Thoughtless* to students through an amatory timeline prevents a teleological reading that begins with the mid-1700s and works backward. I've argued elsewhere that the domestic novel owes a debt to amatory fiction, one that is central to understanding *Betsy Thoughtless* ("Marriage"). Therefore, I teach experience over repetitive virtue in order to link Haywood's amatory genres to her advice literature and domestic novels. I then place Haywood's interpretation alongside the virtue-rewarded narrative in *Pamela*. Essentially, I am interested in reforming the narrative of reform in the classroom: I want students to see how values asserted by amatory fiction manifest in and are central to the supposedly oppositional and elevated domestic novel.

I do this work in my Amatory Fiction and the Rise of the Novel course. Its description emphasizes an alternative discourse to the rise of the novel, one that refocuses the pre- and post-1740 novel as a continuum rather than identifying any point as a watershed. I use a lecture-discussion model, with historical and biographical contextualization, small-group discussion, a daily discussion board post, and analytical essays. While I offer lectures to support students' readings by placing each author in the context of historical events and contemporary criticism, we do this work predominantly through close reading. The reading list includes works by Aphra Behn, Jane Barker, Mary Davys, Delarivier Manley, Frances Burney, and Richardson, but Haywood is at the core of the course. The issue of "reform" as genre and cultural discourse focuses on four texts: *Fantomina*; "The Lady's Revenge," from volume 3 of *The Female Spectator*;

Pamela; and *Betsy Thoughtless*. These texts encourage students to see a trajectory of approximately thirty years of change in writing style and audience expectation. I focus on the question, How would students understand *Betsy Thoughtless* if reform were not the dominant discourse?

I begin the course by establishing a vocabulary for amatory fiction through students' close readings and my guidance. For the purposes of these texts, we focus on the following issues:

the protagonist as amatory heroine: usually orphaned or has ineffectual or unavailable guardians; always youthful, beautiful, intelligent (the texts use the word "wit"), well-off (but usually not independent), and sexually innocent, but romantically inclined;

a tale of (self-instigated?) seduction and the physical, psychological, and social fallout of the end of this relationship;

the protagonist's negotiation of how to retake control of her narrative, regain reputation, exact revenge, or otherwise overcome her situation, and (typically) a lack of clear systemic punishment or reward for her actions.

With these concepts in mind, students begin to see the structural similarities between Haywood's earlier and later works. Importantly, students feel that amatory works focus on how the protagonist takes control of her plot, rather than explaining the consequences of her succumbing to seduction or the rewards of her inviolate virtue.

The class's daily dialogue begins by reviewing students' posts on a discussion board—short responses addressing text-specific questions. Students are encouraged to make connections between the texts they have already read and the one they are reading. Additionally, I provide semester-long thematic threads for them to follow: the tension between action and reputation; the use and meaning of the word *virtue*; and the protagonist's ability or inability to learn and act. What follows are reactions from one iteration of the class, which took place at a nonelite university in the American South. About half my students were returning or delayed-enrollment students, with dependents, jobs, or both—students typically referred to as "nontraditional" (Choy 23). More than half were first-generation university students.

My students, who began with *Fantomina*, observed the amatory heroine's ability to control her identity and the plot of the novel. Some students, such as Walter Elmore, quoted here, saw the progression of her character choice as revealing a sense of self, because "every disguise brings 'Fantomina' one step closer to revealing her true nature to Beauplaisir. On the very first page she is the whore at the playhouse, where she is just another face. . . . Near the end, she has revealed as much of her real person as she dares without giving away her identity." For Elmore, the lady's progression from one character to another becomes a creation of her identity. Elmore understood the heroine's character as developing from her desire to demonstrate her actual rank and wealth to Beauplaisir. Her resulting experience with him implies that if she should reveal herself, the story would turn into the marriage-as-reward plot. She doesn't, of course, and many students remarked upon the abrupt ending, though none could see how to remedy that particular problem of plot without making very clear choices about punishment and reward. But none seemed to think that Haywood judged her heroine; if anything, they felt Haywood was endorsing distinctive approaches to the problems of being female in the eighteenth century. One student, Benjamin Sasser, offered this interpretation: "I got the impression that Haywood was promoting both intelligence/wit and costume play together, as something that should be admired and reveled in." Students felt that the heroine could, and should, do something to control her story and that moral judgment was absent.

By the time we moved to *Pamela*, students had read several amatory tales and were particularly interested in tracking plot and character. Students were unsatisfied with the emotional turn that Pamela takes. They saw her as frustratingly ignorant and inactive compared with the other protagonists we had discussed. One post, by Sasser, titled "I Don't Buy It," wrestled with Pamela's decision to return to Mr. B. once he has finally allowed her to leave the estate: "I don't think that Richardson gives us enough of a reason to believe Pamela's sudden change of heart or Mr B's 180-degree change of character. . . . I'm shocked that, given the fact that the novel is 400 plus pages, this transformation wasn't a slower development, or a more natural evolution by degrees." Students found this emotional change frustrating after having read the amatory works. But the amatory works have many of the same kinds of abruptness and lack of verisimilitude; students described *Fantomina*'s ending as confusing and ambiguous, but they had fewer problems with the heroine's disguises than with Pamela's emotional change of heart. Because they had about six weeks of amatory reading behind them, and about half of that with Haywood as author, students were inclined to attribute these hard-to-swallow plot changes to Richardson's lack of authorial ability, even arguing that his inexperience as a writer must account for Pamela's lack of motivation. Having learned to read the amatory heroine as an agent in her own plot, they found *Pamela* unsuccessful. Though the plot arranged itself into a careful denouement of reward by underscoring Pamela's passive behavior, they couldn't see the narrative in terms of Mr. B.'s reformation or of the reformation of the novel more generally. They read *Pamela* as a failed amatory fiction rather than as an exemplar for elevated reading, writing, and behavior. For these students, *Pamela* wasn't marking anything in particular; it was a tale of a victim struggling with uncontrollable forces rather than a protagonist trying to control her plot.

When we moved to "The Lady's Revenge" in *The Female Spectator*, they saw a difference between the two Haywoods, but the tonal shift from licentiousness to morality was not nearly as pronounced for them as was the repetition of the amatory character doing her best to control her plot and thus her reputation and desires. Sasser saw the protagonist Barsina's development as advocating judgment over emotion: "More than anything to me, this story advocates the pursuit of logic and reason rather than an explosion of whole-hearted passion." For students, the didacticism of Haywood's tale was not as concerned with moral behavior as it was with taking the appropriate kind of action. Another student, Savannah Smith, noted,

> Haywood was telling women to stop grieving and take matters into their own hands. . . . She seems to be saying, "Look, acting like a lady while showing the world the evil nature of the man will prove to be the better course in the end," [that the result is more] satisfactory to the woman because her revenge will be fulfilled and everyone will love her more dearly for the knowledge of his affairs and retaining her reputation and honor.

Despite the self-serving nature of Barsina's revenge, students read her control of the plot as an example of appropriate behavior for a woman living in a society that gives her little to no legal power.

If they didn't find Pamela amatory because she lacked agency, they didn't find Betsy amatory because she learned slowly and didn't control her plot as soon as she could have. Students concentrated far more on the plot of experiential learning in *Betsy Thoughtless* than in any of the other texts. This was not a reformed coquette narrative to them; while they saw her behavior as foolish, they didn't see her as reforming her ways so much as eventually succeeding through active experience rather than passive resistance. Betsy differs from her amatory sisters, though, because the manner of her education is less dramatic. As Sasser noted, "In almost every chapter she learns some lesson about life and love and thus seems to be growing in the 'ways of the world.' This does not seem like the classic amatory female to me, who learns about life in a more immediate and brutal manner." Betsy's lack of realization in the first couple of books eventually began to annoy my students. Elmore claimed, "It seems like everyone, even total strangers, can see the danger signs except Betsy herself." Sasser finally became so irritated that he wrote his own letter to Betsy:

> My Dear Miss Betsy:
> Allow me to educate you on your missteps in the ways of love. It is not for you to take your time as you are, and seek to get to know such as seek to win your favour. That you continually put off making a choice among the many eligible suitors that wait on you is an advertisement of your own tendency towards inconstancy. My dear, when such fine men meet on the field to duel for your affection you must play the role and to the winner be as fair a trophy as already you are an object of adoration. In fine, when you do not adhere to the accepted manner of courtship, you show in the parlance of our text-messaging times, "ur doin it wrong." Until you mend your ways, I will serve as your conscience in such billets as this.

This student saw not a narrative of the coquette reforming but a narrative of experiential (if slow) learning. Students understood that Betsy's failure to take courtship rules seriously placed her in big trouble when it came to her marriage.

Their perspectives of domestic fiction changed when they reached book 4 of *Betsy Thoughtless*, which presents the ugliness of Betsy's marriage to Munden. Taking the conventional conduct-book advice from her guardian's wife, Lady Trusty, Betsy carefully keeps accounts and remains patient—acts as the elevated domestic heroine, in other words. Then she learns that none of that advice actually works with a self-centered and abusive husband. Students therefore read the novel as a lesson in the importance of decision in courtship: Betsy's experiences underscore the idea that marriage can be just as disappointing and destructive as an illegitimate affair. They picked up on Haywood's questioning the infallibility—proving the fallibility, they felt—of marriage as a reward for virtue. As far as students were concerned, Betsy learned that she chose the wrong husband, because the text mocked the traditional conduct-book advice.[2] By the end of the book, students read Betsy as someone who learned the art of self-representation within the confines of societal requirements. Students recognized that *Betsy Thoughtless* was in many ways a *Female Spectator*—a piece of advice fiction in long novel form: an establishment of character, a mistake made, a lesson learned (or not), and then an opportunity to try again. If *Pamela* shows that heroic virtue reforms, *Betsy Thoughtless* takes that neat narrative to task. Students saw Betsy as a character in a narrative experience—a dynamic, faulty person, like themselves, who fumbles toward subjectivity through mistakes and then accepts the consequences and makes corrections. By focusing on the idea of the amatory narrative and the domestic narrative, they found Betsy to be an heiress of amatory writing and that Haywood had extended her technique rather than reformed her plots and characters.

Building on lectures, class discussions, and blog posts, these responses can be shaped into a more formal critical outcome through a project that engages primary sources from the era. Book 2 of *The Female Spectator*, for instance, is an issue dedicated to marriage choice. After reading this text and others (like *The Spectator* or *The Ladies Calling*), students write essays analyzing the implications of Betsy's behavior according to her contemporary guidelines. Projects built around these primary comparisons encourage students to see conversations between the individual texts, the novel as genre, and prescriptive rules of conduct, in addition to criteria for aesthetic evaluation of texts.

While the narrative of two Haywoods offers a tidy account that fits within an orderly historical trajectory of the novel's rise from morally dissolute to culturally elevated, it is a false narrative. It minimizes the similarities and continuities among Haywood's early and late works while reifying morality as an aesthetically superior interpretation of fiction. When read through the lens of amatory fiction, *Betsy Thoughtless* provides an account of the forging of subjectivity, not through the internalization of moral precepts, but rather through a narrative of experience. Students can learn to assess easy assumptions critically and can be invited to reassess conventional readings by reforming the reformation narrative. When they are encouraged to do so, an alternate and parallel discourse of the novel emerges: the elevation of the novel rests side by side with the experiential power of the heroine.

NOTES

[1]Backscheider, "Story"; Hultquist, "Haywood's Re-appropriation"; King, "Afterlife"; Potter, "God-like Sublimity"; and Spedding, "Shameless," dispute the mythology of two Haywoods.

[2]For more on *Betsy Thoughtless* and conduct-book advice, see Nestor; Stuart.

"Manfully Resolved": Haywood's Masculinities and *Betsy Thoughtless* in the Eighteenth-Century Fiction Course

Christopher F. Loar

In Eliza Haywood's novel *The History of Miss Betsy Thoughtless*, her bluntest suitor describes himself as "no courtier,—no beau." Praising himself for his fortitude and lack of polish, the seaman Hysom compares himself favorably to the "pampered landmen" who compose the bulk of the heroine's suitors (129); they in turn ironically praise his ludicrous persistence, describing him as "manfully resolved" (140). Hysom's self-consciousness about his own manhood makes *Betsy Thoughtless* a useful classroom text for exploring the historical vagaries of gender and its stylization in eighteenth-century fiction. Haywood's novel features a virtual catalog of masculine types: men polite and rough; men duplicitous and straightforward; cynical men and men of feeling. This catalog replicates and parodies versions of manhood found in other fictions in the period, such as Samuel Richardson's Mr. B., Henry Fielding's Joseph Andrews and Tom Jones, and Daniel Defoe's con artists and castaways. The opportunity to explore this panoply of manhoods is an excellent reason to devote classroom time to this lengthy novel.

In my courses on eighteenth-century fiction, gender history plays a prominent role. I frequently remind students that scholars work to historicize masculinity as well as femininity. I point out that, as Stephen Gregg has argued, masculinity as a category, in the way we think of it today, did not exist in the eighteenth century, since manliness in this period was effectively invisible: in the sense that men served as baselines for human behavior, they were not understood to "carry" their gender in the same way that women did (1–2). However, I also encourage students to recognize a concern—even an anxiety—about manliness throughout the century; many writers understood modernizing social, economic, and political events to threaten normative ideas about the male personality. The emergence of desire-driven consumer markets, for example, encouraged men to consume, to spend, and to adorn themselves in ways that did not comport well with more austere notions of masculinity derived from a civic humanist tradition (Barrell 64). A developing sense of British nationhood and an emergent empire also challenged masculine conventions (Wilson 185–205; Colley 164–72, 257–58). Masculinity at the time that *Betsy Thoughtless* was published was thus enfolded in an array of issues related to social status, nationalism, and politics.

Fiction writers of this period played a critical role in propagating and revising ideas about masculinity, imaginatively stitching together practices and performances that would contribute to the creation of new forms of masculine self-discipline, gentlemanliness, and exemplary behavior (Solinger 17–39; Mackie

1–21). My courses draw attention to the forms of masculinity made visible by male writers of the period, especially Defoe, Richardson, and Fielding. These authors are also frequent interlocutors with Haywood, whose fictions both inspired them and responded to them (W. Warner, *Licensing Entertainment* 192–99; Hultquist, "Marriage" 141–43). In this ten-week course, which meets four or five hours a week, I encourage students to scrutinize male figures in the novels on the syllabus—currently *Moll Flanders*, *Pamela*, and *The History of the Adventures of Joseph Andrews*, though there are, of course, many other options; a longer course could opt for the abridged *Clarissa*, *Tom Jones*, or both, for an even richer array of masculine types.

Defoe's *Moll Flanders*, though most memorable for its striking heroine, offers some surprisingly close parallels with *Betsy Thoughtless*: Moll's many suitors anticipate Haywood's masculine pantheon, and Defoe's protagonist is involved with many men before finding her match. Her story is, in part, one of education in masculine duplicity—an education that begins when she is a servant girl seduced by her master's son, only to be pawned off as wife to his younger brother (63–71). Her next marriage offers a notable moment of misreading; her husband initially seems perfect in his ability to combine the traits of the tradesman and the gentleman, but he is actually a "fop" (92). As Gregg notes, this gentleman tradesman erroneously believes that he can spend his way to gentility rather than cultivating a virtuous inner self, thus highlighting one of the key problems in gender in this period: the problem of seeing through the polished surface to the "real" man within (18). Carter identifies the troubling of gender epistemology as central to transitions in masculinity in the later eighteenth century, though this problem had clearly already surfaced well before that point (78–81).

This problem of duplicity also appears in Moll's later relationship with Jemy, her favorite husband, despite his dubious status as a gentleman con artist. "Bred a gentleman but reduced to low fortune," Jemy dupes Moll into a marriage, not realizing that the duping is mutual and that Moll is no more prosperous than he (164–68). Jemy is charming but unable to surrender his gentlemanly distaste for labor and trade, preferring the more genteel pastimes of robbery and hunting. Gregg underscores the way Jemy's class prejudices and habits have persisted; his training as a man makes him ill-suited for the changing world in which he finds himself (41–42). For students, these characters underscore the need to treat manly performances with a discerning eye and suggest that different masculinities may be appropriate for different social and economic conditions.

Richardson's *Pamela*, on the other hand, has only a single serious suitor. Although Mr. B. styles himself as a libertine, I encourage students to see that Mr. B. is, at bottom, a sentimental man, susceptible to Pamela's positive feminine influences. Christopher Flint has noted that Mr. B. is torn between his desire to emulate the heroes of romance and the appeal of the libertines of his own day (191). With some encouragement, students can locate Mr. B.'s references to characters from romance and then track not only certain transformations in Mr. B.'s orientation toward Pamela but also the literary and cultural as well as personal sources of his performances (Flint 189–91). Mr. B.'s emotional susceptibility also anticipates the development of the man of feeling. When Pamela weeps, Mr. B. finds it difficult to master his own sympathy, and it is in part his deepening awareness of Pamela's suffering that leads him to release her from captivity.

Fielding also offers students an opportunity to discuss literary manliness. Joseph Andrews, as Jill Campbell has argued, blends the masculine and the feminine in ways that make it impossible to read him in terms of any straightforwardly idealized manhood (109–15).[1] Parson Adams, on the other hand, works both as a moral exemplar and as a skeptical portrait of the learned man; in my class, we spend time discussing the ways in which his unworldly and desexualized virtue can mark him as an ineffectual—and in this sense unmanly—male (Marshall 230–31). On the other hand, some critics have preferred to emphasize the title character's intermittent displays of "robust masculinity" (anticipating the more complex presentation of manhood in *Tom Jones*) that, with its energetic virtue, provides a sharp contrast to Adams (Hammond and Regan 100). A more developed portrait of masculine virtue is found in the tale of Mr. Wilson, whose story of dissipation followed by reform offers students a secularized spiritual autobiography that renders him a more complete version of his offspring (Campbell 99). I also ask students to recall more pointedly satiric portraits found in the novel's minor figures: the country squire's cruelty and unpolished and unfeeling masculinity, or Beau Didapper's foppish contrast with the narrative's less polished characters (Campbell 71–75, 100–01).

In this course, *Betsy Thoughtless* is the second of Haywood's works we explore. We first study *Fantomina*, which students read at the beginning of the quarter as a way of highlighting several of the course's key topics, including masculinity. *Fantomina* is perhaps most commonly read for its intriguing commentary on feminine agency, but it also allows students to think about manhood, since the narrative is structured around the protagonist's ability to learn what libertines want. Students also need to learn what libertines want—and how they come to want it. They often recognize (and threaten to universalize) Beauplaisir's libertinism. After all, the students recognize the type of the philanderer who seduces women and then moves on. This connection, though, helps prompt a discussion of masculine types: students recognize that not all men are "players," any more than all eighteenth-century novelistic characters are libertines. We consider factors that enable Beauplaisir to play this role, such as his gender, his class privileges, and his lack of strong family supervision. As Juliette Merritt has suggested, the protagonist uses her capacity for disguise to carefully observe Beauplaisir's behavior, becoming a "theorist of masculinity" (*Beyond Spectacle* 61). The novella's focus on a single man, however, limits the range of masculine gender norms and performances presented, especially in comparison with Haywood's other fiction.

Betsy Thoughtless, on the other hand, presents readers (and the protagonist) with a masculine menagerie. Representing a range of personalities and social positions, these characters force Betsy to carry out two tasks: first, to discern the truth beneath various false demeanors; and second, to select the proper type of man who will lead to eventual happiness. Her choice is guided by others, most whom are men themselves. Indeed, the novel as I teach it emphasizes the relational nature of gender: Betsy's education as a woman is centered on her education about men. Though she is an orphan, she receives advice on her potential suitors from a surrogate father, Mr. Goodman, and from her older brothers, the hot-tempered Francis and the libertine Thomas. All of these figures are problematic, despite their virtues. Mr. Goodman and Francis are apparently benevolent, but they are highly effective in pushing Betsy toward sexual norms; after her refusal to settle down with her most attractive suitor, they pressure her into marriage with the duplicitous Mr. Munden. These men continually remind the reader of the way that masculine social economies shape and limit women's autonomy, even if the men who replicate these economies are kind in nature and believe that they act for the best.

But while these men constrain Betsy's social world, they don't force Betsy to choose among them—and this forcing of choice is where the novel truly excels as a site for considering gender and masculinity in the undergraduate classroom. I like to use Captain Hysom to start this discussion. The captain not only refers self-consciously to his own and others' masculinity and presents himself straightforwardly as a male type in competition with other male types; he also highlights a sort of directness that students might expect, in a different context, to be attractive. After all, the novels they've been reading are full of pompous and self-important men and duplicitous libertines; why not try someone who presents himself forthrightly? But, as readers know, this approach is unsuccessful and, for those familiar with the class politics of this period, could hardly be expected to succeed with someone of Betsy's standing. Why is that? Encouraging students to identify problems with Captain Hysom's attempts at courtship allows them to see the necessary traits that men of Betsy's class must present: a certain politeness, sophistication, and polish.

Other men appear in the novel as tests of Betsy's perspicacity and wisdom—tests in which she has an imperfect track record. Though she quickly dispatches brazen libertines (or "rakes of quality" [401]) like Miss Airish's associates, who attempt to drag her into worlds of debauchery, she struggles more with those who put on an appearance of submissiveness and abjection. Consider her dealings with Fineer: he appears to her as a self-abnegating and slightly ludicrous admirer—but one she cannot completely ignore, owing to his purported wealth. She feels that she can easily master him with her superior wit, but her cavalier attitude nearly produces disaster. Concocting a scheme to ensnare her (and her fortune), he feigns a suicide attempt and uses emotional blackmail to attempt to force her to marry him before he dies—an event, he claims, that cannot be far distant (421). This recourse failing, he resorts to attempting rape, from which Betsy is rescued by the heroic intervention of Trueworth. Only then do readers learn that "Sir" Fineer is really a servant. This scene presents students with the opportunity to consider the signs of Fineer's falsity (his lack of poise and wit, for example) and the ways Betsy misreads him; the outer trappings of a superior masculinity are called into question by the character's witlessness, but while Betsy perceives the latter, she misses the former, taking Fineer for a hapless aristocrat rather than the class-crossing deceiver he is.

Though there are many other characters to consider, the most consequential difference in manliness is exhibited by Betsy's two husbands: the first, Munden, whose almost detached approach to courtship makes him resemble Fineer, but in a more dangerously credible register; and Trueworth, her aptly named soul mate, whose attentions she is ready to welcome after her traumatic marriage to the sadistic Munden ends with the latter's death. Betsy correctly recognizes Trueworth's merits early on, but the pleasure she takes in keeping her options open outweighs the attractions of marriage; as she says, she prefers her coquetry to the love of any one man. Trueworth's true worth is repeatedly emphasized, mostly without irony, throughout the novel. His desirable masculine traits include not only his handsome appearance, his financial resources, and his social standing, but also his "sense and honor" (291). His honor is clearly demonstrated at many points in the novel; he scrupulously follows the highest forms of male conduct when forced to duel, for example (170–71). He also has all the social graces requisite of his class, such as a fine singing voice and experience taking the Grand Tour (153). His behavior corresponds to his inner traits, which is why his eventual marriage to Betsy promises to be a happy one.

This happiness is, of course, in sharp contrast to Betsy's horrific first marriage. The reader is given many explicit marks of Munden's insincerity and heartlessness early on. He is, the narrator notes, concerned to give the impression of being devoted to Betsy, but his heart isn't really in it. He is a "courtier . . . accustomed to attend at the levees of the great." This association with the court as a man in waiting is a mark of his untrustworthiness, as it has accustomed him to offering flattery in exchange for marks of favor from his betters. He sees Betsy in a similar light and considers "the case of a lover with his mistress, as the same with one who is soliciting for a pension, or employment." Indeed, his cynicism is all too apt for Betsy at this stage in the narrative; the narrator reminds us that she is a sovereign or a "tyrant" of sorts, toying with her lovers much as a prince might torment or reward his fawning toadies in court (295). Unhappily for Betsy, Munden is better at this game than she: "he could act over all the delicacies of the most tender passion, without being truly sensible of any of them" (296).

It is, of course, Munden's inherently unfeeling and self-serving character that renders their marriage entirely unhappy; until his deathbed conversion, he reveals himself as increasingly uncaring, unsentimental, and even abusive. What's interesting about Munden, though, is that Betsy initially views him with nothing but indifference; he is not her first marriage choice but only persuades her to consider him after she wrecks her courtship with Trueworth. Why does Betsy acquiesce? In the case of Fineer, she sees through his duplicity only at the final moment and is rescued by a Trueworthian deus ex machina, but here, in the face of pressure from her family to settle down, there is no chivalric knight to come to her aid—only her own wit. And that wit, though well honed for verbal combat, is vulnerable to the flattery of potential suitors—a skill that Munden has in spades.

It is the novel's interest in the way manhood can deceive that encouraged me to develop an assignment asking students to adopt Betsy's position as a judge of men and their masculinities, encouraging them to see how Betsy's education as a woman necessarily incorporates knowledge about masculinity. What information does the narrative give us about her suitors? How does she use that information? How do we, as readers, use this information? At the opening of our last day of discussion about the novel, I ask students to place themselves in the position of trusted advisers to Betsy and to identify the clues that Haywood gives us, as readers, regarding the virtues and vices of Betsy's suitors (setting aside, as much as possible, the narrator's own direct commentary). Beginning with this prompt, students work independently at first and then move into collaborative groups to compare notes. In my class, this assignment is part of an in-class discussion (typically in a two-hour class block, which allows ample time for groups to process these questions and produce written responses). I ask students to follow up their group discussions with short, in-class reflections, but this general approach could be adapted to other assignment formats, such as essay prompts or take-home exam questions. If so, a general class discussion that takes students from first impressions toward more settled claims would be part of a scaffolded process leading toward a more precise critical position.

Framing a discussion of the novel this way accomplishes a few different things. First, it helps students become more attentive to details. Second, it allows students to consider whether the novel is, as many critics have claimed, didactic—and, if so, what role the range of manhoods on display plays in this educational mission. Third, it encourages students to think about Betsy's advisers: What are their interests? Do they really perceive things that she does not? What is Haywood's text suggesting about the role of these advisers (male and female alike)?

These questions not only allow students to consider the novel in its historical moment as a document of shifting notions of manhood; they also allow students to consider gender relationally, as Betsy's education as a woman is centered on her education about men, and the masculinities on display in the novel are all responsive in various ways to women or to women's influences. This approach also encourages students to consider the novel not just as a record of these interrelated shifts but also as an intervention—an effort to change the way that femininity and masculinity are understood. Aleksondra Hultquist has argued, for example, that Betsy's *bildung* ("education") is to be understood as a reappropriation of amatory fiction—one that seeks not to deny the passions but to explore a feminine subjectivity that is not centered on virtue ("Haywood's Reappropriation" 39–43). Learning to become a savvy reader of men is perhaps an important aspect of that subjectivity. In short, among the many reasons to make *Betsy Thoughtless* a part of a course on the eighteenth-century novel is the opportunity it gives to explore Haywood's treatment of masculinity—a treatment that responds to and revises her literary predecessors, even as it offers ambiguous advice and guidance on the question of how to discern, from a character's masculine appearance, the heart of the man within.

NOTE

[1]In a graduate version of this course, I found that *Tom Jones* offered an even richer exploration of masculine virtues and values. Jones blends passion, frankness, and rank in ways that allowed students to consider the continuities and discontinuities between Jones and his antecedents while also looking ahead to his descendants in the world of men of feeling (see Potter, *Honest Sins* 2–5, 122–23). Manushag N. Powell has suggested *Jonathan Wild* as an excellent teaching text; certainly it would offer ample opportunities to discuss satiric portraits of masculine misbehavior and duplicity ("*Jonathan*" 163–69).

Eovaai and the Fiction of Fantasy in Eighteenth-Century England

Ros Ballaster

Eliza Haywood may not seem an obvious contender for inclusion in courses on the fairy tale, orientalism, or science fantasy. This essay describes teaching Haywood's oriental tale *The Adventures of Eovaai, Princess of Ijaveo* in the context of the burgeoning teaching area of fantasy studies. I teach *Eovaai* alongside Samuel Johnson's *Rasselas* and William Beckford's *Vathek* as part of a suite of texts that challenge the presumption of realism in the eighteenth-century novel. The unit on the oriental tale could easily be included in general eighteenth-century fiction courses and fits equally well into a course on the history of fantasy or on Enlightenment orientalisms. The students who sign up for the course have, like myself, a strong interest in fantasy fiction in print and on-screen, sometimes as makers as well as consumers. Familiarity with generic conventions and styles in texts as various as *Game of Thrones* and *The Arabian Nights* informs our discussion despite the primarily historicist focus of the course. We are often surprised and delighted to see the continuities—especially the tendency to ironic reflection on the business of trafficking in fantasy itself—between this past and our present.

My course, The Fiction of Fantasy, 1660–1780, aims to test the apparently simple hypothesis that fictions of fantasy from the emergence of the fairy tale in Europe onward signal a consistent resistance to what has been termed the rise of the novel and its attendant realism. Most students and even teachers in eighteenth-century studies still operate within the framework of Ian Watt's 1957 definition of "formal realism," which he sees as emerging in the mid-eighteenth century. The survival, indeed thriving, of fantasy forms alongside the fictions of domestic courtship and national realism has only recently garnered attention.

The course comprises four units, each of which explores a specific fantasy genre. Two units look at fairy tales and oriental tales, both modes of writing that were, as I argued in my book *Fabulous Orients*, for English readers of the period identified with entertainments designed to placate absolutist rulers and courts (French, Ottoman, Persian, Mughal). Two further units turn from the more obviously fantastic regions of fairyland and the ancient Orient to the pseudorealism of the imaginary voyage, which draws on the traditions of travel writing and the hyperrealism of the it-narrative or narrative of circulation. I remind the students early in the course that fantasy genres thrive alongside and speak in the language of the new ethnographic and travel writing associated with expanding English trade in the Ottoman Empire, Persia, and India. Fantasy speaks very pointedly to its contemporary moment, to immediate political and ideological contexts; it seeks to master that strangeness and to manage the otherness of foreign landscapes and peoples.

I offer here three paths to teaching *Eovaai*: first, I demonstrate how a reading of *Eovaai* as fantasy can be illuminated with brief explanations of eighteenth- and twenty-first-century theories of fantasy and fiction. Second, I elaborate on the relation between fantasy and orientalism in the eighteenth century; central to this relationship and to its playing out in *Eovaai* is the ambivalent function of the Orient as analogy or opposite to the Occident in this period. Third, I invite students to compare *Eovaai*, *Rasselas*, and *Vathek* to see how temporal and geographical dislocations enable eighteenth-century writers to comment on contemporary English culture and on both gendered and cultural difference through stories that set before the protagonist a choice or series of choices about a path in life. In class we concentrate on three scenes of the flight of fancy in the oriental tale to point to ways in which it also comes back home.

Eovaai *and Theories of Fantasy*

Readings in Joseph Addison's *Spectator* papers of June 1712 titled "The Pleasures of Imagination" (nos. 411–414) and "On the Fairy Way of Writing" (no. 419) position students to recognize that for early eighteenth-century readers fancy was not—as it was for later readers, influenced by Wordsworth and Coleridge's later mythologizing of the imagination—the degraded or inferior form of the imagination. Addison argues that the pleasures of the imagination stem from three causes: the great, the beautiful, and the new (no. 412). The great gives a feeling of vastness; the beautiful, of harmony; and the new, of curiosity. Students recognize that Haywood's *Eovaai* falls into the third of these aesthetic categories, also termed by Addison "the uncommon" (no. 412) and closely associated with the novel (in the sense of the new as well as that of an extended prose fiction). *Eovaai* uses a wayward, eccentric, often comical narrative form; it is defined by its uncommonness, its acrostically playful departure from conventional paths. The conceit is that the story is an ancient preadamite tale fragment from Australia, originating from a longer tale sequence never fully translated by a group of seventy Chinese philosophers at the bequest of their fifth-century emperor. The modern translator, a young Chinese man living in London, often comments ironically on the old-fashioned and prejudiced opinions of the stuffy cabal. The fact that one of those ancient translators is named Hahehihotu (the name sounds like a titter) lets us know that we are expected to laugh at him. The authoritative sources of reason and virtue are subject to irony. *Eovaai*, as a political satire—in the introduction to the Broadview edition, Earla Wilputte describes its sustained critique of the corruption and self-interest of Robert Walpole's ministry under George II—encourages us to look for understandings of fantasy as a means of political expression.

For advanced students, bringing Slavoj Žižek's provocative thinking about the political valence of fantasy into dialogue with fantasy works of earlier periods is productive. In class I encourage students to identify several key points in Žižek's essay "Fantasy as a Political Category" that help to interrogate our assumptions about fantasy. Žižek suggests that fantasy does not "cover" or "substitute" for a hidden desire; it constructs it (92). Fantasy thus does important work for political propagandists in making its contemporary readers feel they recognize a political reality in a myth. Hence, Haywood presents her opposition politics in terms of an ancient mythic tale in which we recognize elements common to fantasy narrative in general: evil magicians, transformations of state from human to animal, a young and promising generation overcoming the tyranny of the old. What fantasy screens is not a hidden real horror but the void in consciousness or subjectivity itself. *Eovaai*'s satirical argument suggests that rational government by a mature consciousness may itself be a kind of fantasy: Eovaai's eventual happiness and restoration as a ruler is the result of her violent attraction to a young prince, Adelhu, who rescues her from the predatory magician Ochihatou. She rationalizes her feelings as a responsible adult choice of one now fit to govern.

Eovaai is, then, the target of irony as well as the vehicle for it. Here too Žižek's theory of fantasy can be helpful in guiding students to more advanced readings and especially to a focus on aspects of form and narration. Readers of fantasy do not, Žižek asserts, identify with the protagonist in the narrative. We identify rather with the position of the gaze itself. Indeed, fantasy "creates a multitude of 'subject-positions' among which the (observing fantasizing) subject is free to float, to shift his identification from one to another" (99). The play of ironic subject positions—in the form of different embedded narrators who comment on Eovaai's experiences, reactions, and consciousness—allows us to enjoy this freedom. Moreover, some of the inset stories that leave Eovaai's story behind ("The History of Yximilla" and "The History of Atamadoul") encourage fantasy identifications across a range of subjectivities rather than with a single protagonist (as is the tendency of the picaresque and the sentimental or domestic novel).

Eovaai, *Eighteenth-Century Fantasy, and Orientalism*

The great sequences of fairy tales (e.g., works by Charles Perrault or Countess d'Aulnoy) and oriental tales (Galland's *Arabian Nights*) were first translated from the French into English at the end of the seventeenth and the beginning of the eighteenth century to great popular success. My class on the oriental tale opens with staging a contrast between the argument of Srinivas Aravamudan in his *Enlightenment Orientalism* and my own in *Fabulous Orients*. Where Aravamudan sees the oriental tale as a transcultural allegory or flight of fantasy that resists the rise of national realism, I tend to characterize it as a mode that shapes fictions of national identity and allows fantasy to remain a buoyant presence within the increasingly legitimate mode of the novel. Aravamudan and I agree, however, that a study of these earlier oriental tales complicates the significant insights of Edward Said about imperial orientalism from the later eighteenth century onward: in this earlier period, occidental states such as England and France were more often in supplicant positions for trade with oriental powers than in a place of nascent or realized imperial ambition. Hence students can be guided to recognize that oriental cultures can serve not only as other but also as analogue.

For eighteenth-century English writers, absolutist forms of government in Chinese, Mughal, and Ottoman states often serve as parallels for their near neighbor, enemy, and political opposite, France. But the more philosophical forms of the oriental tale can also simply use oriental locales as spaces for thought experiments about universal traits in human behavior: as analogues. In *Eovaai*, the genre of the oriental tale has a monitory force. English readers are being warned by an opposition writer that their country runs the risk of becoming like an oriental or French state, governed by an absolute ruler in the grip of self-interested counselors or viziers; those readers must be on their guard to protect their contractual form of government and to call their rulers to account (they govern to serve their people, not to exploit or neglect them and pursue their private interests). The world of English government can be played out in the fantasy space of another culture set in the distant past or in a distant geography. Drawing on the material on attitudes toward China in *Fabulous Orients*, we establish that China has a special status in the oriental pantheon: both celebrated as a source of rational wisdom and abstract thought and condemned for its difficult language and inflexible scholarly traditions, both of which were often impenetrable to traders and travelers. *Eovaai* speaks to these characterizations of China as both *specula principum* ("mirror for princes," the genre originating in the Middle Ages of texts that instruct potential rulers in rational and virtuous government) and satire on false learning (mocking the pedantry of translation and annotation).

Eovaai *Brought Back Home*

The oriental tale often overlaps with the philosophical tale, especially the *specula principum* genre. We look in our class at two other oriental-philosophical tales that concern the "choice of life" for a young ruler-in-waiting being prepared for government. *Eovaai* is unusual in that it puts at the center of its story a single female protagonist with the "choice of life." All three of the works we consider are uncommon, wayward, and surprising, and it is not my intention to suggest that *Eovaai* is especially sophisticated or self-conscious. But it does help to recognize the comic and ironic valence present in much of this writing from an early stage. These "choice of life" oriental tales often appear to conclude that the conviction that wishes can be realized and will improve the world is itself the fantasy of an absolute imagination. Hence, in Johnson's *Rasselas*, the young Abyssinian prince who leaves the Happy Valley with his sister and companions to explore the oriental states beyond it comes to discover that there is no happy state in solitary wishes—it is companionship and mutual love that sustain us through life's inevitable disappointments. Beckford's *Vathek* appears to have been written to some extent as a spoof inversion of Johnson's homely domestication of the oriental tale. Rather than the thoughtful and reserved but still ambitious prince of Johnson's tale, Beckford gives us an extravagant, violent, willful young ruler whose own insatiable appetite for knowledge and power leads him, in exchange for the promise of supernatural powers, to submit to the depraved demands for the sacrifice of innocents made by a mysterious stranger to his court, a giaour (the word is a now obsolete insult in Turkish for an infidel, a non-Muslim). Vathek begins a career of vice—sexual, political and physical—that leads to his eventual punishment, confinement in Eblis, a hell of eternal flames. Setting *Eovaai* alongside Johnson's and Beckford's tales invites students to look to the positioning of female characters. We recognize that both Johnson and Beckford give us intelligent, ingenious young princesses who learn (or, in Beckford's case, learn better) alongside their male counterparts how to manage rebellious desires or at least recognize how difficult it is to contain those desires and to be watchful of them. Johnson's Nekayah and Beckford's Nouronihar have much in common with Eovaai in their search for domestic happiness to set alongside their responsibilities as the daughters of rulers.

I conclude the unit by inviting students to concentrate on three parallel scenes that help us explore further the ways in which fantasy's apparent departure from the real often brings us back to earth with seemingly new and better knowledge of how to negotiate present space and time. The mythographer Marina Warner points to the association of fantasies of flight with thought experiments in oriental tales and fairy tales. She provides a prompt we use to consider these scenes: "Long before flight became a reality and a commonplace way of traveling, it was part of the world of the mind and experienced, unconsciously, through phantasmata, pictures, and stories. The idea of flying—like birds, like angels—opened a vista of metaphorical meanings for the human subject" (331).

We look at depictions of flight and its capacity to represent the mix of sublimity and bathos so characteristic of the oriental tale. Flights by definition must come back down to earth, but in the political-philosophical-satirical tradition of which *Eovaai* is a part, they often come to earth with a bump. They demonstrate hubris and its inevitable downfall, but also the ambition of the imagination itself. However, they also point to an important distinction between women's and men's access to that imaginative hubris: women are taken in flight or fly in the shape of birds to escape predators. Men fly to express their ambitions, the reach of their imagination beyond the limit or horizon.

Chapter 6 of *Rasselas* (13–17) introduces us and the prince to an ingenious designer who insists he can design a flying machine that will allow the "pendent spectator" (15) to watch the scene move below. He agrees to spend a year building a flying machine to enable an escape from the Happy Valley if Rasselas will keep the secret of construction to himself, since it would be a dangerous weapon in the hands of the enemy. In a year "the maker appeared furnished for flight on a little promontory; he waved his pinions a while to gather air, then leaped from his stand, and in an instant dropped into the lake" (16). The wings hold him up in the water, however, and Rasselas, ever considerate, gets him to land "half dead with terrour and vexation" (17). Johnson mocks the belief that one can rise above others and take a view from such a height, and the fall is comic. This bathos relates to the steadfast refusal in his work of oriental trappings and machinery. Magic powers and talismans have no place in Johnson's tale.

In *Vathek*, the chief eunuch of Vathek's court, Bababalouk, is placed on a great swing above a bath in the harem at the subterranean palace of Fakreddin on the orders of Nouronihar, daughter of the emir (57–59). The naked harem ladies push him on the swing until he is filled with terror. The cord snaps and he finds himself flying in the air before falling into the bath. The women flee, and he tries to get out of the bath but decides to stay there until light. When he recounts the story to Vathek the next day the prince only laughs. There is a playful and fantastic eroticism about this depiction of the harem women teasing the eunuch. It also, however, chimes with the story's contrasting of an airy asexual sublimity (the boy-child Gulchenrouz is saved from the appetites of the giaour by being whisked into a heaven for presexual children) with the dark underground appetites that Vathek increasingly serves and services.

Eovaai taps into a different tradition of thought experiments and flight in fairy tales and oriental tales: the transformation of protagonists into birds, whether to escape predation or as punishment. The novel opens and closes with the flight of birds. Eovaai's precious jewel, which will allow her to protect her people and to govern well, is stolen by a bird from the necklace in which it is kept (57–58). At the end of the novel, Eovaai is obliged to strip naked in order to be transformed into a dove by the magician Ochihatou, who promises to return her to her kingdom (148). He adopts the shape of a vulture and carries her in his talons to a deserted forest, where he threatens to rape her. She breaks his wand before his face in an act of defiance of his (phallic) power, but she still requires rescuing by the young prince Adelhu, who hears her screams when the vengeful Ochihatou ties her by the hair to the bough of a tree and threatens to scourge her with bundles of stinging nettles and thorns (152). Ochihatou dashes his own brains out against a tree in frustration (153).

This scene, my students often observe, resonates with previous depictions of abducted princesses in romance. I point out that it certainly parodies romance conventions, but it also associates those romance conventions with contemporaneous political events: a historical moment when the Patriot opposition, a group of young Whig parliamentarians, imagined a young generation overcoming the repressions of the old. The darling hero of the Patriots in opposition to George II and Walpole was Frederick, Prince of Wales, who married Princess Augusta of Saxe-Gotha-Altenburg a few months before Haywood published her novel in 1736. Here the magical world of the oriental tale is brought back down to earth and to the context of eighteenth-century Georgian politics (see Ballaster, "Secret History"). What seems a flight of fancy is a way of directing readers to recognize the immediate political context of a young prince's challenge to his father's authority and the wider debates of the seventeenth and eighteenth centuries around the best balance of power between Parliament and the monarch. We discuss too how different this allegory of female flight and eventual triumph is from the more peripheral but still significant roles given to the women of *Rasselas* (Nekayah and her maid, Pekuah) and *Vathek* (Nouronihar and the harem women) in bringing down the false sublimity of empty claims to political authority and power.

While students often have a good understanding of modern fantasy conventions, they require a good modern edition of *Eovaai*, such as Wilputte's, in order to understand the work's explicit political references. However, political design in the oriental satire goes beyond allusions to contemporary persons and events. I design class discussion around these related scenes in order to enable students to connect apparently politically neutral tropes of the oriental tale to the parodic and satirical purposes of the work: here flight is a matter of content, a familiar trope of the oriental tale and fairy tale, and part of an overall design not only to puncture the pomposity and authority of a political enemy, but sometimes also to warn against similar hubris among one's political allies.

Literary Communities: *The Tea-Table* and the Hillarian Circle

Earla Wilputte

Teaching Eliza Haywood's *The Tea-Table; or, A Conversation between Some Polite Persons of Both Sexes* offers an opportunity to demonstrate how an eighteenth-century literary community explores literary works and social behaviors through polite conversation. By extension, it can teach students how they too can discuss literature both inside and outside the classroom. *The Tea-Table*'s participants are five intelligent young men and women who come together to talk sociably, without any given agenda. The fictional tea table is patterned upon the sociable interactions of Aaron Hill's real-life coterie, the Hillarian circle, to which Haywood belonged from 1720 to 1724. Teaching Haywood's *Tea-Table* by itself provides students with a model of how to talk about literature; teaching it within the context of Hill's coterie gives students an appreciation of the communal and collaborative nature of literature and life in the eighteenth century as well as in the modern-day classroom.

The Tea-Table, like many of Haywood's works, is a hybrid genre modeled on periodical writing; imitative of conversation; and comprising conduct literature, an amatory novel in miniature, and the meta-novel. A very short work (occupying only thirty-three pages in Broadview's Fantomina *and Other Works*), it is a compact piece about a group of people casually but critically discussing love and literature. The epigraph and advertisement set the tone. The epigraph states that "A faultless Virtue's to be found in [no one]" (73)—no one is perfect—so readers and students should be put at ease that perfection is not expected in their class discussion. The advertisement makes clear that the author is not intent on satirizing "any particular Persons, or Families"; her design is "to expose those little Foibles which disgrace Humanity" and to lead readers to improve themselves (73). In this way Haywood separates herself and Amiana's tea table from the stereotypically feminized and trivialized tea table where the "Curious," "Criticks in Fame," "prying Eyes," and "inquisitive Fleerers" revel in gossiping about the "Scandal, and Ridicule" of others (73–74). Whereas those scrutinizing tea tables aim to expatiate on "any Irregularity in Conduct, any Indecorum in Behaviour or Dress, any Defect in Beauty," at Amiana's tea table it is "Wit and good Humour," as well as "useful Topicks," that make up the conversation (74). Talk does not devolve into the personally vindictive, and subject matter and decorum remain civilized and respectful.

My particular approach to teaching Haywood's *Tea-Table* involves awareness of three literary communities: the Hillarian circle, Amiana's tea table group, and our own classroom. First, I introduce students briefly to Haywood's onetime literary community, the Hillarian circle, which met at the homes of the Hills or the Sansoms to discuss and offer critiques of one another's manuscripts as well as to talk about philosophy, love, and human nature. I focus primarily on Hill, Haywood, Martha Fowke Sansom (hereafter referred to as Fowke, her maiden name and the one associated with her published poetry), and Richard Savage—their personalities, relationships, and major works, but especially their fraught interrelations. Next, we examine how the five men and women at Amiana's ideal tea table converse about love and literature. We focus our discussion specifically on love (78–85) and the novel (103–06), with references to the novella Brilliante reads to the assembly. Finally, *The Tea-Table* is "a narrative about reading narrative" (Gevirtz 103), and when students discover this, the work can be used effectively to develop their critical thinking in reading literature. I encourage students to think about how our discussions of *The Tea-Table* and the Hillarians make our classroom like Haywood's idealized tea table and how we too are a literary community gathering to discuss and analyze literature.

I begin by pairing our reading of the successful dialogic gathering in *The Tea-Table* with number 11 of Joseph Addison and Richard Steele's *Spectator*, which describes the tale-telling duel between the hostess Arietta and her impertinent male guest. To encourage students to recognize elements of a productive conversation, I ask them to bring to class a list of each tea table's main characteristics, including the personalities of the participants (speakers and listeners), their primary topics of conversation, and their apparent goals. Students are quick to point out that the conflict between the *Spectator*'s incessant talker and the protofeminist Arietta does not result in a dialogue; rather, the talker is interested in the sound of his own voice as he repeats the story of the Ephesian matron, and Arietta is intent on teaching him a lesson and shutting him down by telling her story about the profit-minded Inkle. Students are also aware of Mr. Spectator's bias; he obviously dislikes the "Common-Place Talker" and wants Arietta to trounce him (1: 48).

Turning their attention to Haywood's *Tea-Table*, students point out the impertinence of the coxcomb and the coquette, the performance of the hypochondriac, and the malice of her friend as disruptive to good conversation. Students don't often remark on the narrator's behavior without some prodding. The narrator crosses the room to avoid the rude women and must be brought back to the company and reminded of the social responsibility to participate at the tea table. I mention that this is much as a successful class works: each member must participate by speaking, interacting, and listening actively. Students find that when the five members of Amiana's table do not agree (as often happens) they politely voice their own opinion after the other speaker is finished; they do not aim to silence or shame each other but to educate and persuade the others to their view. As Karen Gevirtz describes it, "Haywood models the use of amicable conflict as a tool for uncovering truth, showing a collection of independent thinkers working together to tease out and articulate authoritative insight" (122). In some cases, no definitive answer is arrived at, but the subject is examined from a number of perspectives. *The Tea-Table* demonstrates how people can disagree without being combative or rude and how polite disagreement can result in mutual edification—a good lesson for any classroom.

This assignment and discussion can be developed into a major essay about the elements of a good conversation, using examples like those found in *The Spectator*, number 225 of Steele's *Tatler* on polite conversation, Jonathan Swift's "Hints towards an Essay on Conversation," the good and bad conversations in *The Tea-Table*, and the conversations between author and reader in a major novel (e.g., *Joseph Andrews* or *Tristram Shandy*).

The Hillarians

Once students are aware of how fictionalized conversations can unfold, we turn our attention to the real-life Hillarian circle, which did not conduct itself as amicably as Amiana's tea table assembly. Even a brief exploration of the Hillarians' relationships, poetic and passionate, reveals a tempestuous, eventually destructive series of love affairs and literary conflicts. Tall, handsome, blue-eyed Aaron Hill was thirty-five when he began the coterie in 1720. By that time, he had been married to Margaret Morris for ten years and had had eight children with her. A playwright, poet, periodical writer, and prolific letter writer, Hill was constantly encouraging young authors. Christine Gerrard notes that "the most important part of his 'patronage' was the spirit of disinterested advice, support, and friendship which he extended to many writers" (*Aaron Hill* 63). In number 11 of Hill and William Bond's *Plain Dealer* there is "an idealized account of the Hillarian circle" as "a public space for a civilized relationship between men and women untainted by outmoded rituals of female coquetry and male pursuit" (*Aaron Hill* 76). Unfortunately, Hill's real-life circle of young writers of both sexes became encumbered by messy emotions exacerbated by the presence of the beautiful and unconventional Fowke.

Fowke's poems "Clio's Picture" and "The Innocent Inconstant" reveal how she "presented herself as an object of erotic fascination" as well as a woman who deserved to have her desires satisfied (Gerrard, *Aaron Hill* 78; Wilputte, *Passion* 90–93). Fowke writes,

> Well! an Inconstant, let me then be thought;
> Nor can I help it, if it *be* a Fault.
> No solid *Lead* is in *my* Atoms mix'd,
> *All Mercury!* too sprightly to be fix'd! (Savage 100–01)

Fidelity and feminine submission were not Fowke's style, but she could play the persecuted damsel when it served her purpose—as she seems to have done when Haywood began to publicly resent what she saw as Fowke's manipulation of the Hillarian men.

Hill and Fowke were married to other people—Margaret Morris and Arnold Sansom, respectively—but they engaged in a fervent clandestine affair between 1721 and 1723. Hill sent Fowke erotic letters and poetry to initiate their affair (see Guskin 168–90); and in 1723 the subsequently abandoned Fowke wrote "Hillarius" (Hill's poetic name) a long prose letter about her life, outlining all her previous lovers but describing how he surpassed them all. Fowke's letter ends with a series of increasingly pessimistic and emotional poems expressing her desire that Hillarius love her again to prevent her death by a broken heart and hinting at a possible pregnancy. Fowke died in 1736; her letter to Hillarius was not published until 1752, two years after Hill's death. Its title was sensationalized into *Clio; or, A Secret History of the Life and Amours of the Late Celebrated Mrs. S—n—m.*

Savage also features in a relationship with Fowke; however, its details remain unclear. Hill certainly seems to have encouraged a speculative romantic pairing between the two poets, perhaps hoping they could publish together just as Fowke and Bond had collaborated to produce the poetic dialogue *The Epistles of Clio and Strephon*. Haywood insinuates a more insidious, pandering relationship between Fowke and Savage in her novel *The Injur'd Husband*, and in her scandal novel *Memoirs of a Certain Island Adjacent to the Kingdom of Utopia*, she depicts Fowke as "that big-bone'd, buxom, brown Woman," guilty of incest and adultery, bearing three bastards, and morally corrupting the youthful "Riverius [Savage]" (43; 183–87). When a manuscript copy of *Memoirs* was read by some of the Hillarians, it purportedly led to Haywood's being dropped from the group in 1724. Scholars have been unable to account definitively for Haywood's hatred of Fowke, many speculating that she was jealous of Fowke's affair with Hill or with Savage. Kathryn R. King has essentially exploded the story that Haywood was in love with Savage or had a child with him; but the rumor that Haywood was in love with Hill and jealous of his attentions to Fowke has not been entirely discounted. She certainly admired Hill, and her poetry to and about Hillarius celebrates him as godlike in his writing and his mentorship (Wilputte, *Passion* 98–113).

When time permits, my class explores some of the Hillarians' poetry as it appeared in Savage's *Miscellaneous Poems and Translations by Several Hands*. "Clio" definitely features as the muse of the group, with many poems written to her—by Hill, Savage, John Dyer, and David Mallet—celebrating her beauty and talent. A comparative study of Fowke's earlier published poem "Clio's Picture" and Hill's "To the Author of the Foregoing Verses, a Painter, on His Attempting a Lady's Picture" or Savage's "To Mr. John Dyer, a Painter" in the *Miscellany* provides an effective reflection on the gender roles against which Fowke was rebelling even as she played with them. An examination of "Sleep," by Margaret Hill (as "Miranda"), with Fowke's reply, "Clio to Miranda, Occasion'd by Her Verses on Sleep," and Miranda's response, "In Answer to the Foregoing," reveals a brief poetic dialogue about sexual jealousy, suggesting that Margaret was aware of her husband's affair with Fowke.

Haywood's work is glaringly absent from the *Miscellany*, although there are two poems addressed to her. She published *Poems on Several Occasions*—seven poems written while she was part of Hill's coterie—in the final volume of her collected works in 1724, the year Savage's *Miscellany* was originally scheduled to be published. A comparison of Haywood's "The Vision" with Hill's "The Vision" in the *Miscellany*, or of Savage's "Unconstant" with Fowke's answer, "The Innocent Inconstant," brings to light the differences between a woman's—particularly a female author's—self-perception and her image in the eyes of men. The initial discussion among Haywood's *Tea-Table* participants about how love and society treat men and women differently can be effectively compared with the groupings of the Hillarians' poetry that explore gender difference.

Amiana's Tea Table: On Love and Novels

The fictional polite young people who attend Amiana's tea table do not accurately correspond to real-life Hillarian coterie members; however, similarities can be found. I ask students to consider their earlier list of characteristics of *The Tea-Table*'s four main conversationalists in relation to the topics discussed over the course of the work to aid them in perceiving how personalities affect interpretations of the novella Brilliante reads to them.

Amiana, the hostess, magnifies others' virtues and conceals their faults. Her aim is to gather a congenial and intellectual group of men and women at her table for edifying discussion. Students discover that Amiana is a bit of a prude who cannot appreciate the didactic value of Brilliante's novella. Students pick up immediately that Philetus is based on Hill. Of Philetus (whose name, from the Greek, means "amiable" or "beloved"), the narrator says, "[T]here is in him nothing wanting that one would wish to find in a Lover, a Husband, a Brother, a Companion, or a Friend" (77). Brilliante may be a novelist, like Haywood, for she brings the manuscript of the amatory tale "Beraldus and Celemena" to share with the company. She is "distinguished by the Title of the *Lovely*, by others the *Witty*" (77). I like to ask about this dialectic, especially in the light of the poems by Haywood and Hill, Fowke and Savage. Can a woman be both lovely and witty, or are these mutually exclusive traits? Do these titles indicate something about Brilliante, or about how the world categorizes women?

Nothing much can be gleaned about Dorinthus, the friend who brings the narrator to Amiana's house, apart from his supporting Philetus's view that love is "unavoidable" (78). And finally there is the narrator, who observes and listens, and who tries to be physically separate from annoying or self-centered visitors. Discussion about the narrator arises when I ask what the narrator's gender is. Since Haywood's name appears clearly on the title page, do we assume that she is the narrator? Scholars do not agree on whether the narrator is a man or a woman. Can the narrator function as an avatar for any reader of *The Tea-Table*?

The four speaking participants at Amiana's table, like the *Plain Dealer*'s mixed assembly and the real-life Hillarian circle, easily converse about the passions, literature, and their interrelation. They have poems in their pockets or learned by heart to lend authority to their arguments, to punctuate their conversation, to emphasize a point, or to provide an example of behavior. In response to Philetus and Dorinthus's view that love's errors should be excused, Brilliante quotes Nicholas Rowe's she-tragedy *Jane Shore*, about how women are not pitied when they succumb to love (79–80); Amiana reads a copy of verses by an acquaintance—"XIMENE fearing to be forsaken by PALEMON, desires he would kill her"—to illustrate "the Extravagance that [love] inspires" in some people (81); and Philetus relates an anecdote about one Arabella, who languishes and finally dies for fear that her great happiness with her husband will not last (82–84). (The extravagant melodramatics of Ximene and Arabella may be allusions to Fowke's behavior and her poetry at the end of her "Letter to Hillarius.") We discuss whether this debate is resolved. Do Amiana and Brilliante change the men's romantic (or naive or privileged) opinion about love and women?

The Classroom

Brilliante reads to the little assembly "Beraldus and Celemena," an amatory tale that precipitates a discussion among the tea table participants about the value of novels. For our discussion of the novella and the assembly's responses to it, I break the class up into groups to enact their own tea table conversations. This assignment requires some preparation on my part and on that of the students. In each group of four or five, each person adopts a specific persona from among Amiana's tea table participants; her visitors—the coxcomb, coquette, malicious friend, or fashionable lady; or even Martha Fowke. Then the students prepare a defense or criticism of the novella based upon the personality and views (some expressed in the *Tea-Table* discussion) of their adopted character. I provide beforehand some questions they can discuss. Is Celemena sympathetic? Amiana says no and gives her reason, but can the others provide evidence that she is? Would the narrator, who is inclined to draw apart from the group, sympathize with Celemena's self-imposed isolation at court? Amiana disapproves of Beraldus's characterization, but Brilliante defends it. How would Dorinthus respond? Or Fowke? None of the assembly speaks about Lamira or the Princess. What is their relevance?

Upon reviewing Philetus's defense of the novel genre (104–05), each group continues the conversation by discussing some contemporary views about the novel (provided beforehand). Good discussion starters include Haywood's statement that her novels' purpose is "to remind the unthinking Part of the World, how dangerous it is to give way to Passion" (*Lasselia* 105), number 4 of Samuel Johnson's *Rambler*, and David Hume's "On the Study of History." The tea table reenactment can be brought back for critical discussions of other works in the course too.

By approaching Haywood's *The Tea-Table* as one model among three literary communities, we can demonstrate and discuss how those communities reflect upon and influence one another. Knowledge of the Hillarians serves to color and historicize our reading of *The Tea-Table*; reading the *Tea-Table* characters as an example of how to have a classroom discussion about literature shows how the introduction of different perspectives and even disagreement can facilitate our understanding and enlighten our interpretation of a work; and, last but not least, *The Tea-Table* helps bring an awareness to our students that they are members of a diverse literary community and are responsible for generating and developing knowledge through interactive discussion.

A Spectator View: Narratives of Sex, Consent, and Rape in *The Female Spectator* and *Love in Excess*

Emily Dowd-Arrow

> [I]t is literature that inhabits the very heart of what makes sexuality problematic for us speaking animals. . . . [It is the] thwarted investigator but also the incorrigible perpetrator of the problem of sexuality.
>
> —Barbara Johnson, *The Critical Difference*

As a feminist teacher-scholar, I strive to construct a reading list capable of capturing the literary conflict of sexuality in a historically enriching way. But once one has chosen to include Eliza Haywood, the sheer volume of works to consider and the limited availability of her texts often lead us to predictable selections: *Fantomina* or *Love in Excess*, two readable and available fictions that, unfortunately, cannot alone represent the complexity and range of their author's preoccupation with women's sexual and intellectual lives. In this essay, I hope to tempt my fellow teacher-scholars to broaden their representations of Haywood—not by adding more of her works, but by selecting from one of her most successful works: *The Female Spectator*. I hope this essay serves as both inspiration and guide to teaching an oft ignored but always intriguing periodical that, in my view, encapsulates so much of the author herself. Indeed, whatever you are looking to teach, *The Female Spectator* probably has an essay or story all about it.

Of course, to know that is to have made a serious commitment. The twenty-four books of *The Female Spectator* are a veritable tome; their volume alone can discourage pedagogical ambition, and the inexpensive 1999 *Selections from* The Female Spectator, edited by Patricia Meyer Spacks, culls some of Haywood's most fascinating passages. Yet, even (and perhaps especially) for students new to historical literatures, *The Female Spectator* can be accessible and enriching. After ten years of teaching from *The Female Spectator*, I have learned this: One teachable moment is worth ten scholarly or interesting ones. I no longer attempt to be representative of the periodical as a whole. Instead, I decide what literary and historical moment I want to capture with my course and select the passages that can best represent the way *The Female Spectator* approached that moment. In this way, I am using Haywood's most successful periodical venture much as it might have been experienced in its own day—as one voice among many in a cacophonous and thriving London print culture (King, *Political Biography* 111–32; Powell, *Performing Authorship* 131–92).

What follows is a brief overview of teachable moments from *The Female Spectator*, with suggestions for textual couplings and an extended example of a module on Haywood and her complex and often contradictory representations of sexual violence. It goes without saying that to venture into this area involves risk. Rape is not a vehicle or a teaching tool, and neither the legal history nor the narrative fiction can be separated from the fact that its subject is, essentially, a traumatic event. Interestingly, the Spacks edition does not include the rape narrative I teach, which raises the question, Why not? In no other event are victims more silenced than in instances of sexual assault. That Haywood chooses to give them a voice may help her readers and our students better understand the implications of that silence in eighteenth-century contexts.

Periodicals, Voices, and Debates

I have taught *The Female Spectator* at both two-year and four-year institutions, and introducing *The Female Spectator* as a popular, feminocentric voice in eighteenth-century media resonates with students at all levels. Historically organized courses, for example, can use books 1 and 8 to capture Haywood's protofeminist vision for the venture and her characterization of the Mrs. Spectator eidolon, as well as a feel for the often Dear Abby–esque relationship she constructs with her audience and the implied conversation with other publications. In Joseph Addison and Richard Steele's earlier periodical, *The Spectator*, numbers 1 and 2 introduce the purpose and eidolon of Mr. Spectator and his coffeehouse society of six; the first book of *The Female Spectator* uses *The Spectator* as both template and point of departure to introduce its own unified body of contrasting female voices. In another inviting comparison, reading *The Female Spectator*'s book 18 inclusion of a supposed reader's travel narrative against *The Spectator*'s "Inkle and Yarico" tale from number 11 serves both as a general site for examining the broad interests of the times and as a specific one that illuminates Haywood's subtly subversive representation of other cultures and of influential women.

Students tend to enjoy comparing *The Female Spectator* with thematically related selections from *The Spectator*, especially when detecting Haywood's resistance to the sexist assertions of her "learned Brother of ever precious Memory" (2: 17).[1] One example of such conflicts with *The Spectator* arises in book 5 of *The Female Spectator*, when Sarah Oldfashion begs for Mrs. Spectator's advice about how to tame her daughter's rage for frivolous pursuits (2: 153–56, 166–69). Mrs. Spectator's clear approbation for French society's influence on young ladies flies in the face of Mr. Spectator's anti-French rhetoric in Addison's "On French Fashions and Fopperies" (no. 45).

In a related example, Mr. Spectator's Theophrastian construction of female foibles and the periodical's clear desire to objectify them are exemplified in "Spectator's Plan" (no. 4) and "To Whom *The Spectator* Is Most Useful" (no. 10). Virtually any selection from *The Female Spectator* can be used to contrast this sense, including Mrs. Spectator's response to Sarah Oldfashion. Fuller rejection of the kind of mocking regard for women promoted in *The Spectator* can be found in Haywood's books 10 (the final third), 11, and 15. While Mr. Spectator mocks "female orators" (no. 247), Mrs. Spectator and her correspondents present an argument for a robust female education (2: 352–367) and suggestions for curricula and practical application (3: 82–106). Women's and gender studies instructors who bookend their courses with Mary Astell and Mary Wollstonecraft will find that these passages can fill the gaps in the complex history of the century's growing feminist consciousness. Those preferring fiction can examine book 22's novella, *The Triumph of Fortitude and Patience over Barbarity and Deceit*, in dialogue with Mary Hays's *The Victim of Prejudice* or Wollstonecraft's *Mary*.

The pedagogical value of Haywood's periodical is not limited to senior specialist courses, however; there is an important place for *The Female Spectator* in British literature and even world literature survey courses: to students, Haywood the author and *The Female Spectator* the periodical feel *real*. At my predominantly two-year college, the majority of students hold multiple jobs, support families, or are single parents. Most are women whose status as working mothers or caregivers seems underrepresented in the typical survey canon. They embrace the notion of a brilliant and successful single mother of two carving out a space for herself in the male-dominated print market, and they are both surprised and impressed that a female author in the eighteenth century would be bold enough to address sexually controversial issues facing women.

Contextualizing Rape Culture

One of the most profound examples of such a module is one I present to my students as a historical exploration of rape culture.[2] Sexuality, sexual double standards, and the resurgence of sexist rhetoric in twenty-first-century political discourse all suggest the value in introducing our students to texts that, according to legal historians, formed the "origin story" of our contemporary legal approach to and accompanying attitudes about rape (Simpson, "'Blackmail'"). I foreground my students' reading of a single vignette, Erminia's story, from book 1 of *The Female Spectator* with brief explanatory notes added as comments to the PDF I provide them. In these notes, I situate the story within the periodical's context with quotations; I also provide trigger warnings and brief historical context addressing the problems and tendencies when narrating rape in contemporary novels (the fortunate rescues of comedies; the delicate omissions of tragedies) and in the media (such as the popular court transcripts published in the *Old Bailey Sessions Papers* [*OBSP*]). In order to give students a comparative reading experience through which they can begin to develop their own ideas about Haywood's depiction of sexual consent and assault, I pair *The Female Spectator* vignette with another text, such as *Fantomina*, *Love in Excess*, or the *Gentleman's Magazine*'s teaser excerpt from Haywood's later novel

The Invisible Spy, titled "Affecting Masquerade Adventure." Each adds a more complex view of Haywood as a writer unafraid of breaking the sexual silences enforced upon eighteenth-century women, yet playing her role as "incorrigible perpetrator" of sexual double standards (B. Johnson 13).

In order to think critically about consent and assault in eighteenth-century texts and contexts, students first need a clear understanding of the cultural and institutional frameworks that defined sexual norms and responses to violations of those norms. Legal and literary historians of the period document a perfect storm for sexual misadventure and assault, tracing its foundations to shifting social attitudes about the minds and bodies of women, with little legal structure to prevent wide judicial interpretation (Simpson, "'Blackmail'" 103–04). Five elements of these nuanced and complex circumstances lend themselves to particularly fruitful classroom discourse: the conflict between the emerging sense of women as semiautonomous creatures and a legal system that defines women as property; the softening attitudes toward a heteronormative libertinism (Potter, *Honest Sins* 155–62); the rise of seduction as an attempt to make sense of women as sexual agents still socially subjugated by men (Staves, "British Seduced Maidens" 116); the cultural fetishization of female innocence and simplicity (116); and the eroticization of rape and defloration as the epitome of male sexual satisfaction (Mills 141). Combined with traditional misogynistic ideologies maintaining that "[f]orce is pleasing to girls" and that they say "no" when they mean "yes" (qtd. in Bowers, *Force* 11), one can hardly wonder that seduction and attempted rape flooded the public imagination (Staves, "Fielding" 86).

Inadvertently, or perhaps not, the literature of seduction also served as a tool for silencing real victims of rape. Antony E. Simpson and Laurie Edelstein both argue that literature and media played a stronger role than ever before in capturing and influencing attitudes toward rape. One might ask why attempted rapes and seductions predominate over actual rapes in eighteenth-century literature. As Susan Staves writes of the period, "[rape] itself was close to being unnarratable" ("Fielding" 105). It was very close to being unprosecutable as well. An imaginative backlash effectively suppressed reporting and convictions for rape. Jennie Mills writes that "if [women] were virgins they provoked violent desire," but if they were "overpowered," they could prove innocence only by testifying to a purity they no longer possessed (162). Between 1730 and 1830, only 294 cases of rape and 81 cases of attempted rape were heard in the Old Bailey and the City of London Quarter Sessions. Of those, only 51 (seventeen percent) resulted in a conviction (Edelstein 366); between 1700 and 1750, eighty-five percent of rape and attempted rape cases resulted in acquittal (Mills 151). The *OBSP*, one of the only popular media depicting reported assaults and transcribing actual court proceedings, give some insight into why rape may have been so underreported. Victims who testified were rarely treated as truth tellers, whether the charge was rape, for which the penalty was death, or attempted rape, a misdemeanor fine.

It was the victim's story that was the problem. In order to legally establish rape, a victim must be able to prove "force" and to attest to "carnal knowledge" and to both penetration and ejaculation (Simpson, "Popular Perceptions" 51). The *Proceedings of the Old Bailey* Web site can show students how and why a victim's story and reputation first became the focus of a rape trial. They can see the *OBSP* themselves as salacious commodities, in which judges miss no opportunity to punctuate the victims' stories with insinuations of sexual promiscuity, collusion, extortion, and even prostitution. Dramatic representations of rape, like Henry Fielding's play *Rape upon Rape*, echo this format, sexually exciting the audience by attacking the victim's testimony with questions and accusations that press for details and that stupefy her into silence. Like Samuel Richardson's depiction of rape in *Clarissa*, Haywood's narratives shield their victims from skepticism and allow them to represent their experience and to condemn their attackers. Rather than cast blame on her victims in these examples, Haywood indicts social forms and popular institutions seemingly designed to manufacture female victims for male pleasure. At the same time, her narratives echo the hopelessness of ever finding justice.

Teaching The Female Spectator, The Invisible Spy, *and* Love in Excess

Comparisons between Erminia's story, published in *The Female Spectator* in 1745, and "Affecting Masquerade Adventure" yield productive class discussions. From the start, the *Invisible Spy* episode is so obviously cannibalized from the earlier periodical that students cannot miss it and never fail to raise questions about opportunism in the eighteenth-century print marketplace. But the obvious parallels in the stories also facilitate critical reading by focusing attention on what has changed, what has not, and how those parallels and discrepancies influence their understanding of Haywood's historical imagination.

Both stories stage rapes facilitated by the libertinistic and enigmatic atmosphere of the Haymarket masquerades. The masquerade setting, of course, perfectly distills period anxieties about female sexuality, innocence, and vulnerability, as does the villain of the tales. Indeed, one might ask whether scholarship has overshadowed depictions of assault and rape at the masquerade in categorizing them by their setting, as masquerade tales, rather than by the event they narrate, in other words, as rape narratives. In both *The Female Spectator* and "Affecting Masquerade Adeventure," the villain is a man of rank and fortune who is either conveniently masked identically to the victim's own brother or calculatingly changes his original costume in order to match that of a beloved husband. As a character, he is literally a libertine in disguise, sexually stimulated either by the virgin terror of his victim or by the prospect of using force to instruct a woman in the "true interest of [her] sex" (Haywood, "Affecting"

627). Both rapes take place in the neighborhood of Covent Garden and stage a distraught victim wandering the streets alone near where Haywood lived and kept her shop, the Sign of Fame, in the early 1740s.

The plot similarities invite students to examine core plot concerns about rape, its victims, and eighteenth-century notions of virtue. For example, Haywood's depiction of rape is decidedly feminocentric and, unlike those written by her contemporaries, refuses to upstage the victim's suffering with that of a father or brother. And both narrators conclude their story with a sharp critique of society's—especially men's—hypocritical notions of female virtue, which require that the victim be removed (voluntarily or involuntarily) from society. The plot differences help highlight Haywood's examination of female vulnerability in the eighteenth century, both sexually and in the court of popular opinion.

An exercise I call "He Said, She Said" helps students historicize the events and think critically about Haywood's presentation of them. Prior to class discussion, I distribute a perspective-in-context handout, divided into quarters, to help students conceptualize the eighteenth-century sexual worldview as they read. In the upper left quarter, I list beliefs and expectations about men typically held by eighteenth-century gentlewomen, and in the upper right, I list eighteenth-century beliefs typically held by gentlemen about women. Erminia's context might contain ideas like "unsupervised interaction with men is forbidden," "gentlemen are protectors of female innocence and sexuality," "women create desire in men," "gentlemen don't seek extramarital sex from good women," and so on. One might also include pertinent information, such as the evidence required to swear a warrant for rape, or how many rapes were sworn, prosecuted, or acquitted, in London between 1730 and 1830. In the lower half, I ask students to document and analyze the characters of Erminia or Matilda on one side and of their unknown attackers or their husbands on the other, with brief quotations or references to the passages they draw from.

I divide the classroom down the middle and ask the students in each half to discuss their character analyses and to collaborate on an analysis of one of the two narrators: Mrs. Spectator or Explorabilis. As full-class discussion unfolds, this game illustrates the impact of narrative differences, such as the sex of the narrator (Mrs. Spectator is a woman; Explorabilis, probably a man), the marital status of the victim, and the use of dialogue (Mrs. Spectator offers little, while Explorabilis offers an interrogation scene between Matilda and her husband). It forces students to consider the impact upon characterization when the victim narrates her own story (as Matilda does) and when her story is narrated for her (as Mrs. Spectator does for Erminia). Charting in relation to cultural contexts also helps students notice shifts in notions like female virtue and shame. For example, Erminia demonstrates her steadfast virtue by electing to leave society in *The Female Spectator*, while in the "Affecting Masquerade Adventure," it is the husband who forces his wife, Matilda, into social exile after her assault.

Haywood's *Love in Excess* provides a site for expanding the class discussion into perceptions of masculinity, as well as a counterpoint with the novel's flirtation with rape. Indeed, as a seduction story, *Love in Excess* forms a perfect opening to a discussion of an eighteenth-century paradox: how can women defend their sexual purity when the very men charged with protecting it are the ones most likely to threaten it? Since D'Elmont is the hero of *Love in Excess*, the perspective-in-context handout charts a deeper sense of male perception while steadily constructing a female fantasy of ideal masculinity. It can be used to direct students' attention to male and female perceptions of masculinity in the text. For example, while D'Elmont struggles against his libertine presumptions about male sexual prerogative, his friend D'Espernay is there to confirm all his errors and to bully him into raping the object of his love, perpetuating the assumptions that women "are taught by custom to deny what most they covet, and to seem angry when they are best pleased" (113–14). When students compare their completed perspective-in-context handouts for *The Female Spectator*'s Erminia episode and the intimate scenes of *Love in Excess*, even deeper critical discussion emerges about the complex nature of eighteenth-century sexual villainy. D'Elmont's words reveal deep-seated fears that sexual "tameness" is unmanly and that even Melliora herself may "justly . . . scorn" him (117). As students look for differences between D'Elmont's perception of Melliora and the unknown nobleman's perceptions of Erminia, they quickly pick up on D'Elmont's perception of Melliora's "panting with equal wishes" (117), while Erminia's attacker (as interpreted through Mrs. Spectator) is enflamed by Erminia's "Shrieks and Cries," "Tears and Entreaties" (2: 42). They also note, however, that D'Espernay leads D'Elmont to reinterpret his object's response to sexual advances: "the foolish girl does not know her own mind"; he pushes D'Elmont to "make her happy in her own despite" (136). The result is often that the distance between D'Elmont and the unknown nobleman narrows.

The Female Spectator's depiction of rape is so intentionally troubling that comparing it with *Love in Excess* brings Haywood's illustration of masculinity, the female sexual imagination, and eighteenth-century rape culture into better focus for students. Despite many stock opportunities and constant near misses, rape, both in act and word, is conspicuously absent from *Love in Excess*. When Alovysa and D'Espernay are alone together in part 2, her threat to "proclaim thee for what thou art, a monster!" if he forces her is sincere (148). The scheming Melantha too has a perfect opportunity to follow the Fielding-style comedy script by "crying rape" to save her virtue when D'Elmont is discovered in her bed, but she hides beneath the bedclothes instead. In fact, though the "comedy of attempted rape" would appear to have been at its height in Haywood's day (Staves, "Fielding" 87)—a popular way to satirize prudes and add spectacle to botched romantic encounters—Haywood eschews the trope. When *Love in Excess* is read beside *The Female Spectator*, it is possible to suggest why this is so: for Haywood, rape is not a laughing matter. With its breadth of female experiences and its interest in communicating those experiences beyond the coterie of women, *The Female Spectator* offers instructors a trove of such insights.

My goal has been to present Haywood's *Female Spectator* as more than just a token example of a periodical written by a woman, for women, and instead to demonstrate that its rich, teachable moments and surprisingly diverse perspectives can highlight or complicate course themes. Whatever one's pedagogical goals, the periodical once considered "too ticklish to meddle with" (3: 178) can be a compelling addition to any eighteenth-century reading list.

NOTES

[1]The edition of *The Female Spectator* quoted in this essay is published in *Selected Works of Eliza Haywood*, edited by Kathryn R. King and Alexander Pettit.

[2]On the links between modern and eighteenth-century rape cultures, see Dowd-Arrow and Creel, "'I Know You Want It': Teaching the Blurred Lines of Eighteenth-Century Rape Culture."

Women, Sex, and the Law in Eighteenth-Century Popular Media: *The Invisible Spy* and the Elizabeth Canning Case

Kathryn R. King

This essay makes a pitch for teaching *The Invisible Spy* in a range of undergraduate classes and then describes in some detail a class project that brings together Eliza Haywood and Henry Fielding to take students more deeply into the London media ecosystem at midcentury. Not so long ago the idea of teaching *Invisible Spy* would have been laughable. True, Haywood's near contemporary Clara Reeve thought it one of two works by which she would be remembered (the other being *The Female Spectator*), but as recently as 2005 this massive, four-volume text, Haywood's last major prose fiction, was "almost completely neglected" (Reeve 1: 121; Backscheider, review 142). Pickering and Chatto's publication, in 2014, of *The Invisible Spy*, splendidly edited by Carol Stewart, marked the passing of the era of neglect.

Told from the point of view of a magic-enabled, sometimes invisible male narrator who is able to penetrate intimate domestic spaces but also to mix freely with other men in coffeehouses and on the streets, this to-the-moment narrative of contemporary life offers an excellent introduction to Haywood's late-career activities as a politically engaged journalist. The topicality of *Invisible Spy*, not least its scoffing treatment of Elizabeth Canning's cause, challenges students to rethink an inherited image of Haywood as luscious celebrant of a quasi-timeless realm of female desire. It also presents for study a veteran author's long-considered (and decidedly jaundiced) meditation on the power and dangers of the new print media.

Many students will be unaware that early in the 1740s Haywood operated a Covent Garden pamphlet shop from which she vended the period equivalent of breaking news (King, *Political Biography* 95–110). From the mid-1740s she was editor and chief author of three distinctive works of the periodical essay kind—*The Female Spectator*, *The Parrot*, and *The Young Lady*—experiments that form an important context for the curiously periodical-like *Invisible Spy* (see Powell, "Eliza Haywood" 174–81). Part spy story, part amatory fiction, part political commentary, this generically elusive work can be productively approached as a sustained reflection on the new world of print: a critique of the seductive power of productions of the press and the political corruptions they spawn; a satiric treatment of the period's pamphlet skirmishes, electioneering, party politics, and coffeehouse whisper campaigns; and—the focus of the teaching approach described below—a response to the press sensation surrounding the midcentury's most febrile legal controversy. The affair of the alleged abduction of the maidservant Elizabeth Canning in January 1753 remains to this day one of London's great unsolved crime stories. The media event to which it gave rise holds special interest for the way it brought Haywood into dialogue with Fielding in what can be seen as a final salvo in her late-career political dispute with her onetime friend and ally, now a Westminster magistrate who championed Canning as an injured innocent.

The Canning case, compelling on so many levels, is eminently teachable in a wide variety of contexts and lends itself to a class project that in my experience is a surefire success: a retrial of Canning on the charge of perjury. Students love the enigma of Canning's disappearance and want to figure out what "really" happened, even though this means they must hack their way through a tangle of difficult (but exceptionally rewarding) primary sources. Since these materials are readily available online and in print, the project can be incorporated into a number of undergraduate courses, ranging from histories of popular media culture to studies of representations of law, female sexuality, domestic servants, and the racialized other in the eighteenth century (in this instance Roma people, or "Gypsies," as they were then known). Touching as it does debates over the "problematic sexuality of female domestic servants" stirred by Samuel Richardson's *Pamela* some years earlier (Straub 3), it might find a place in courses on the development of the novel or other topics in literary studies. Within a variety of pedagogical frames, then, the Canning project invites students to make discoveries about the interplay of law, gender, sexuality, narration, and the power of print in the mid-eighteenth century.

The Canning Story

For those unfamiliar with the case, an overview is in order. The Canning affair was a cause célèbre, a pair of trials at the Old Bailey that loosed a storm of public speculation early in 1753 and generated upwards of forty pamphlets over the next two years, including what were in effect position papers by Fielding and Haywood.[1] Canning, an eighteen-year-old maidservant, disappeared the evening of 1 January 1753. She reappeared nearly a month later, filthy and dangerously emaciated, with a bizarre story. She had been abducted by two men and taken to an obscure house of ill repute, where, when she refused to "go their way" (that is, become an in-house prostitute), she was robbed of her stays and thrust into an attic or back room. There, half naked in the dead of winter, with no fire, she subsisted for four weeks on a jug of water, a quarter loaf of bread, and a few bites of mince pie and then made her escape through a window and returned home on foot. The story was improbable, to say the least, but Canning was a good girl of irreproachable character, and good character was thought to entitle her to protection (Straub 70–72). Her family and outraged neighbors believed her and sought legal redress. At this point Fielding, justice of the peace for Westminster and Middlesex, enters the story.[2] An interview with Canning convinced Fielding that she was a "poor, honest, innocent, simple Girl" deserving of his advocacy. Her story was odd, unaccountable, even surreal; but why would a simple girl of good repute concoct a story "scarce credible" (Fielding, *Clear State* 58, 13)?

The authorities, on dubious evidence as it turned out, apprehended two women: Mary Squires, described in an early newspaper account as "an old Gipsey Woman" (Rabin 38), and Susannah Wells, proprietor of the brothel where Canning claimed to have been confined. Her abductors were never identified. In February 1753 the two women were tried at the Old Bailey and found guilty: Squires was condemned to death; Wells was sentenced to branding and six months' imprisonment. At this point events took a dizzying turn that would place Fielding and Haywood on opposite sides of "an interpretive struggle" (Straub 66). Powerful people began to doubt the truth of Canning's story and demanded the case be reopened. Following new investigations, in April 1754 Canning was charged with perjury, tried, and found guilty; she was transported to Connecticut, where she married and became a mother. Squires and Wells were released. Canning never recanted or offered a word of explanation regarding the events of January 1753.

Teaching Canning as Part of the Haywood-Fielding Story

I developed the Canning project for an upper-division literature course that set out to read novels by Haywood and Fielding side by side. My frankly polemical aim was to dismantle the view of Haywood's novels as market driven, opportunistic, and derivative—a view Paula Backscheider taught us to distrust in her influential "The Story of Eliza Haywood's Novels." That essay pairs beautifully with John Richetti's "Histories by Eliza Haywood and Henry Fielding: Imitation and Adaptation," a near perfect exemplar of the critical condescension that typically inhabits her story: Haywood's "eye for the main chance" enables her to produce, writes Richetti, "what is in some ways a perfectly good imitation of Fielding" (248). The chief exhibits in the critical smackdown that I envisioned were the two great "histories"—*The History of Tom Jones* and *The History of Miss Betsy Thoughtless*—framed as bildungsromans featuring good-natured protagonists whose progress toward worldly wisdom moves across differently gendered territory, with *Betsy Thoughtless* posited as a creative reply to (rather than an imitation of) *Tom Jones*. The hope, of course, was that students would come away persuaded of Haywood's originality and skeptical of narratives passing her off as Fielding lite. In this I had been overly sanguine. My students loved *Betsy Thoughtless* but were not prepared for the syntactic complexities of Fielding's sentences, the layered irony, the twists and turns of his plot; and we were obliged finally to resort to the very good five-part BBC adaptation of *Tom Jones*. This certainly helped them get down the basics of Fielding's novel—characters, settings, story line, and so on—but limited the depth of our comparisons of these two long and complex novels.

A more manageable vehicle for reading Haywood and Fielding side by side is provided by the Canning materials, and happily the relevant sources are not only of lesser compass but also readily at hand. Fielding's pamphlet *A Clear State of the Case of Elizabeth Canning* is available in a well-introduced and well-annotated text prepared by Malvin R. Zirker. Haywood's representation of the Canning case is found in volume 4, book 8, chapters 1 and 2 in the Pickering and Chatto edition of *Invisible Spy*, which boasts reliable notes and a careful introduction that is especially good on the political contexts. Some half of the Canning materials are reprinted in *Selected Fiction and Drama of Eliza Haywood* (Backscheider 287–98), alongside additional selections from *Invisible Spy*. Alternatively, both *Invisible Spy* and *Clear State* can be accessed via *Eighteenth Century Collections Online* (*ECCO*). Students will discover that Fielding and Haywood took sharply opposed positions on the question of Canning's innocence—Fielding regarded her as a victimized innocent; Haywood, as a calculating liar—but that both condemned the Canning affair as what today we would call, following William Warner, a media event that "feeds upon itself, producing a sense that [it] has become an ambient, pervasive phenomenon" (*Licensing Entertainment* 178). Early in *Clear State*, Fielding expresses a legal professional's misgivings over the way "inflammatory Libels" purveyed by papers and pamphlets had moved the case out of the justice system into "the Bookseller's Shop" (5). His attempt to reclaim the case for the professionals was to prove futile, however; Canning's cause would become the subject of a voluminous paper war between the "Canningites" and the "Egyptians" (supporters of the "Gypsy" Mary Squires), which can be tracked by motivated students across the electronic archives of *ECCO*.

Haywood was late coming to the controversy. By the time *Invisible Spy* came out in November 1754 (the title page has 1755), Canning had already been convicted. Stewart suggests *Invisible Spy* was first written with the intention of influencing the spring 1754 general elections, but for some reason publication was delayed until later that year (Haywood, *Invisible Spy* xv, 364). Haywood's account reflects with tart astringency on the power of the press to manipulate a "credulous, infatuated, deluded multitude" (437). On this point she and Fielding are not far apart. But she sees Fielding as implicated, if unwittingly, in a network of electioneering corruption in which the Canning media event amounts to a distraction engineered to "*amuse* and divert the attention of the public from what most demands its regard" (Haywood, *Invisible Spy* 427; emphasis mine). Students who look up *amuse* in the *Oxford English Dictionary* will find that in midcentury usage it meant to cause another to "muse" or stare; an amused public is a public confounded, distracted, and designedly bewildered. A productive discussion might address the parallels between Haywood's satiric representation of political campaigns and the so-called fake-news campaigns in recent years that also rely upon a combination of rumor, scandal, and conspiracy theory to deliver an intoxicating brew of "amusement," equal parts entertainment and deflection.

Some knowledge of the history of professional relations between Haywood and Fielding may help students understand their responses to the Canning case. It was once thought they were adversaries from the start (Elwood). Recent accounts have stressed the friendly nature of their relations in the 1730s, when Haywood the actress collaborated with Fielding the playwright and theater manager at the politically edgy Haymarket Theatre, the two sharing a kind of devil-may-care jauntiness when it came to ridiculing everyone's favorite political target, Sir Robert Walpole (King, "Henry and Eliza"). In the early 1740s they were comrades in their shared dislike of *Pamela*: both entered that epochal media event from the satirical side, he with *Shamela* and *Joseph Andrews*, she with *Anti-Pamela*. It was during the post-Walpole political realignments of the mid-1740s that their relationship soured, almost certainly for political reasons (King, *Political Biography* 65–72; Stewart, Introduction to *Invisible Spy* xiv–xix). Haywood, an oppositional writer to the end, would continue to write against the government, usually from a Tory-Patriot perspective; Fielding would propagandize on the government's behalf, championing the Duke of Cumberland in his virulently anti-Jacobite *Jacobite's Journal* (1747–48), for example. Haywood, if not a Jacobite herself, often showed considerable sympathy for the Jacobite cause; she excoriated Cumberland in her daring (and rapidly closed down) periodical *The Parrot*. In 1748, through the interest of his friends George Lyttelton and the Duke of Bedford, Fielding was appointed justice of the peace for Westminster (and later Middlesex), cementing his alliance with the Pelham ministry Haywood consistently assailed. In short, conflicting allegiances and probably patronage systems pulled them in different directions from at least the mid-1740s, and, in spite of a mutually beneficial literary relationship—Stewart makes the case that they were learning novel craft from each other throughout the 1740s and 1750s (Introduction to *Rash Resolve* xvii–xix)—they remained adversaries in print. The famous swipe at Fielding's "scandal-shop" in *Betsy Thoughtless*, which recalls his Haymarket "invectives" against the Walpole ministry in order to impugn more generally his motives as a writer, speaks to the persistence of their political enmity into the 1750s:

> There were no plays, no operas, no masquerades, no balls, no public shews, except at the little theatre in the Haymarket, then known by the name of F——g's scandal-shop; because he frequently exhibited there certain drolls, or, more properly, invectives against the ministry: in doing which it appears extremely probable, that he had two views; the one to get money, which he very much wanted, from such as delighted in low humour, and could not distinguish true satire from scurrility; and the other, in the hope of having some post given him by those whom he had abused, in order to silence his dramatic talent. . . . [The town] has since seen him, with astonishment, wriggle himself into favour, by pretending to cajole those he had not the power to intimidate. (66–67)

The following year Fielding charged *Betsy Thoughtless* with dullness in his periodical *The Covent-Garden Journal.* This history of political difference, combined with Fielding's early and conspicuous advocacy of Canning's innocence, helps explain why Haywood would devote two chapters of *Invisible Spy* to a denunciation of Canning's story as a romance and an imposture, a "heap of wild absurdities" (431), in which she showers scorn upon Fielding for his susceptibility to a "preposterous and ridiculous" story (428), and why she would insinuate that a credulous Fielding was the tool of powerful political interests pursuing their own electoral and legislative ends. Comparison of their positions on the Canning affair casts a strong light on the political hostilities that marked the final stage of a complex and shifting professional relationship.

The Canning Perjury Trial Retried

The trial itself takes students outside the texts by Haywood and Fielding and asks them to investigate a range of additional primary and secondary source materials. Canning's perjury trial occupies more than four hundred pages in the thirty-three-volume *Complete Collection of State Trials* (Howell 283–692), and, while students should be aware of this source, most of their needs can be met by the *Proceedings of the Old Bailey* Web site. This easy-to-use, open-access online resource provides not only searchable accounts of the criminal court's proceedings but also a wealth of explanatory materials and additional readings that enable students to place the two Canning trials within a variety of eighteenth-century contexts. It includes, for example, a useful introduction to Romani communities in eighteenth- and nineteenth-century London with suggestions for further readings, to which should be added Dana Rabin's invaluable "Seeing Jews and Gypsies in 1753." These materials confront students with the fragmentary and ambiguous nature of courtroom testimony. I have used the *Old Bailey* online tool in several classes now, and students are often enthralled by what can feel like an unmediated brush with experience encountered in the transcribed depositions of witnesses—in the case of Canning, a thicker than usual cloud of witnesses.

A classroom staging of the trial of Canning on perjury charges requires, at a minimum, counsel for the prosecution and for the defendant as well as witnesses. Because there were so many—twenty-seven testifying on Canning's behalf, forty-one on Squires's—it is probably best to assign a student or a team of students to summarize the testimony under questioning from counsel. In my class the most eye-opening presentations came from expert witnesses and special investigators, the latter a strategic anachronism devised to deepen engagement and, somewhat paradoxically, to foster the critical distance encouraged by twentieth- and twenty-first-century perspectives. Two proved especially illuminating. A presentation on stereotypes of Roma in the eighteenth century provided context for the harsh punishment initially meted out to Squires; contemporary illustrations of her with swarthy skin, swollen lips, and a prominently hooked nose gave a visual face to the stereotyping process (see Rabin). A presentation on the period obsession with female servants' sexuality (good starting points are Straub 47–82; Bowen) provided context for the tendency of pamphleteers to spin out (with no evidence) scenarios of Canning's imagined sexual misconduct. A pair of expert witnesses guaranteed to rivet student attention are the two medical men, Daniel Cox and James Solas Dodd, who examined Canning's body in search of signs of rape, aborted pregnancy, and venereal disease as well as evidence to substantiate her story of starvation and exposure. Each published a pamphlet; the contents are summarized by Judith Moore in *The Appearance of Truth* (116–22) and further discussed in Moore's "Whose Story Is This, and Who May Tell It?"

Following the trial proper, the students reconstituted themselves as jury members and, somewhat to my surprise, found Canning guilty as charged of "Wilful and Corrupt Perjury" (Howell 283). They rejected Canning's abducted-and-confined claims for the more familiar maidservant-gone-bad story advanced by the majority of contemporary pamphlets. They thought it likeliest that a secretly pregnant Canning had betaken herself to a lying-in house, where she had miscarried or given birth. I was glad to see them reject the assumption of criminality among the Roma that did much to doom Squires in the 1753 trial but somewhat disheartened by their punitive reaffirmation of the stereotype of the sluttish maidservant. Looking back, I wish I had given more time to critical scrutiny of that hardy perennial assumption that servant girls were "inherently prone to sexual misconduct and consequent deception" (Moore, "Whose Story" 228) and in the future might introduce into the discussion insights about victim blaming.

Why was the Canning case so fascinating to so many people in the eighteenth century? Many answers have been offered, but inevitably scholars return to the mystery at its core: the unresolvable contradictions and improbabilities in Canning's story. The episode beckons, now as then, as a problem in interpretation that offers opportunities to introduce students to important aspects of English legal and public-sphere culture at midcentury. Fielding often satirized the inadequacies of the English courts, and Haywood could be quite scathing on the cruelties of a legal system that disadvantaged women. The accounts of the two trials on the *Proceedings of the Old Bailey* Web site enable students to observe for themselves the workings of the justice system and the roles played by gender, race, class, and ethnicity in shaping media-driven cultural narratives of crime and punishment. They see firsthand the problem of witness reliability; weigh the credibility of the accuser and of her alleged abusers; confront the difficulty of sorting through conflicting stories and trying to determine truth based upon fragmentary evidence and multiple voices—all without the assistance of an authoritative narrator to guide them to an interpretation. They learn something, then, about the role of narrative convention in mediating reader interpretation. By way of their encounter with *The Invisible Spy*, students are introduced as well to a side of Haywood ripe for further exploration: her critical stance on the London media culture in which she had played so robust a part.

NOTES

[1] See Moore (*Appearance*, "Elizabeth Canning," "Whose Story"); Straub; Wilner; and Zirker.

[2] For overviews of Fielding's legal career, see Bertelsen; Rogers. For his involvement in the Canning case, see Zirker xciv–cxi.

An Overview of Haywood's Digital Humanity

Laura Runge

In *A Political Biography of Eliza Haywood*, Kathryn R. King describes the vast and multigeneric productions of Eliza Haywood's pen as well as the complex workings of her often invisible networks. Belying centuries of negative publicity, King's research suggests that Haywood was the quintessential agent of media rather than the object of its manipulation. Though Haywood is primarily taught in today's classroom as a novelist, in the eighteenth century she was also known as an author of poetry, plays, translations, pamphlets, and essays; she acted on the stage and worked as a book publisher. Though elusive and private, she nevertheless appeared everywhere that media allowed. Unsurprisingly, she has been reincarnated in digital media of the twenty-first century, and she exists in diverse forms and nodal points of our digital world. The digital framings of her eighteenth-century media presence make her an enticing subject of digital humanities inquiry.

Digital humanities (DH) is a notoriously ambiguous and contentious label that nonetheless is useful for identifying a set of practices and critical options related to digital media (Svensson 476). DH is commonly understood as research and learning at the intersection of digital technologies and humanities, with reciprocal influence on those key terms. This essay first provides a tour of Haywood's current presence in the constantly evolving digital landscape, with extended visits at a few key sites. Then it focuses on teaching students how to use digital corpora to become skilled readers of the literature. Using the relatively simple tool of text mining with word clouds, I demonstrate how data sets can be used to analyze thematic questions of individual texts (such as the sample here, *Fantomina*). The essay then outlines investigations of how early and later Haywood texts compare in their use of language. Computational documentation can then be used to support discussion of how alterations in style are constituted linguistically. Finally, the essay establishes how these methodologies can invite students to situate Haywood's texts in the context of other writers—for example, Jane Austen—in new and informative ways.

Haywood's Digital Presence

King's biography takes pains to separate biographical facts available to us now from the centuries of rumor and conjecture. We ultimately know very little of Haywood's life. This, however, does not stop the Internet from recirculating the rumors and conjectures that, repeated often enough, attain the patina of fact. The digitization of out-of-copyright print materials means that out-of-date scholarship finds a new audience; thus, especially among students unfamiliar with the feminist recovery of Haywood's reputation, obsolete references may come to appear legitimate. Rather than dismiss the Internet as an unreliable source, instructors can use the state of scholarship on Haywood as an opportunity to teach students important lessons in digital literacy.

When a student uses *Google* to search for Haywood, the first result inevitably will come from *Wikipedia*. *Wikipedia* has one of the highest scores in domain authority on the Internet, which indicates that it is most likely to track in search engines. In this case, the result is advantageous, because the *Wikipedia* article on Haywood is the most up-to-date online source of biographical details at present. Students will find several other biographical entries on Haywood in their searches, some of which may appear authoritative: the *Notable Names Database*, *Encyclopedia Britannica*, *Encyclopedia of World Biography*, *ThoughtCo*, and *Lumen: English Literature 1*, an online course with a chapter on Haywood. At the time of this writing, all of these circulate false, disproven, or misogynistic claims. The *Oxford Dictionary of National Biography* article by Paula R. Backscheider, available only to subscribers, is substantially more informed, but it depends upon the biographical facts available in 2004. The growing knowledge on Haywood makes it difficult to keep print materials current.

To develop digital literacy, students need at the very basic level to become critical consumers of digital media. A simple exercise is to evaluate the biographical resources on Haywood. Instructors can begin by having students read King's biographical prolegomenon and introduction in order to establish the limited facts and the textual record (*Political Biography* xi–16). Students then trace the representation of fact in the various Internet biographies (either one source per student as part of a collaborative analysis or all the sources together for a more substantial individual project). For example, the scandalous story of Haywood's marriage to the Reverend Valentine Haywood, exploded by Christine Blouch in 1991, appears undocumented as fact in most of the digital biographical entries on Haywood, as do popular conjectures, refuted by King's research, about the paternity of Haywood's two children. Another questionable biographical practice is the uncritical repetition of misogynistic quotations about Haywood by famous men like Alexander Pope and Jonathan Swift. The comparison of biographical entries immediately opens questions about what is true and what is reliable, and it creates the opportunity for the instructor to demonstrate the role of the archive, the research process, and human judgment in the circulation of knowledge. At the very least it underscores the need for citation, a practice we are often at pains to make relevant to our students.

For more advanced illustration of information literacy, students can explore the *Wikipedia* article in more depth. Many teachers avoid *Wikipedia* because "anyone can write it" or because the content can change from day to day. I would argue that given the state of scholarship on Haywood, the responsiveness of a crowd-sourced public information project puts *Wikipedia* in a good position to become authoritative. The quality of the information in the articles is only as good as we make it. If we care about our subjects, then scholars of Haywood can participate in the production of reliable knowledge for publication on this frequently visited site.

On the surface, the text of the Haywood article reads like a regular encyclopedia entry, guided by rules of neutrality, citation, and significance.[1] Unlike most resources, though, each *Wikipedia* page provides a record of its own construction in its "Talk" and "View History" pages. The "Talk" page is a discussion among editors, all volunteers, to decide what information should be in the article. For Haywood, the editors weigh the merits of featuring the quotations from Pope most prominently in the article. As a result of the discussion, Pope was demoted at one point to a reference in the critical reception section. All the choices were supported by an understanding of significance and with reference to current information. The "View History" page records exactly what changes have been made, by whom, and when. The *Wikipedia* community is rule-based and orderly, and it is vigilant about acts of sabotage, should they occur. Students can trace the changes to the article over time and evaluate the quality at different stages. Most important, they can begin to understand that people like them are involved in this process.

Digital literacy involves critical participation in digital culture, and *Wikipedia* offers an excellent opportunity for involving students in public knowledge production on the Web. The Wiki Education Foundation provides detailed, structured support for teachers who want to use *Wikipedia* in the classroom. Through an easy automated process (with helpful live support from the Wiki Education staff), instructors can establish a course page with an individual dashboard customized for their needs. They can review learning modules on how to design and assess *Wikipedia* assignments for students at all levels, from creating and editing full articles on Haywood's works and contemporaries to checking references, adding illustrations, or fixing grammatical or citation errors. The unique course dashboard is especially helpful for organizing, monitoring, and evaluating the contributions of all the students.[2]

Two additional nodes of digital information on Haywood should be recognized, though they are both behind paywalls. Haywood appears to advantage in both *Orlando: Women's Writing in the British Isles from the Beginnings to the Present* and *Women Writers Online*, a subscription database in the Women Writers Project. Laura Mandell praises these sites as rare and welcome examples of digital projects that "reconceive the infrastructure of women's writing" by offering deep contextualization through the affordances of digital media (518). A student of Haywood will find ample, accurate information in the *Orlando* database, including an easily navigated overview with highlights, an informative list of her writings, a lengthy sketch of her life, a combined life and writing time line, and links to related *Orlando* entries on other women, men, and works that either mention Haywood or are mentioned by her. The web of information available is complex, and it allows for envisioning Haywood in various ways and relationships. In *Women Writers Online*, subscribers have access to ten TEI-encoded, edited digital texts by Haywood, including a full set of *The Female Spectator* and *Love in Excess*.[3] The public-facing, open-access *Women Writers Project*'s "Women Writers in Context" page contains three essays by Earla Wilputte on Haywood, linked to sources, a time line, and a web of connections between Haywood and other works. Both sites are active research projects that continue to be updated.

Patrick Spedding, Haywood's bibliographer, has posted a *Blogspot* entry entitled "Eliza Haywood Texts, Links, etc." This post is the closest thing to an online bibliography of Haywood. While not a substitute for his *Bibliography of Eliza Haywood*, published by Pickering and Chatto in 2004, it includes a partial list of online references to scholarship (not full texts). Most valuable is Spedding's extensive list of digital texts of Haywood's works available online and coded to his bibliography. The "facsimile texts and downloadable pdf" links return to *Google Books* for free e-copies. The "electronic texts" links yield digital editions from various sites, including *Project Gutenberg*. Instructors assigning these texts should first examine the chosen work's imprint and digital representation and determine its reliability. As is true of the original imprints, not all digital facsimiles are equal.

Haywood's digital footprint is by far the greatest in digital reprints or transcriptions of her numerous publications. In addition to Spedding's list, there are external links at the end of the *Wikipedia* article to connect visitors to several sites that feature Haywood or her works. Significant lists of e-texts can be found at the following open-access sites: *Project Gutenberg*, *HathiTrust*, *Internet Archive*, and *Google Books*. Most of these sites have digital scans of print copies, but some include OCR renderings for download, which can become part of a personal digital corpus.

Accessibility for vision-impaired students will be aided by audio files. Both *Betsy Thoughtless* and *The Fortunate Foundlings* are available for download on *LibriVox*, a resource for public domain audiobooks. These and other Haywood works are also available on *YouTube*, along with a growing number of student projects.

Using Computational Methods for Literary Analysis

The availability of machine-readable versions of Haywood's texts offers the opportunity to establish digital corpora that students can use to practice basic linguistic analysis using word counts and concordance. To conduct word counts and related visualizations, one first needs a digital corpus, the simplest being a collection of Haywood literature in separate plain-text files. There are many ways to establish a digital corpus, but for beginners I have provided a set of sixteen novels and four plays by Haywood in plain text at *GitHub* (lrunge.github.io/Haywood-Digital-Corpus). If you want to establish your own, instructions for making a corpus can be found online; it is not hard, but it takes time and attention to detail. Free concordance software that can be used in the classroom includes *AntConc*, *Intelligent Archive*, and the most classroom-friendly, *Voyant Tools*.[4] In her online tutorial for beginners, Heather Froehlich helpfully delimits the uses for corpus analysis:

> Corpus analysis is a form of text analysis which allows you to make comparisons between textual objects at a large scale (so-called "distant reading"). It allows us to see things that we don't necessarily see when reading as humans. If you've got a collection of documents, you may want to find patterns of grammatical use, or frequently recurring phrases in your corpus. You also may want to find statistically likely and/or unlikely phrases for a particular author or kind of text, particular kinds of grammatical structures or a lot of examples of a particular concept across a large number of documents in context. Corpus analysis is especially useful for testing intuitions about texts and/or triangulating results from other digital methods.

Computational corpus analysis is a set of methods that can introduce students to analysis of style, diction, themes, plot structure, and their development over time by breaking down Haywood texts in structured, mechanical ways.

To begin, we have the lowly word cloud. Trivialized by overuse, the word cloud is a simple visualization of the word frequency of a corpus: the size of the type used for each word directly relates to that word's frequency. Word clouds work better than lists of most frequent words (MFW) because they use size to emphasize the priority given to the highest frequencies—the MFW clearly dominate. The word cloud is prominent in *Voyant*'s suite of visualization tools, so instructors have easy access to it, but the range of visualizations available in

Voyant goes well beyond the word cloud, and users can customize their windows to feature those they find most useful.

My sample exercise begins with *Fantomina*, the most frequently assigned of Haywood's texts. The user uploads a text file of *Fantomina* into *Voyant*, and the reveal presents a dashboard with a word cloud, a text reader, the trends of MFW across the segments of the text, key words in context, and a summary of general text features. Being simple, the word cloud provides the easiest entry point for classroom DH. *Voyant*'s default setting removes the stop words (small, common words) from the word cloud, called "Cirrus" in *Voyant*. The cloud visualizes the fifty-five most frequently used words, but the user can adjust that figure up or down. The word cloud invites students to make observations about the meaning of the most frequently used words in the text (fig. 1).

Immediately one is struck by the largest words: *Beauplaisir, time, manner, lady*, and *Fantomina*. An instructor could begin by questioning why *Beauplaisir* has greater textual presence than *Fantomina*. More intriguingly, why is *time* so prominent? *Voyant* provides a tool to show the words in context that, when clicked, will highlight the passage in the text reader. The Links visualization, available in a pull-down menu of visualization options, reveals the collocates,

Figure 1. Cirrus for *Fantomina*. Created by the author based on works in the public domain.

or words appearing most frequently in proximity to the MFW; for *time* the collocates are *manner, oblig'd, going, country*, and *house*. These tools offer more information on the meaning of MFW and encourage students to examine specific passages in close reading. The research question shifts in the light of the visualizations to the understanding of a theme: time. Haywood uses the word thirty-two times in total; the word-use trends indicate that it is most heavily used in the first and final segments of the novel. Students might then hypothesize the reason for the frequency in the structure of the plot.

We can explore more complex questions by increasing the number of texts in the corpus, and *Voyant* helpfully allows users to upload single or multiple texts to be revealed. To continue our pursuit of the research question, we might seek to discover whether *time* continues to be a frequently used word in Haywood's novels in general. My archive includes a corpus of sixteen prose narratives published between 1720 and 1753, which might arguably represent the author's career as a novelist. The resulting concordance indicates, indeed, that *time* is second only to *said* in the corpus overall (fig. 2). The Trends tool in *Voyant*

Figure 2. Cirrus for Haywood's prose narratives. Created by the author based on works in the public domain.

defaults to relative frequencies (percentage of the whole), which provides a more accurate way of comparing texts of varying length. Because the text files are titled with dates of publication preceding alphabetic titles, the visualization demonstrates the trends across time as well as across novels. There is a general trend upward in Haywood's use of the word *time*, suggesting that it became a more important theme as she progressed in her career and, indeed, her life.

Textual analysis, as Froehlich says, is best used for testing intuitions and triangulating research with other digital methods. Scholarship on the novel from Ian Watt forward has recognized that novels, as distinct from romances, directly confront both formally and thematically the diurnal activities of actual lives. Time, therefore, is a signature element of the emerging genre in which Haywood played a critical role. We can test this hypothesis, to a certain extent, by comparing Haywood's fictional corpus with her dramatic corpus (fig. 3). Interestingly, *time* appears only sixty-one times in the dramatic corpus of 58,117 words, which is significantly less than in the novels. We can say that this information supports the claim that time is a distinctly novelistic preoccupation, but the insight emerging from the digital analysis can direct fruitful paths for text-based comparisons and close readings.

Figure 3. Cirrus for Haywood's dramatic texts. Created by the author based on works in the public domain.

Given Haywood's chronological range of literary production, computational analysis can provide some insights into differences between early and late Haywood. By separating the corpora into prose narratives published before and after 1740, we establish two sets of text to run through the *Voyant* visualization. Each visualization can be exported and saved so that you can isolate the visualizations you want to compare (*Voyant's* help button explains useful options for each tool). Below are the images that summarize the general information about the corpus: document length, vocabulary density, average words per sentence, MFW, and distinctive words. By setting early and late Haywood side by side, students can begin to see documented evidence of changes in style as well as links to specific textual examples by which to pursue any insights with close reading (figs. 4 and 5).

For more advanced study, you might compare a Haywood corpus with that of other writers to identify patterns of difference and commonality. For example, *Voyant* contains the corpus of Austen novels, a comparison of which

This corpus has 11 documents with 426,277 total words and 12,331 unique word forms.

Document Length:

- Longest: 1720- Haywood, Eliza,... (89227); 1726- Haywood, Eliza,... (78286); 1723- Haywood, Eliza,... (56823); 1722- Haywood, Eliza,... (49689); 1722- Haywood, Eliza,... (40469)
- Shortest: 1725- Haywood, Eliza,... (11949); 1724- Haywood, Eliza,... (11986); 1724- Haywood, Eliza,... (13153); 1724- Haywood, Eliza,... (17273); 1723- Haywood, Eliza,... (22132)

Vocabulary Density:

- Highest: 1724- Haywood, Eliza,... (0.184); 1725- Haywood, Eliza,... (0.184); 1724- Haywood, Eliza,... (0.176); 1724- Haywood, Eliza,... (0.162); 1723- Haywood, Eliza,... (0.144)
- Lowest: 1720- Haywood, Eliza,... (0.070); 1726- Haywood, Eliza,... (0.078); 1723- Haywood, Eliza,... (0.091); 1722- Haywood, Eliza,... (0.098); 1722- Haywood, Eliza,... (0.100)

Average Words Per Sentence:

- Highest: 1725- Haywood, Eliza,... (83.0); 1723- Haywood, Eliza,... (71.9); 1723- Haywood, Eliza,... (62.1); 1720- Haywood, Eliza,... (52.0); 1723- Haywood, Eliza,... (51.2)
- Lowest: 1724- Haywood, Eliza,... (45.3); 1722- Haywood, Eliza,... (48.9); 1722- Haywood, Eliza,... (50.3); 1726- Haywood, Eliza,... (50.4); 1724- Haywood, Eliza,... (50.4)

Most **frequent words** in the corpus: little (900); said (859); make (844); love (836); time (836)

Distinctive words (compared to the rest of the corpus):

1. 1720- Haywood, Eliza,...: d'elmont (185), melliora (152), alovisa (130), frankville (127), count (327).
2. 1722- Haywood, Eliza,...: lysander (74), belinda (57), courtal (37), worthly (33), cleomira (30).
3. 1722- Haywood, Eliza,...: beauclair (181), montamour (115), du (93), lache (92), baroness (68).
4. 1723- Haywood, Eliza,...: idalia (158), myrtano (83), abdomar (70), mulyzeden (50), ferdinand (48).
5. 1723- Haywood, Eliza,...: amye (72), lasselia (54), valier (26), douxmourie (24), montespan (20).
6. 1723- Haywood, Eliza,...: emanuella (135), emilius (57), berillia (56), pedro (41), don (90).
7. 1724- Haywood, Eliza,...: anadea (64), blessure (31), marquis (34), count (45), roche (11).
8. 1724- Haywood, Eliza,...: philecta (49), dalinda (44), dorimenus (40), philecta's (6), masquerade (4).
9. 1724- Haywood, Eliza,...: bellamant (49), alinda (42), euphemia (20), ellmour (19), alinda's (4).
10. 1725- Haywood, Eliza,...: beauplaisir (34), fantomina (21), bloomer (7), celia (6), bath (7).
11. 1726- Haywood, Eliza,...: ismonda (171), marmillio (128), aridanor (94), theodore (88), adrastus (86).

Figure 4. Document summary pre-1740. Created by the author from databases.

This corpus has 5 documents with 640,201 total words and 13,992 unique word forms.

Document Length:
- Longest: 1751- Haywood, Eliza,... (230324); 1753- Haywood, Eliza,... (165656)
- Shortest: 1748- Haywood, Eliza,... (68353); 1741- Haywood, Eliza,... (73110)

Vocabulary Density:
- Highest: 1748- Haywood, Eliza,... (0.081); 1741- Haywood, Eliza,... (0.070)
- Lowest: 1751- Haywood, Eliza,... (0.038); 1753- Haywood, Eliza,... (0.050)

Average Words Per Sentence:
- Highest: 1748- Haywood, Eliza,... (67.3); 1741- Haywood, Eliza,... (67.3)
- Lowest: 1751- Haywood, Eliza,... (40.8); 1744- Haywood, Eliza,... (56.6)

Most **frequent words** in the corpus: mr (2000); said (1970); miss (1593); time (1527); lady (1300)

Distinctive words (compared to the rest of the corpus):
1. 1741- Haywood, Eliza,...: syrena (253), tricksy (90), vardine (26), mamma (70), syrena's (22).
2. 1744- Haywood, Eliza,...: horatio (284), louisa (244), charlotta (140), plessis (99), dorilaus (91).
3. 1748- Haywood, Eliza,...: natura (340), elgidia (43), charlotte (32), abbess (67), page (18).
4. 1751- Haywood, Eliza,...: trueworth (544), betsy (870), munden (388), goodman (267), flora (215).
5. 1753- Haywood, Eliza,...: jemmy (394), jenny (423), jessamy (207), speck (157), lovegrove (139).

Figure 5. Document summary post-1740. Created by the author from databases.

yields striking similarities between the MFW in Austen and Haywood's post-1740 novels, but not the pre-1740 test set (remember that the stop words have been excluded). *Time* is the eighth-most-frequent word in Austen's corpus. Most notably, the average length of sentences drops significantly from early to late Haywood and even more for Austen. Novelistic style indeed becomes nimbler over time. *Voyant* also contains the plays of Shakespeare, and drama students may want to compare Haywood's dramatic works with those of the Renaissance playwright.

Computational literary analysis aided by tools like *Voyant* will never replace close reading, but it does offer reasonably stable data allowing students to compare and analyze literary texts. These classroom strategies emphasize for students that literature is structured and literary criticism is evidence-based. Once the students have obtained the results of these analyses, the pedagogical question will always be, So what does this mean? For Haywood, the research has only begun, and the classroom can serve as a wonderful lab for new discoveries about this prolific, shape-changing denizen of multimedia.

NOTES

[1] On how *Wikipedia* operates, see en.wikipedia.org/wiki/Wikipedia:About.

[2] For more information on the Wiki Education classroom program, see wikiedu.org/teach-with-wikipedia.

[3]TEI is text-encoding initiative, "a consortium which collectively develops and maintains a standard for the representation of texts in digital form. Its chief deliverable is a set of Guidelines which specify encoding methods for machine-readable texts" (tei-c.org).

[4]*AntConc* was developed by Laurence Anthony (www.laurenceanthony.net/software/antconc); *Intelligent Archive*, by the Centre for Literary and Linguistic Computing at the University of Newcastle (www.newcastle.edu.au/research-and-innovation/centre/education-arts/cllc/intelligent-archive); and *Voyant*, by voyant-tools.org.

Nonfatal Inquiry: *Love in Excess*, Print, and the Internet Age

Tonya-Marie Howe

When I teach Eliza Haywood, my central thematic concern is the status of women writers in literary history. *Love in Excess* offers important opportunities to reflect on the power of affect (as discussed by Stephen Ahern in this volume), the rendering of female desire, and the intersection of public and private in women's lives. It also offers, however, an important opportunity to explore gender asymmetry in the literary marketplace. Despite a deck stacked against them, women writers in the eighteenth century took full advantage of the new thirst for print entertainment and the rise in literacy rates—and Haywood was particularly adept at this, as Catherine Ingrassia has shown. During her lifetime, she was valued as a publishing powerhouse. Haywood's debut novel showed just how commercially viable women's writing could be, opening the literary marketplace to notably larger numbers of women (Ingrassia, *Authorship* 77). She deftly navigated the world of print, making her work a fascinating site for students exploring what it means for a woman to be a public writer, with a public voice, writing about human intimacy in a particular material context.

I teach at a four-year, private Catholic university serving a diverse population. Sixty-six percent of students are commuters, and the demographics of the school as a whole hold true in my classroom: sixty-four percent of students are women, just over one-third identify themselves as white, and roughly another third identify themselves as either black or Hispanic. While thirty-five percent of students identify themselves as Catholic, there are significant populations of Protestant, Muslim, and nonreligous students ("Perspectives"). The course featuring Haywood's work is Women Writers before Austen, an upper-level, writing-intensive liberal arts core class. The course has only one prerequisite, composition. It is therefore rare to have English majors in the course, and even were the mythic creatures to appear, they won't have encountered Haywood—or Aphra Behn, or Charlotte Lennox, or Frances Burney. I need to help students invested in college primarily as a means to a non-humanities-focused career connect with distant literary material in a way that feels significant.

What can we learn from bringing this example into the contemporary marketplace of print, the Internet? What might it look like to translate the erotic spaces of amatory fiction into the public and collaborative spaces of the Web? Drawing implicitly on insights from digital humanists like Mark Sample about the value of sharing and Bethany Nowviskie's call for both "hack" and "yack" in the humanities, I introduce three interrelated digital options for teaching Haywood's novel as an intervention in the public sphere: optical character recognition (OCR) correction with *TypeWright*, *Wikipedia* editing, and audio recording each offer scalable frameworks within which students can explore the materiality of women's writing. [1]

Reading the Text: Audiobooks

As Sharon Harrow points out, Haywood was successful in part because "she turned to account stories of sexual and emotional investment" (298). Known for hyperbolic amplifications, lush and verdant imagery, and breathless breaks that suggest the limits of language as a vehicle to give form to passion, Haywood's *Love in Excess*, a "laboratory of feeling" (Hultquist, "Bringing Order" 80), emphasizes the epistemological value of passion and love (Lubey, *Excitable Imaginations* 95–96). The novel's notorious eroticism impresses even savvy twenty-first-century students. Because none of my students have any experience with eighteenth-century diction or syntax, the audiobook project introduces the language while foregrounding its intimate physical effects. Corollary benefits abound: plot comprehension, introduction to the genre of amatory fiction, engagement with the epistolary additions to the novel, preparation for close reading. This text does not yet exist in audiobook format, so creating a complete book would be a real service to the community—and to the students who so often read along to them. A scaled-up project might involve a collaborative recording for *LibriVox*, which has strict production standards.

To allay students' fears about using unfamiliar technologies, I frame the project as a low-stakes assignment within the course's larger multimedia and participation component of ten to fifteen percent of the total grade. I introduce a variety of tools students might use to generate their recording, including *SoundCloud*, *TwistedWave*, even a cell phone with a good microphone; I guide students to free editing platforms like *Audacity*; and I show students how to get help from our audiovisual technologist on campus. I complete the project myself with *SoundCloud*, from which I create a step-by-step handout. Emphasizing students' freedom while clearly defining the project's goals empowers students to use their voices—and to hear their voices as public interventions. While my recording is always available online, I show students how to download and delete their work from *SoundCloud* for upload to *Canvas*, a learning management system, enabling them to assert control over their public voices.

Worries about accented speech can be connected to Haywood's experience in the public print marketplace. I use other recordings, such as a collaborative *LibriVox* recording of *Wuthering Heights* (Martina), to highlight the beauty of accented speech and create a teachable moment—we must strive to embrace our voices, in all their rich variety, while realizing that it may not always be easy. By the same token, one must prepare and do the work. Students read their selection aloud several times, noting difficult areas, before recording. The goal is to complete the reading in one shot, because a low-stakes project demands

Table 1. Sample excerpts

Pages	Start–End Points	Key Topic / Significance
55–60	"D'Elmont knew the power"—"'my shameful breach of it'"	Scene between Amena and D'Elmont in the garden showcases the erotics of amatory fiction
84–93	Beginning—"last of her tranquility"	Emphasizes D'Elmont's changing character as a result of Amena's epistolary revelation
113–18	"The Baron was"—"opened the door"	The Baron's instigation emphasizes homosocial masculinity; D'Elmont assaults Melliora in her room
139–59*	"At last the hour"—end	The confusions of the bed trick and Alovisa's death are integral to the plot; D'Espernay's response reveals gender ideology
163–70	Beginning—"with which he entered"	Dramatizes the exoticization of Italy and the trope of concealed identity
204–13	"These new made friends"—"from his heart"	D'Elmont visits "Camilla," who is exotically, aggressively sexualized
241–45*	"The next day found"—"carefully attended"	The cross-dressed Violetta/Fidelio provides another model of amatory engagement
256–66*	"My impatience to behold you"—end	Conclusion emphasizes the value system of the novel

*Particularly recommended for teams.

simplicity. Grades, which I assign according to accessibility, accuracy, style, and initiative, are typically above eighty percent.

Using David Oakleaf's Broadview edition of *Love in Excess*, students choose from preselected passages that are particularly telling of Haywood's style or contain representative tropes (table 1). All passages are appropriate for either teams or individuals; because they have clear beginnings and endings, they also focus class discussion.

Students also complete a two-page reflective analysis in which they explain what they learned about Haywood's writing style, her appeal, and their own voice, using specific examples. In their reflective writing, comments about the act of reading itself leads to critical analysis. Karina Garcia, a student who worked on a collaborative reading, wrote, "It may seem obvious, but it is very different to read something in one's mind and actually reading with one's voice." Such self-awareness helps get at the what and the why of close reading, and it is especially helpful in a writing class where nearly a third of students speak

English as a second language. Virtually every reflection showed awareness of the physical experience of reading, especially the elaborately phrased sentences that generated a need, as Kaya Hampton wrote, "to control breath." Others, like Kirsten Pettaway, made interesting connections between the long, multipart sentences and the dramatic, "over-the-top and exciting" quality of the genre, explicitly singling out how the "lavish" use of language leads to readerly investment; for Garcia, the "constant use of semicolons . . . makes readers . . . even more engrossed in the novel"; and Margaret Baer wrote that Ciamara's "outfit alone" was so descriptively explored that almost anyone would "be enamoured by her." Other students saw Haywood's use of gendered violence in vivid detail—D'Elmont and D'Espernay's conversations made one student angry, which in turn rendered the recording process difficult. Alexandra Pedroza, however, described growing "closer to the characters" because of Melliora's "intelligent, passionate retorts to the constant finesse that D'Elmont pursued her with." Such responses offer inexperienced readers clear ways to participate in theoretical discussions of the dangerous allure of novel reading (W. Warner, *Licensing Entertainment* 4–6), for instance, or the power of gendered voice (Potter, "Language").

The Politics of Public Writing: Wikipedia

Each time I use *Wikipedia* in the classroom, I learn something new—about *Wikipedia*, about my students, and about the act of writing in public. Because *Wikipedia* is a site of collaborative authorship, while it is incumbent upon us to be correct, our words are also not the end of the story. This fact minimizes some of the concern students often have about putting their words into the public sphere. Given that my students typically struggle both with writing and with reading archaic prose, I emphasize that this project is about exploration and making a beginning. The assignments I create around *Wikipedia* are incorporated into the multimedia and participation course component. I have also incorporated this as an individually motivated extra credit project, especially for weaker writers who lack confidence.

Before beginning *Love in Excess*, students will have read *Fantomina*, at which time I discuss Haywood's reception, emphasizing her embeddedness in the world of the professional writer. I ask students to read the *Wikipedia* entry on Haywood, raising issues of the sort outlined in Laura Runge's essay in this volume. Students compare Haywood's entry with those of Alexander Pope and Jonathan Swift, which leads us into a discussion of canonicity and gender bias on *Wikipedia* (see "Worrying Consequences" and "Wikipedia:WikiProject").

Despite being one of the first and most often consulted Web sites, *Wikipedia* has a well-known gender bias, visible both in content and in demographics. According to a 2011 report by the Wikimedia Foundation, the typical editor is a thirty-year-old, college-educated male (only eight percent identify as female, and less than one percent as transgender) who resides in the United States, a relatively small part of "the West" ("Wikipedia Editors"). Women who do contribute make fewer edits, and women of color are even more underrepresented. People who look like the people I teach, in other words, are not writing *Wikipedia*. Because the essays populating *Wikipedia* foreground the values and interests of its writers, it is unsurprising that those about women are less visible. At time of writing, the page on *Love in Excess* is an orphan, meaning it can be accessed only by direct search; it is disconnected from internal links to related and more visible topics. *Wikipedia* articles about women also disproportionately emphasize their subjects' femininity, unlike articles about men ("Computational Linguistics"). Further, recent controversies highlight the dangers of using gendered subcategories for women while omitting them for men (Filipacchi). It is essential that more women, and more people of color, contribute.[2]

Students at all levels of skill benefit from interacting with *Wikipedia* in a more critical, participatory manner. As the list below demonstrates, projects can be organized around writing and criticism, around gender and the public sphere. Such assignments offer a rich context for students not only to see their own writing as potentially public, but also to assess the politics of women's writing in a society that continues to be shaped by masculinist values often treated as neutral, unmarked, and invisible.

Criticism and rhetorics of valuation: Compare the *Wikipedia* page for Shakespeare's *Midsummer Night's Dream* or *Winter's Tale*, works that overlap thematically with Haywood's novel, to the page for *Love in Excess*. Notice links from and to each page, subcategories, sources, and the writing style of each page. Write a summary of the differences you note, and then draw a logical inference about the comparative cultural status of these texts.

Summary and critical dialogue: Draft a summary of the novel that covers the entire plot but clearly distinguishes between necessary and tangential information. Then revise a peer's work, being sure the piece conforms to *Wikipedia* guidelines. Select the best summary and incorporate it into *Wikipedia*.

Critical approaches: Locate one *Wikipedia* page that should link to *Love in Excess* but doesn't and one page that *Love in Excess* should link to but doesn't. Add the links.

Critical approaches: Incorporate an appropriate scholarly source. Working with a partner, locate, read, and discuss your source, being sure you understand its content. Identify possible places to incorporate your new information into the page and choose the best way to do so. Write two to three sentences, correctly cited according to *Wikipedia* rules, that incorporate your new information into the page.

Academic writing and rhetorical analysis: Examine the rules that guide writing on *Wikipedia*, paying particular attention to "Neutral Point of

View" and "How to Write Simple English Pages." What universal rules for academic writing can you draw from these pages? Comparatively evaluate your own writing for this class.

Academic writing and revision: Wikipedia has several "templates," or standardized messages, that can be added to pages to indicate what additional editing or content is needed ("Wikipedia:Template Messages"). An example appears on the *Wikipedia* page for "*Henrietta* (novel)," which identifies the page as too long and in need of reorganization. Look through the available templates and, working with a partner, identify which two or three might best apply to the page on *Love in Excess*. Insert the most important into the page.

Grappling with Print: Optical Character Recognition

A third point of contact for students new to the eighteenth century and eager to forge a real-world connection is the material text itself. This assignment asks students to correct faulty OCR in the full text of *Love in Excess* (available outside of *Eighteenth Century Collections Online* through *18thConnect*'s *TypeWright* tool), a task that invites them to interact physically with the text. Such engagement with even facsimile copies of early printed works materializes the reading process, an important opportunity for students with no experiential map of earlier printed books. It also emphasizes broad goals of access and accuracy, enabling students to see themselves as engaged in impactful scholarly work. In a class that meets twice a week for ninety minutes each period, students do hands-on in-class work for two days and finish the work on their own over the next two weeks.

Homework due during the first hands-on period is a reflective writing exercise about their experience with online texts. I ask students, What are the benefits and the challenges of online texts? What different sources for online texts have you used? What is it like to use these sources in a classroom discussion or for writing an essay? What differences do you notice between online and print texts, or between different online texts? On the first hands-on day, we discuss these reflections. Most will describe having not purchased a printed book required for the course, instead choosing to read it online in one of the various corrupted, unpaginated, unreliable, or otherwise divergent versions available. We talk about the purpose of printed books in our class (being on the same page, access to notes, portability) and in history, which reintroduces concepts about asymmetrical, gendered access to the marketplace of print. This leads us to discussions about what gets recorded, edited, and reprinted over time, which we connect to Virginia Woolf's hypothetical Judith Shakespeare, Samuel Johnson's "test of time," and feminist scholarship of recovery. To conclude, I encapsulate the major positives and negatives of the way the Internet has made texts available for students and scholars.

I then spend twenty minutes introducing *TypeWright* and sketching out the assignment. *TypeWright*, a tool that enables users to engage in what Kenneth Price terms "social scholarly editing" (137–38), is online in accessible, no-cost versions. Automatically scanned books from the early modern period have challenging typographical features, and therefore the searchable text generated from OCR is notably incorrect, or "dirty." Therefore, scholars using full-text digital archives like *ECCO*, owned by Gale, cannot necessarily rely on search results. Among its mission goals, *18thConnect*, the Web site that houses *TypeWright*, works to improve access to proprietary digital archives and helps scholars "negotiat[e] new modes of publication and scholarly production" ("What Is *18thConnect*?"). Once a text has been corrected, the text and the page images are made available by the scholar for further use and publication, including the production of more accurate digital editions. I describe *TypeWright* as a tool that allows everyone, not just people with PhDs or universities with large budgets, to participate in the scholarly project.

In the assignment, students work individually to correct the dirty OCR generated by the automatic scanning process in the first edition of our novel. Our goal is twofold: to learn about the material page as Haywood's readers might have encountered it, and to make the work of a marginalized author more accessible for other scholars. After completing their pages, students write a focused reflective essay describing their experience and, through it, what they learned about any or all of the following subjects: the eighteenth-century book, problems with online texts, what it means to contribute to the scholarly project in this way, and feminist recovery work. This project can also be scaled up, culminating in the production of a digital edition or articulated over several terms. For a small correction project, I emphasize that generating accurate text is our central task. It is essential for scholars to have at their digital disposal accurate renderings of the content; otherwise it cannot be relied upon, much less effectively searched. The optional markup guide (OMG) addresses how to generate machine-readable texts that account for more complex typographic features that also carry meaning, like italics or small caps, catchwords, printers' ornaments, different typefaces or colors, and so on. More advanced projects could incorporate more complex descriptions of the material page, accompanied by a reflection assignment asking students to assess their reading experience or to compare this facsimile edition with their modern one. The buddy system, whereby students work in pairs and each reviews the work of the other, is a useful tool for quality control.

Finally, I spend twenty minutes walking the class through the *18thConnect* Web site, modeling activities such as creating an account, finding (and bookmarking) the text they're to work on, navigating the site, and correcting a few lines. Students take notes or set up an account and follow along on their own computers. Recording the process using a screen capture tool provides a resource students can turn to after class. At the end of the period, I hand out a fuller assignment sheet and ask students to explore *TypeWright* either individually or with a partner (students ultimately correct twenty to twenty-five pages and write a five-page reflective analysis about the process as a public, digitally collaborative academic endeavor, providing specific evidence from their experience). Before the next class, students must have signed up and logged in to the site, navigated to the text, corrected an assigned page, and noted down at least five questions.

When we next meet, I bring sample printed books from special collections so students can ask the inevitable questions about the physical nature of a book from the eighteenth century (*Internet Archive* offers an alternative). *TypeWright*-specific questions are also discussed, and we spend the rest of the class working on the project with a few minutes of reflective writing time at the end. Students complete their projects independently, though I encourage co-working. On the due date, I ask students to share the most interesting thing they learned or a question for further exploration, whether about the novel, online books, eighteenth-century printed books, or another related topic.

Seen as a scandalous woman and a hack writer, Haywood persisted with dogged determination. Yet her amatory work fell out of fashion in a world increasingly invested in the sentimental novel and moral domestic fiction, and it has only been through the efforts of feminist scholars working since the 1980s that some of her vast output has become available in anthologies and scholarly modern editions. Inquiry-based projects like these give students the opportunity to put their reading and writing into a real-world environment that resonates across centuries, from print to digital and back again. By physically engaging students in the production of accessible, public knowledge, such projects enable young writers to begin to see themselves as having a role to play in ongoing conversations about literature, access, and power. My goal is not to transform students into youthful experts on Haywood or even on just one of her works, but to awaken their curiosity about eighteenth-century literature and to help them come to terms with the ways their own voices have a history and a future.

NOTES

[1] This idea emerged from the model provided by *Eighteenth-Century Audio*, a project led by Marie McAllister at the University of Mary Washington. Omar Miranda of the University of San Francisco is currently developing a collaborative, social, web-based platform called *Recited Verse* for similar projects.

[2] I am grateful to Adrianne Wadewitz for her advocacy of diversity on *Wikipedia*.

Social Reading Practices: Teaching *The Female Spectator* with Twenty-First-Century Feminocentric Digital Periodicals

Kirsten T. Saxton and Cassie Childs

Teaching Eliza Haywood's periodicals in a senior literature course is addressed elsewhere in this volume; our essay offers a module for using digital tools to teach Haywood's periodical *The Female Spectator* in a generalist course. The assignment introduces Haywood, periodical literature, and some digital humanities tools. Specifically, we pair Haywood's periodical content with content from a twenty-first-century feminocentric digital periodical for a comparative analysis. By *feminocentric* we mean a text that is generally associated with or focused on women and curated or edited by women, although its authors and readers span genders. The unit introduces students to the ways in which *The Female Spectator*, one of the earliest woman-authored periodicals, created a textual space of dizzying formal and topical diversity, shaped authorial practice across genders for a variety of readers, and presented writing as a viable option for women.

Our assignment spans roughly a month (or twelve to fifteen contact hours, which may expand or contract as needed) and includes a directed analysis of a selection, of the student's choice, from *The Female Spectator*; a directed analysis of a selection on the same topic from a twenty-first-century digital periodical; a digital visualization of the two selections; and an original, thesis-driven comparative post for inclusion in a class blog, available to the public or to the campus community. Haywood's periodical allows students to consider an array of topical themes, such as curatorial reviews of current events and media, as well as decor, disability, food, emotional management, hostessing, illness, manners, politics, reading material, and romance. The close readings invite students to consider tone, topic, presumed audience, authorial persona, syntax, diction, and so forth. The assignment creates a public community of readers and writers that itself produces the effects it analyzes.

Teaching *The Female Spectator* in the context of today's digital periodical culture introduces students to the historically expansive legacy of social reading practices. Haywood's popular and influential periodical is a terrific choice for students immersed in a culture that, in Manushag N. Powell 's description, "emphasizes social reading and new forms of rapidly disseminated periodical publications" ("New Directions" 240–47). Eighteenth-century periodical reading practices resemble those of our students, and of many twenty-first-century readers navigating a variety of digital content that is meant to be read in short installments. *The Female Spectator* advertises that it does not wish to "tye any Person down to engage for a longer Time than is agreeable to themselves" (qtd. in Powell, "Eliza Haywood 168"). The module emphasizes how reading practices in the eighteenth century and our own are not limited to novels but include complex multivocal and generically, rhetorically, and thematically rich texts.

It is perhaps this conceptual frame of reading practices that most critically informs the success of the assignment across institutions—with different sizes, populations, and resources—and in a range of general education courses, whose goals vary but include critical thinking, reading, and writing. Our experience (including quantitative and qualitative assessments) indicates that the module works well with diverse curricular models, populations, and archival and digital resources. Cassie Childs is a visiting instructor at the University of South Florida, a large, regional, public university in Tampa. The library system includes more than 930 databases and vast, well-funded special collections. Kirsten Saxton is professor of English at Mills College, a small liberal arts women's college in Oakland, California, with fewer than one thousand students, where she directs the MA and first-year composition programs and cochairs a small, underresourced digital humanities working group. The library has strong special collection holdings but no access to *Eighteenth Century Collections Online* or extensive digital resources. This essay arose from our desire to cocreate an assignment that placed feminist eighteenth-century content and digital humanities pedagogies in conversation to meet general education goals at both campuses. We are delighted that our cowriting also enacts the feminist collaborative creative process that the assignment series explores.

Haywood's is one of the first periodicals written by a woman, and it is "at the center of a cultural matrix" (Wolf 76). Taking an intersectional feminist and cultural studies approach, we focus on the complex formal and vibrant affective and aesthetic potential of the feminocentric periodical, both in the eighteenth century and in our own moment. The assignment attends to the specifically gendered ways in which women writers are read and invites students to engage in critical and rigorous analysis of the intersections of gender, genre, and rhetoric. We pay particular attention to how Haywood's periodical constructs models of women's authorship. As Kathryn R. King reminds us, Haywood's political journalism, including *The Female Spectator*, is remarkable "for advancing a distinctive and at the time almost utopian feminism that calls out for exploration" (*Political Biography* 113). For students, part of this "exploration" involves considering and contextualizing Haywood's brand identity[1] and their own branding in our technological age. Haywood's use of personae, or eidolons, in *The Female Spectator* is a rhetorical tactic that allows her to maintain "credibility as a social commentator, educator or moralist" (113). The concept of the eidolon is particularly timely for students navigating their own authorial personae as they write for and in the classroom and on the Web. Thinking critically about the uses and effects of the eidolon offers a key entry point for discussions of gender and genre, in Haywood's text and era and in our own moment. Through their comparative close readings, students not only practice important text-specific formal and analytical skills but also begin to see the long history that informs authorship, literary networks, and the collaborations of and within textual spaces with which they are familiar.

The assignment serves as a low-stakes introduction, not only to Haywood and periodicals, but to digital tools as well. The assignment lets students (and teachers) engage and play with digital spaces and tools without requiring that they be experts. As the digital humanities scholar Adeline Koh reminds us, we are already digital humanists, because we "all use technology in [our] daily lives." Digital humanities activities in general education courses, particularly at colleges that do not have richly funded labs or faculty development funds, should be easily accessible and should make inherent pedagogical sense. Digital humanities assignments are important for the undergraduate classroom not because they are trendy, please administrators, or teach career readiness (although all these things are helpful), but because they afford meaningful teaching and learning opportunities. But this is not an essay about the pleasures and dangers of digital humanities practices, which are always only as good as the questions that inform them and the pedagogies that motivate them. Rather, we hope this essay helps readers avoid some of the pitfalls we have encountered in our attempts to include eighteenth-century material in general education courses and to introduce digital tools as, or to, nonspecialists.

The module outlined here includes ten parts, of which elements can be extracted, condensed, or expanded as an instructor chooses: Context: Terminology, Genre, and History; Introduction to the Archive and Digital Tools; Choosing a Topic and the *Female Spectator* Selection with Reflection; Digital Annotation of the *Female Spectator* Selection with Reflection; Contemporary Periodical Selection; Digital Annotation of the Contemporary Periodical Selection with Reflection; Visual Text Analysis; Thesis Chart; Blog Post; and Reader Responses.

Context: Terminology, Genre, and History. One unexpected roadblock that we encountered was that students could not identify or define a periodical. We now include a brief discussion of the genre and its expectations and mutations across time and place. Before digging into the archive, students should engage with the historical context in which *The Female Spectator* was produced.[2] This contextual piece may be brief, but we suggest prefacing the module with information about eighteenth-century print culture; periodical literature; and social, economic, and cultural history, with particular attention to gender and its intersections with nation, race, and social position.

Introduction to the Archive and Digital Tools. Next, students visit the library to interact with eighteenth- and nineteenth-century periodicals. Students can see material similarities and differences among archival periodicals and begin to analyze the historical genre: Who was the audience? What types of articles, advertisements, and images are included? Were the periodicals cheap or expensive? If your institution does not have access to archival periodicals, or if your course is online, you can share scanned images, easily obtainable through open-access sites such as *Internet Archive*, *Google Books*, and *HathiTrust*.

During this session, students learn how to use a database to access *The Female Spectator*. They learn to navigate the periodical digitally, including how to search within the text for key words and phrases and how to save selections of texts and images as PDF or JPEG files. They practice these skills using keywords they choose. A librarian can facilitate this introduction, or students and teachers can study the guidelines on each archival site. The session should include time for instruction and provide support as students navigate Haywood's text and play with new digital tools or literacies. After this session, students write a two-page reflection, which includes

image from *The Female Spectator* saved as a PDF or JPEG
description of something engaging about the session
explanation of one new thing learned
two observations about the archival periodicals
description of the most difficult part of navigating the database
keywords attempted, noting least and most successful
reflection on readiness to complete the next stage of the assignment

Our students overwhelmingly found the library session more valuable and engaging than they had anticipated. They were excited to engage with the materiality of the archive, characterizing their access to and handling of the periodicals as significant markers of privilege and as important for their understanding of and interest in the content. Students are often frustrated and put off by eighteenth-century typography and find the databases daunting and the texts confusing; the group introduction resulted in students reporting they felt less intimidated and more capable.

Choosing a Topic and the Female Spectator *Selection with Reflection.* Students choose a topic and a relevant selection from *The Female Spectator*, using keywords to guide their research. They may choose a topic related to an interest or major; our students' keywords included *gambling*, *marry*, *happiness*, *young lady*, *partner*, *fortune*, *education*, *virtue(s)*, *conversation*, *correspondence*, *family*, *knowledge*, *passion*, *reputation*, *illness*, *plants*, *cooking*, and *travel*.

They write a reflection on their independent research, including

the topic and *Female Spectator* selection and citation
report of any problems using the database on their own
description of what was interesting or enlightening about using the database

account of how they found the selection
two other topics or selections considered
explanation of most intriguing thing about the final topic

This reflection frames them as active and successful researchers and highlights their self-directed choice.

Digital Annotation of the Female Spectator *Selection with Reflection.* Students grapple with the complex rhetoric and form of Haywood's text by digitally annotating a short section of their selection. We introduce a free digital annotation tool, such as *Annotation Studio* or *Prism*, and sites such as *Google Drive* or *Lit Genius*, which allow students to annotate Haywood's text, marking it up with definitions, historical and cultural references, and questions and confusions, using comment bubbles, highlighting, and various colors and fonts. We first collaboratively annotate in class. The selection can be pulled from a text-only Internet site, such as those mentioned above, or students can retranscribe the paragraphs into the program. Students preferred the transcription process because it helped them better grasp the material; pedagogically, transcription enacts the rereading practice essential to close reading. The annotations in the margins include words, phrases, or sentences that are confusing or need more explanation (often content, cultural, historical, or language references), along with research and definitions of those elements (fig. 1). Students then write two paragraphs that begin their close reading: the first explores how the annotation influenced their understanding of and reaction to their Haywood selection; the second includes transcription of two sentences from the selection, a paraphrase of their literal meaning, a detailed description of their style (word choice, sentence length, tone), and an explanation of why they were chosen.

Contemporary Periodical Selection. Students choose a contemporary article from a feminocentric periodical (published in print or online) or blog that addresses the same topic or theme as their eighteenth-century selection. We created a student-generated list of possible options and required approval of their choices.

Digital Annotation of Contemporary Selection with Reflection. Using the contemporary article, students repeat the annotation assignment and reflection paragraphs (fig. 2).

Visual Text Analysis. Students conduct an initial visual text analysis of their two selections using free digital visualization tools (such as *Wordle* or *Voyant*) to create a word cloud. A word cloud creates a visual representation of the frequently appearing words in a text; the more frequently a word appears, the larger it is in the word cloud. This project allows students to see themes and to notice continuities and differences between their two selections (for more on word clouds, see Runge in this volume).

Students turn in a digital visualization image for *The Female Spectator* and one for the contemporary selection with 250 to 300 words of comparative analysis. We ask them to consider, for example, word frequency, how the words relate to the topic and what is being said about that topic, common words or word forms, and the like. This exercise does not require a thesis and may take the form of a list. More important, it is about creative visual analysis and brainstorming for the final blog post.

Thesis Chart. The three-column chart is a detailed outline that bridges the annotations and visual analyses into a cohesive, argument-driven essay. The columns are "Haywood," "Main Idea," and "Contemporary." The "Main Idea" column contains descriptive claims from earlier work, such as "*The Female Spectator* appeals to logic, while *Teen Vogue* appeals to emotion." The textual evidence for each claim appears in the adjacent columns. Students generate several main ideas to be included in their final blog posts. After finishing the chart, students create a working thesis. This outline provides a good opportunity for peer review and conferences.

Blog Post. Each student produces a blog post on the class site, hosted through either a course management system or a free hosting site such as *Tumblr, WordPress, Weebly*, or *Wix* (all easy to set up without experience). Each student's post includes an image from *The Female Spectator*, the two word clouds, and a narrative organized by a controlling thesis. The length and scope of the blog post are adjustable to fit course goals; our process includes two workshopped drafts.

Reader Responses. Students (following guidelines) publicly comment on their colleagues' blog posts. This practice enacts the sociability and network characteristic of eighteenth-century and contemporary periodical culture. The final class blog may be shared with the department, the larger college community, or the public. Students appreciate and take seriously the large-scale visibility of and readership for their scholarly work. The collected posts create a snapshot of their intellectual community.

Students responded enthusiastically to this module. They enjoyed the combination of archival work and up-to-date digital tools, appreciated the chance to choose their own focus, and found compelling the continuities and disjunctions between the eighteenth- and twenty-first-century discussions of their topics. They reported being intimidated and energized by the wider access to their work.

Students were drawn to discussions of political engagement and activism, histories of war and social conflict, policies on and visions of education, and essays

Selection from bk. 1, in *The Female Spectator*

COULD Fourteen have the Power of judging of itself, or for itself, who that knew the beautiful *Martesia* at that Age, but would have **depended** on her Conduct!—*Martesia*, descended of the most illustrious Race, possess'd of all that Dignity of Sentiment befitting her high Birth, endued by Nature with a surprizing Wit, Judgement, and Penetration, and improved by every Aid of Education.—*Martesia*, the Wonder and Delight of all who saw or heard her, gave the admiring World the greatest Expectations that she would one Day be no less celebrated for all those Virtues which **render amiable that conjugal State, than she at that Time was for every other Perfection that do Honor to the Sex.**

Is it typical for a girl to marry this young in the 18th century? Need to research courtship and marriage.

Define "illustrious": possessing lustre by reason of high birth or rank, noble or lofty action or qualities; distinguished, eminent; renowned, famous (OED)

Define "wit": the faculty of thinking and reasoning in general; mental capacity, understanding, intellect, reason (OED)

Define "judgement": the ability to make considered decisions or to arrive at reasonable conclusions or opinions on the basis of the available information (OED)

Define "penetration": the action of capacity of penetrating something with the mind; keeness of perception or understanding; insight, acuteness, discernment (OED)

Virtues—e.g., wit, judgement, penetration. All about the mind! But does Martesia have these virtues if she is choosing to marry at 14?

KEY

Bold = words or phrases I see as significant and want to discuss

Underlined = words or phrases that I need or want to find specific definitions for

Comment bubbles = my own words and paraphrases or links to Web sites that help me with historical and cultural context

Figure 1. Sample Haywood annotation. Created by the authors.

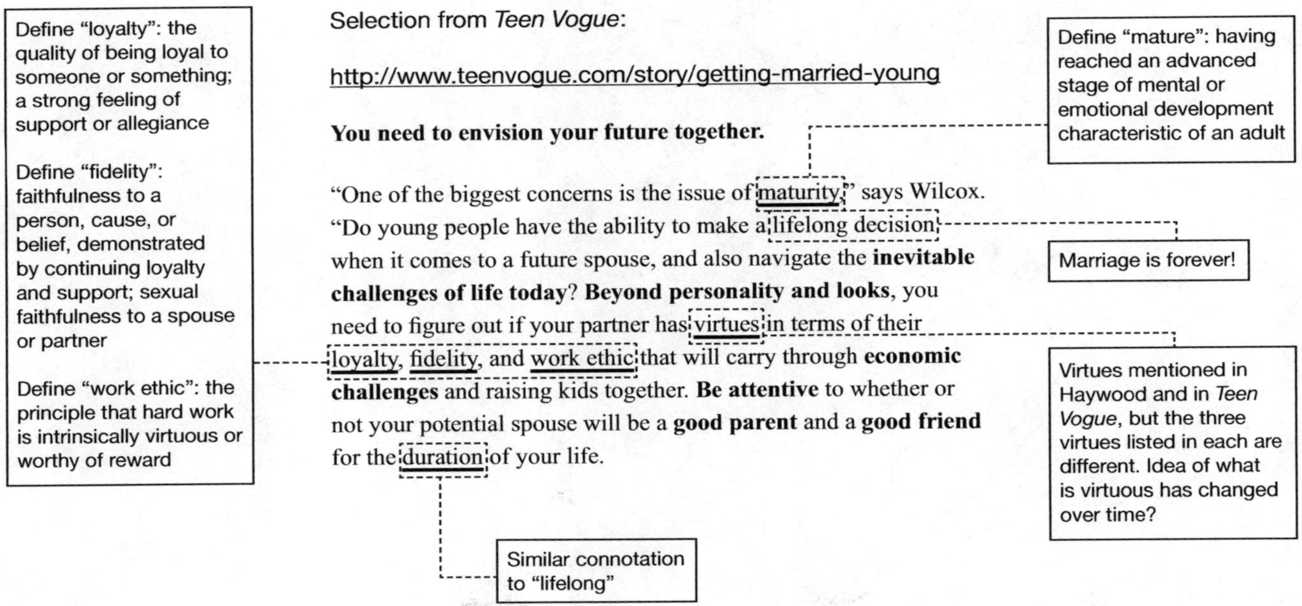

Figure 2. Sample contemporary annotation. Created by the authors.

on gender roles and personal fulfillment—happiness, marriage, health, family, and work. They were fascinated by the ways in which cultural markers such as virtue and reputation have changed over time and the ways they have not. Many students already interested in social media chose pieces on public and private personae or celebrity culture. Students noticed eighteenth-century media's framing of bodies and stories and made links to current media practices on platforms such as *Snapchat* and *Instagram*. They appreciated learning the long history of social constructs around gender, normalcy, happiness, beauty, nation, selfhood, and political agency; they noted the space Haywood gave to subjects they had thought were topical only now because of shifting cultural conceptions of personhood, positionality, and agency or the saturation of social media. Students often pursued topics linked to their academic study; for example, a public health major traced negative stereotypes of mental illness; a biologist put Haywood's discussion of female botanists in conversation with a critique of current representations of women in science; and a sociology major compared how Haywood leveraged the cultural exotic to consolidate a version of English femininity with an essay on white feminism and white fragility.

The assignment allows nonmajor and nonspecialist students a way into the eighteenth century by focusing their research through their current preoccupations. This way in, however, does not mean we seek to make the century un-strange or that we assume students are incapable of engaging with texts outside their own worldviews. Rather, our assignment builds on our assumption that we, as eighteenth-century scholars, are drawn to the century and its rich strangeness always in part because of how it connects to or diverges from our own historically particular presents. We found the assignment engaging and flexible enough that we have adapted it to upper-division literature courses, with some tweaks for more complex writing outputs, contexts, and digital humanities scholarship.

NOTES

The authors welcome communication with instructors who use or adapt this assignment.

[1] For more on branding, see Backscheider's essay in this volume.

[2] See Batchelor and Powell; Italia; Maurer; and Newman and Wright 82–103.

NOTES ON CONTRIBUTORS

Stephen Ahern is professor of English at Acadia University. His work on literature, affect, and the cultural politics of emotion includes three recent books: *Affect Theory and Literary Critical Practice: A Feel for the Text* (2019), *Affect and Abolition in the Anglo-Atlantic, 1770–1830* (2013), and *Affected Sensibilities: Romantic Excess and the Genealogy of the Novel, 1680–1810* (2007).

Laura Alexander is associate professor of English at High Point University. She is the author of *Dangerous Women, Libertine Epicures, and the Rise of Sensibility, 1670–1730* (2011) and *Lucretian Thought in Late Stuart England: Debates about the Nature of the Soul* (2013).

Paula R. Backscheider is Philpott-Stevens Eminent Scholar at Auburn University. She is the editor of more than twenty anthologies and critical editions and the author of nine monographs, including *Spectacular Politics: Theatrical Power and Mass Culture in Early Modern England* (1993), and the forthcoming "Crisis Texts: Staging Wartime Women in the Long Eighteenth Century."

Ros Ballaster is professor of eighteenth-century studies in the Faculty of English, Oxford University, and professorial fellow of English at Mansfield College, Oxford. She has published widely, particularly on women's writing, oriental fiction, and the interaction of prose fiction and theater. She is the author of *Fabulous Orients: Fictions of the East in England, 1662–1785* (2005) and *Seductive Forms: Women's Amatory Fiction from 1684 to 1740* (1992) and editor of *The History of British Women's Writing, 1690–1750* (2010).

Martha F. Bowden is professor emeritus of English at Kennesaw State University. She is the author of *Descendants of Waverley: Romancing History in Contemporary Historical Fiction* (2016) and *Yorick's Congregation: The Church of England in the Time of Laurence Sterne* (2007) and the editor of an edition of three novels by Mary Davys. In 2013 she was awarded Kennesaw State University's Distinguished Professor Award for excellence in teaching.

Toni Bowers is professor of English at the University of Pennsylvania, where she teaching seventeenth- and eighteenth-century British literature and genre studies. Her recent books include the monograph *Force or Fraud: British Seduction Stories and the Problem of Resistance, 1660–1760* (2011) and the collection *Atlantic Worlds in the Long Eighteenth Century: Seduction and Sentiment* (coedited with Tita Chico, 2012).

Cassie Childs teaches at the University of South Florida, focusing on women writers, food studies, material culture, and digital humanities. Her next project examines women's letters and journals from the long eighteenth century, analyzing the implications of food culture on women's identities as they traveled, aged, and wrote.

Catherine Craft-Fairchild teaches women's studies and British and transatlantic literature as professor at the University of St. Thomas in St. Paul, Minnesota. Her most recent research is on Maria Edgeworth, and her earlier work on Eliza Haywood and other female writers includes *Masquerade and Gender: Disguise and Female Identity* *in Eighteenth-Century Fictions by Women* (1993). Her teaching was recognized with the award for Aquinas Scholars Professor of the Year in 2005.

Sarah Creel is lecturer in English at Kennesaw State University. She has published work on Eliza Haywood, printer's ornaments, and portraiture, and her research interests center on Haywood, authorship studies, and visual culture.

Emily Dowd-Arrow is associate professor at Abraham Baldwin Agricultural College, Bainbridge. She has published work on Eliza Haywood and rape culture, and her research focuses on eighteenth-century women writers, with special interest in Eliza Haywood's *The Female Spectator* and the rhetorical construction of the periodical as a conversational female space.

Tonya-Marie Howe is professor of literature and languages at Marymount University. She publishes on both eighteenth-century literature and teaching, with a particular focus on technologically informed critical pedagogies. She is also co–principal investigator of *Literature in Context*, an NEH-funded grant to create a digital platform for providing reliable, classroom-sourced editions of texts typically used in survey courses of the long eighteenth century.

Nicholas Hudson is professor of English at the University of British Columbia. He is the author of *A Political Biography of Samuel Johnson* (2013), *Samuel Johnson and the Making of Modern English* (2003), *Writing and European Thought, 1600–1830* (1994), and *Samuel Johnson and Eighteenth-Century Thought* (1988).

Aleksondra Hultquist is assistant professor of critical thinking at Stockton University and honorary researcher for the Australian Research Council's Centre of Excellence for the History of Emotions. Her work focuses on women writers and the passions in the eighteenth century. She edited *Emotion in the Eighteenth Century* (2017) and a special issue of *The Eighteenth Century: Theory and Interpretation*, and coedited, with Elizabeth Mathews, *New Perspectives on Delarivier Manley and Eighteenth-Century Literature* (2017).

Catherine Ingrassia is professor of English at Virginia Commonwealth University. Her publications include *Authorship, Commerce, and Gender in Early Eighteenth-Century England* (1998), a classroom edition of Eliza Haywood's *Anti-Pamela* (2004), and *The Cambridge Companion to Women's Writing in Britain, 1660–1789* (2015). She also coedited *British Women Poets of the Long Eighteenth Century* (2009) and Blackwell's *Companion to the Eighteenth-Century Novel and Culture* (2005). She won the 2015–16 Innovative Course Design prize from the American Society for Eighteenth-Century Studies.

Kathryn R. King is professor emerita of English at the University of Montevallo. She is the author of *A Political Biography of Eliza Haywood* (2012) and coeditor of Haywood's *The Female Spectator* (2001), and she served on the editorial board for the eight-volume *Selected Works of Eliza Haywood.* She has published numerous articles on Haywood and other women writers in the long eighteenth century.

Christopher F. Loar is associate professor at Western Washington University, where he teaches literatures of the long eighteenth century from both Britain and the Americas. He has published on Eliza Haywood's political theory, James Boswell's melancholy, and Robinson Crusoe's firearms and is author of *Political Magic: British Fictions of Savagery and Sovereignty, 1650–1750* (2014).

Cheryl Nixon is professor of English and associate provost at the University of Massachusetts, Boston. Her research focuses on the rise of the novel and on the literary and legal structuring of the family. Recent works include *The Orphan in Eighteenth-Century Law and Literature: Estate, Blood, and Body* (2011) and *Novel Definitions: An Anthology of Commentary on the Novel, 1688–1815* (2010). She has curated rare books exhibitions at the Boston Public Library that featured Haywood and early-eighteenth-century authors.

Tiffany Potter is professor of teaching at the University of British Columbia. She is the editor of Eliza Haywood's novels *The Masqueraders* and *The Surprize* (2015), Robert Rogers's play *Ponteach; or, The Savages of America: A Tragedy* (2010), and Elizabeth Cooper's play *The Rival Widows; or, Fair Libertine* (2007), as well as the critical collection *Women, Popular Culture, and the Eighteenth Century* (2012). She was awarded UBC's Killam Teaching Prize in 2015.

Cynthia Richards is professor of English at Wittenberg University in Springfield, Ohio. She has published widely on eighteenth-century literature and pedagogy and is coeditor with Mary Ann O'Donnell of the MLA's *Approaches to Teaching Behn's* Oroonoko (2013). She has received teaching awards from the Southwestern Ohio Council for Higher Education and Wittenberg University and won the 2002–03 Innovative Course Design prize from the American Society for Eighteenth-Century Studies.

Laura Runge is professor of English at the University of South Florida. Her publications include *Gender and Language in British Literary Criticism, 1660–1790* (1997) and *Teaching with* The Norton Anthology of Literature by Women (2008). She has won several teaching awards at the University of South Florida and is a founding editor of the online journal *ABO: Interactive Journal for Women in the Arts, 1640–1830.*

Robin Runia is associate professor of English at Xavier University of Louisiana. She is editor of *The Future of Feminist Eighteenth-Century Scholarship: Beyond Recovery* (2018). Her recent research has focused on the idea of race in the work of Maria Edgeworth.

Kirsten T. Saxton is professor of English at Mills College in Oakland, California. She is coeditor of *The Passionate Fictions of Eliza Haywood* (2000) and is scholarly editor at *ABO: Interactive Journal for Women in the Arts, 1640–1830.* She received the 2006 Sarlo Award for excellence in teaching and publishes regularly on eighteenth-century literature pedagogy and research-validated student assessment methods.

Kim Simpson is the Chawton House postdoctoral fellow and lectures in eighteenth-century literature at the University of Southampton. Her research interests include eighteenth-century women's writing; amatory fiction; anonymity, pseudonymity, and attribution; masquerade; the body; afterlives and adaptation; and feminist and queer theories.

Patrick Spedding is a lecturer and associate director of the Centre for the Book at Monash University. He is Haywood's bibliographer of record, the author of *A Bibliography of Eliza Haywood* (2004).

Earla Wilputte is professor of English at St. Francis Xavier University. She has published extensively on eighteenth-century fiction and is the editor of classroom editions of Eliza Haywood's *The Adventures of Eovaai* (1999) and *The Distress'd Orphan, The City Jilt,* and *The Double Marriage,* published as *Three Novellas* (1995). Her most recent book is *Passion and Language in Eighteenth-Century Literature: The Aesthetic Sublime in the Work of Eliza Haywood, Aaron Hill, and Martha Fowke* (2014). She was awarded the St. Francis Xavier University Outstanding Teaching Award in 2005.

SURVEY PARTICIPANTS

Ros Ballaster, *University of Oxford*
Celia Barnes, *Lawrence University*
Toni Bowers, *University of Pennsylvania*
Cecilia Feilla, *Marymount Manhattan College*
Amy Greenstadt, *Portland State University*
Ana Grinberg, *East Tennessee State University*
Catherine Ingrassia, *Virginia Commonwealth University*
Elizabeth Kraft, *University of Georgia*
Elizabeth Kukorelly, *University of Geneva*
Kathleen A. Leicht, *University of Central Missouri*
Kate Levin, *Macaulay Honors College*
Christopher F. Loar, *Western Washington University*
Scott R. Mackenzie, *University of British Columbia*
Precious McKenzie, *Rocky Mountain College*
Leah Orr, *University of Louisiana, Lafayette*
Carrie Shanafelt, *Fairleigh Dickinson University*
Rudolphus Teeuwen, *National Sun Yat-sen University, Taiwan*
Denys Van Renen, *University of Nebraska, Kearney*

WORKS CITED

Addison, Joseph, and Richard Steele. *The Spectator.* Edited by Donald F. Bond, Oxford UP, 1965. 5 vols.

Ahern, Stephen. *Affected Sensibilities: Romantic Excess and the Genealogy of the Novel, 1680–1810.* AMS Press, 2007.

———, editor. *Affect Theory and Literary Critical Practice: A Feel for the Text.* Palgrave Macmillan, 2018.

———. "Nothing More Than Feelings? Affect Theory Reads the Age of Sensibility." *The Eighteenth Century*, vol. 58, no. 3, Fall 2017, pp. 281–94.

Altman, Janet Gurkin. "Teaching the 'People' to Write: The Formation of a Popular Civic Identity in the French Letter Manual." *Studies in Eighteenth-Century Culture*, vol. 22, 1992, pp. 147–80.

Anderson, Emily Hodgson. *Eighteenth-Century Authorship and the Play of Fiction: Novels and the Theater, Haywood to Austen.* Routledge, 2009.

———. "Performing the Passions in Eliza Haywood's *Fantomina* and *Miss Betsy Thoughtless*." *The Eighteenth Century*, vol. 46, no. 1, Spring 2005, pp. 1–15.

Aravamudan, Srinivas. *Enlightenment Orientalism: Resisting the Rise of the Novel.* U of Chicago P, 2012.

———. "In the Wake of the Novel: The Oriental Tale as National Allegory." *Novel: A Forum on Fiction*, vol. 33, no. 1, Autumn 1999, pp. 5–31.

Armstrong, Nancy. *Desire and Domestic Fiction: A Political History of the Novel.* Oxford UP, 1987.

Austen, Jane. *Northanger Abbey.* Edited by James Kinsley and John Davie, Oxford UP, 2003.

———. *Sense and Sensibility.* Edited by Kathleen James-Cavan, Broadview Press, 2001.

Austin, Andrea. "Shooting Blanks: Potency, Parody, and Eliza Haywood's *The History of Miss Betsy Thoughtless.* Saxton and Bocchicchio, pp. 259–82.

Backscheider, Paula R. *Elizabeth Singer Rowe and the Development of the English Novel.* Johns Hopkins UP, 2013.

———. "Eliza Haywood." *Oxford Dictionary of National Biography*, Oxford UP, 2004, doi.org/10.1093/ref:odnb/12798.

———. "The Paradigms of Popular Culture." *The Eighteenth-Century Novel*, vols. 6–7, Aug. 2009, pp. 19–59.

———. Review of *Beyond Spectacle: Eliza Haywood's Female Spectators*, by Juliette Merritt. *Eighteenth-Century Fiction*, vol. 18, no. 1, Fall 2005, pp. 141–43.

———, editor. *Selected Fiction and Drama of Eliza Haywood.* Oxford UP, 1999.

———. "The Shadow of an Author: Eliza Haywood." *Eighteenth-Century Fiction*, vol. 11, no. 1, Oct. 1998, pp. 79–102.

———. "The Story of Eliza Haywood's Novels: Caveats and Questions." Saxton and Bocchicchio, pp. 19–47.

Backscheider, Paula R., and John J. Richetti, editors. *Popular Fiction by Women, 1660–1730: An Anthology*. Oxford UP, 1996.

Baker, David Erskine. *Biographica Dramatica; or, A Companion to the Playhouse.* London, 1782. 2 vols.

Ballaster, Ros. *Fabulous Orients: Fictions of the East in England, 1662–1785*. Oxford UP, 2005.

———. "A Gender of Opposition: Eliza Haywood's Scandal Fiction." Saxton and Bocchicchio, pp. 143–167.

———, editor. *The History of British Women's Writing, 1690–1750*. Palgrave Macmillan, 2010.

———. "Satire and Embodiment: Allegorical Romance on Stage and Page in Mid-Eighteenth-Century Britain." *Eighteenth-Century Fiction*, vol. 27, nos. 3–4, Spring-Summer 2015, pp. 631–60.

———. "Secret History, Oriental Tale, and Fairy Tale." *The Secret History in Literature, 1660–1820*, edited by Rebecca Bullard and Rachel Carnell, Cambridge UP, 2017, pp. 134–46.

———. *Seductive Forms: Women's Amatory Fiction from 1684 to 1740.* Oxford UP, 1992.

———. "Women and the Rise of the Novel: Sexual Prescripts." V. Jones, pp. 197–216.

Bannet, Eve Tavor. "Haywood's *Spectator* and the Female World." Newman and Wright, pp. 82–103.

———. "The Narrator as Invisible Spy: Eliza Haywood, Secret History and the Novel." Hiner and Fowler, pp. 143–62.

Barker, Hannah, and Elaine Chalus, editors. *Women's History: Britain, 1700–1850*. Routledge, 2005.

Baron and Feme: A Treatise of the Common Law Concerning Husbands and Wives. E. and R. Nutt, 1700.

Barrell, John. "'The Dangerous Goddess': Masculinity, Prestige and the Aesthetic in Early Eighteenth-Century Britain." *The Birth of Pandora and the Division of Knowledge*, U of Pennsylvania P, 1992, pp. 63–87.

Barry, Jonathan. Introduction. *The Middling Sort of People: Culture, Society and Politics in England, 1550–1800*, edited by Jonathan Barry and Christopher Brooks, Macmillan, 1994, pp. 1–27.

Barthes, Roland. *Mythologies.* Hill and Wang, 1972.

Batchelor, Jennie, and Gillian Dow, editors. *Women Writers, 1660–1830: Feminisms and Future*. Palgrave Macmillan, 2016.

Batchelor, Jennie, and Manushag N. Powell, editors. *Women's Periodicals and Print Culture in Britain, 1690–1820s: The Long Eighteenth Century*. Edinburgh UP, 2018.

Beckford, William. *Vathek.* Edited by Roger Lonsdale, Oxford UP, 1970.

Behn, Aphra. *The Rover; or, Banished Cavaliers.* Edited by Anne Russell, 2nd ed., Broadview Press, 1999.

Belinda. "To the Author of Pamela." *Gentleman's Magazine*, vol. 15, Feb. 1745, p. 104.

Benedict, Barbara M. *Curiosity: A Cultural History of Early Modern Inquiry.* U of Chicago P, 2001.

Berger, John. *Ways of Seeing.* British Broadcasting Corporation / Penguin Books, 1972.

Bertelsen, Lance. *Henry Fielding at Work: Magistrate, Businessman, Writer.* Palgrave, 2000.

Black, Joseph Laurence, et al., editors. "The Restoration and Eighteenth Century." *The Broadview Anthology of English Literature, Volume 3: The Restoration and Eighteenth Century.* Broadview Press, 2006, pp. xxix–lxiv.

Blouch, Christine. "Eliza Haywood and the Romance of Obscurity." *SEL: Studies in English Literature, 1500–1900,* vol. 31, no. 3, Summer 1991, pp. 535–52.

———. "'What Ann Lang Read': Eliza Haywood and Her Readers." Saxton and Bocchicchio, pp. 300–25.

Bocchicchio, Rebecca P. "'Blushing, Trembling, and Incapable of Defense': The Hysterics of *The British Recluse.*" Saxton and Bocchicchio, pp. 95–114.

Bowen, Scarlett. "'A Sawce-Box and Boldface Indeed': Refiguring the Female Servant in the Pamela-Antipamela Debate." *Studies in Eighteenth-Century Culture,* vol. 28, 1999, pp. 257–85.

Bowers, Toni. "Amatory Fiction." *The Encyclopedia of British Literature, 1660–1789,* edited by Gary Day and Jack Lynch, vol. 1, Wiley-Blackwell, 2015, pp. 40–45.

———. "Collusive Resistance: Sexual Agency and Partisan Politics in *Love in Excess.*" Saxton and Bocchicchio, pp. 48–68.

———. *Force or Fraud: British Seduction Stories and the Problem of Resistance, 1660–1760.* Oxford UP, 2011.

———. "Representing Resistance: British Seduction Stories, 1660–1800." *A Companion to the Eighteenth-Century English Novel and Culture,* edited by Paula R. Backscheider and Catherine Ingrassia, Wiley-Blackwell, 2009, pp. 140–63.

———. "Sex, Lies, and Invisibility: Amatory Fiction from the Restoration to Mid-Century." *The Columbia History of the British Novel,* edited by John Richetti, Columbia UP, 1994, pp. 50–72.

Braunschneider, Theresa. *Our Coquettes: Capacious Desire in the Eighteenth Century.* U of Virginia P, 2009.

Brennan, Teresa. *The Transmission of Affect.* Cornell UP, 2004.

Brewer, John. *The Pleasures of the Imagination: English Culture in the Eighteenth Century.* U of Chicago P, 1997.

Brooks, Peter. *Reading for the Plot: Design and Intention in Narrative.* Harvard UP, 1984.

Buckley, Jennifer. "'Bankrupt in All but My Good Wishes': Speculative Economics in *Cleomilia; or, The Generous Mistress.*" Hiner and Fowler, pp. 79–100.

Burgess, Miranda. "Bearing Witness: Law, Labor, and the Gender of Privacy in the 1720s." *Modern Philology,* vol. 98, no. 3, Feb. 2001, pp. 393–422.

Butler, Judith. *Bodies That Matter: On the Discursive Limits of "Sex."* Routledge, 1993.

———. *Gender Trouble: Feminism and the Subversion of Identity*. Routledge, 1990.

———. "Imitation and Gender Insubordination." 1991. Mann and Patterson, pp. 317–21.

Campbell, Jill. *Natural Masques: Gender and Identity in Fielding's Plays and Novels*. Stanford UP, 1995.

Cannadine, David. *Class in Britain*. Yale UP, 1998.

Cannon, John. *Aristocratic Century: The Peerage of Eighteenth-Century England*. Cambridge UP, 1984.

Carlile, Susan, editor. *Masters of the Marketplace: British Women Novelists of the 1750s*. Lehigh UP, 2011.

Carnell, Rachel. "Eliza Haywood and the Narratological Tropes of Secret History." Hiner and Fowler, pp. 101–21.

———. *Partisan Politics, Narrative Realism, and the Rise of the British Novel*. Palgrave Macmillan, 2006.

Carter, Philip. *Men and the Emergence of Polite Society, Britain, 1660–1800*. Pearson Education, 2001.

Castle, Terry. *Masquerade and Civilization: The Carnivalesque in Eighteenth-Century English Culture and Fiction*. Stanford UP, 1986.

Choy, Susan. *Nontraditional Undergraduates: Findings from the Condition of Education, 2002*. US Department of Education, National Center for Education Statistics, 2002.

Cibber, Colley. *The Careless Husband*. 1705. Edited by William W. Appleton, U of Nebraska P, 1966.

Clery, E. J. "Free Market Feminism? The Political Economy of Women's Writing." Batchelor and Dow, pp. 43–60.

"Cogitation, *N*." *Oxford English Dictionary*, Oxford UP, 2019, www.oed.com/view/Entry/35860.

Colclough, Stephen. *Consuming Texts: Readers and Reading Communities, 1695–1870*. Palgrave Macmillan, 2007.

Colley, Linda. *Britons: Forging the Nation, 1707–1837*. Yale UP, 1992.

Collins, Margo. "Feminine Identity in Eliza Haywood's *The Wife* and *The Husband*." *1650–1850: Ideas, Aesthetics, and Inquiries in the Early Modern Era*, edited by Kevin L. Cope, vol. 14, AMS Press, 2007, pp. 71–88.

Comitini, Patricia. "Imaginative Pleasures: *Fantomina*, Ideology, and Aesthetics." *Studies in Eighteenth-Century Culture*, vol. 43, 2014, pp. 69–87.

The Common Errors in the Education of Children and Their Consequences. M. Cooper, 1744. *ECCO*.

"Computational Linguistics Reveals How Wikipedia Articles Are Biased against Women." *MIT Technology Review*, 2 Feb. 2015, www.technologyreview.com/view/534616/computationallinguisticsrevealshowwikipediaarticlesarebiased againstwomen. Accessed 13 Apr. 2017.

"Consternation." Johnson, *Dictionary*.

"Consternation, *N*." *Oxford English Dictionary*, Oxford UP, 2019, www.oed.com/view/Entry/39829.

Coppola, Al. "The Secret History of Eliza Haywood's *Works*: The Early Novel and the Book Trade." *1650–1850: Ideas, Aesthetics, and Inquiries in the Early Modern Era*, vol. 19, 2012, pp. 134–61.

Corfield, Penelope J. "Class by Name and Number in Eighteenth-Century Britain." *Language, History and Class*, edited by Corfield, Blackwell, 1991, pp. 101–30.

Cotticelli, Francesco, and Paologiovanni Maione. "Metastasio: The Dramaturgy of Eighteenth-Century Heroic Opera." *The Cambridge Companion to Eighteenth-Century Opera*, edited by Anthony R. DelDonna and Pierpaolo Polzonetti, Cambridge UP, 2009, pp. 66–84.

Craft, Catherine A. "Reworking Male Models: Aphra Behn's *Fair Vow-Breaker*, Eliza Haywood's *Fantomina*, and Charlotte Lennox's *Female Quixote*." *The Modern Language Review*, vol. 86, no. 4, Oct. 1991, pp. 821–38.

Craft-Fairchild, Catherine. *Masquerade and Gender: Disguise and Female Identity in Eighteenth-Century Fictions by Women*. Pennsylvania State UP, 1993.

Croskery, Margaret Case. "Masquing Desire: The Politics of Passion in Eliza Haywood's *Fantomina*." Saxton and Bocchicchio, pp. 69–94.

———. "Who's Afraid of Eliza Haywood?" *Literature Compass*, vol. 4, no. 4, 2007, pp. 967–80.

Davis, Lennard J. *Factual Fictions: The Origins of the English Novel*. 1983. U of Pennsylvania P, 1997.

Day, Robert Adams. *Told in Letters: Epistolary Fiction before Richardson*. U of Michigan P, 1966.

Defoe, Daniel. *The Family Instructor: In Three Parts*. E. Matthews, 1715.

———. *Moll Flanders*. Edited by Paul A. Scanlon, Broadview Press, 2005.

DeMaria, Robert, Jr., editor. *British Literature, 1640–1789: An Anthology*. 3rd ed., Blackwell, 2008.

Diamond, David Mark. "Eros and Exchange Alley: Speculative Desire in Eliza Haywood's *Memoirs of a Certain Island*." *Eighteenth-Century Fiction*, vol. 30, no. 1, Fall 2017, pp. 45–64.

Dixon, Thomas. *From Passions to Emotions: The Creation of a Secular Psychological Category*. Cambridge UP, 2003.

Doane, Mary Ann. "Film and the Masquerade: Theorising the Female Spectator." 1982. Thornham, pp. 131–45.

Dowd-Arrow, Emily J., and Sarah Creel. "'I Know You Want It': Teaching the Blurred Lines of Eighteenth-Century Rape Culture." *ABO: Interactive Journal for Women in the Arts, 1640–1830*, vol. 6, no. 2, 2016, dx.doi.org/10.5038/2157-7129.6.2.2.

Drake, Judith. *An Essay in Defence of the Female Sex*. A. Roper, 1696.

Drury-Lane in Tears; or, The Ladies of Pleasure in Mourning. London, 1740[?]. *ECCO*.

Du Bois, W. E. B. *The Souls of Black Folk*. Edited by Henry Louis Gates, Jr., Oxford UP, 2007.

Edelstein, Laurie. "An Accusation Easily to Be Made? Rape and Malicious Prosecution in Eighteenth-Century England." *The American Journal of Legal History*, vol. 42, no. 4, Oct. 1998, pp. 351–90.

Elwood, John R. "Henry Fielding and Eliza Haywood: A Twenty-Year War." *Albion*, vol. 5, no. 3, Autumn 1973, pp. 184–92.

"*Fantomina* Themes." *GradeSaver*, www.gradesaver.com/fantomina/study-guide/themes.

A Farther Essay Relating to the Female-Sex. A. Roper, 1696.

Fielding, Henry. *An Apology for the Life of Mrs. Shamela Andrews*. Ingrassia, Anti-Pamela, pp. 229–76.

———. *A Clear State of the Case of Elizabeth Canning*. Millar, 1753. Zirker, Enquiry, pp. 281–312.

———. *The History of the Adventures of Joseph Andrews and of His Friend Mr. Abraham Adams*. 1742. The History of the Adventures of Joseph Andrews and of His Friend Mr. Abraham Adams *and* An Apology for the Life of Mrs. Shamela Andrews, edited by Douglas Brooks-Davies, revised and introduced by Thomas Keymer, Oxford UP, 1999.

———. *Plays, Volume 1: 1728–1731. The Wesleyan Edition of the Works of Henry Fielding*, edited by Thomas Lockwood, Clarendon Press / Oxford UP, 2004.

———. *The Tragedy of Tragedies*. Edited by Darryl P. Domingo, Broadview Press, 2013.

Filipacchi, Amanda. "Wikipedia's Sexism toward Female Novelists." *The New York Times*, 24 Apr. 2013.

Flint, Christopher. *Family Fictions: Narrative and Domestic Relations in Britain, 1688–1798*. Stanford UP, 1998.

Fordyce, James. *Sermons to Young Women*, 1766. William Pickering, 1996.

Fowke, Martha [Clio]. *Clio; or, A Secret History of the Life and Amours of the Late Celebrated Mrs. S—n—m. Written by Herself, in a Letter to Hillarius*. 1752. Guskin, pp. 168–90.

———. "Clio's Picture." *A New Miscellany of Original Poems, Translations and Imitations*, edited by Anthony Hammond, London, 1720, pp. 257–60. *ECCO*.

———. *Epistles of Clio and Strephon*. 1720. Garland Press, 1971.

Froehlich, Heather. "Corpus Analysis with Antconc." *The Programming Historian*, edited by Fred Gibbs, 19 June 2015, www.programminghistorian.org/lessons/corpus-analysis-with-antconc.

Frye, Northrop. "Towards Defining an Age of Sensibility." *ELH*, vol. 23, no. 2, 1956, pp. 144–52.

Gargano, Elizabeth. "Utopian Voyeurism: Androgyny and the Language of the Eyes in Haywood's *Love in Excess*." *Eighteenth-Century Fiction*, vol. 21, no. 4, Summer 2009, pp. 513–34.

Gay, Roxane. *Bad Feminist*. Harper Perennial, 2014.

Gerrard, Christine. *Aaron Hill: The Muses' Projector, 1685–1750*. Oxford UP, 2003.

———. *The Patriot Opposition to Walpole: Politics, Poetry, and National Myth, 1725–1742*. Oxford UP, 1994.

Gevirtz, Karen Bloom. *Women, the Novel, and Natural Philosophy, 1660–1727*. Palgrave Macmillan, 2014.

Girten, Kristin M. "Unsexed Souls: Natural Philosophy as Transformation in Eliza Haywood's *Female Spectator*." *Eighteenth-Century Studies*, vol. 43, no. 1, Fall 2009, pp. 55–74.

Glover, Susan Paterson. *Engendering Legitimacy: Law, Property, and Early Eighteenth-Century Fiction*. Bucknell UP, 2006.

Gosse, Edmund. *Gossip in a Library*. 2nd ed., William Heinemann, 1892.

Graves, Nicola. "'Injury for Injury'; or, 'The Lady's Revenge': Female Vengeance in Eliza Haywood's *Female Spectator*." Newman and Wright, pp. 155–75.

Greenblatt, Stephen, et al., editors. "Eliza Haywood." *The Norton Anthology of English Literature, Volume C: The Restoration and Eighteenth Century*. 9th ed., W. W. Norton, 2012.

Greenblatt, Stephen, et al., editors. Introduction. *The Norton Anthology of English Literature, Volume C: The Restoration and Eighteenth Century*, 10th ed., W. W. Norton, 2018, pp. 3–33.

Gregg, Melissa, and Gregory Seigworth, editors. *The Affect Theory Reader*. Duke UP, 2010.

Gregg, Stephen H. *Defoe's Writings and Manliness: Contrary Men*. Ashgate, 2009.

Grosz, Elizabeth. *Volatile Bodies: Toward a Corporeal Feminism*. Indiana UP, 1994.

Guskin, Phyllis J., editor. *Clio: The Autobiography of Martha Fowke Sansom (1689–1736)*. U of Delaware P, 1997.

Gwilliam, Tassie. "Disguise, Fantasy, and Misrecognition in *The Belle's Stratagem* and *Fantomina*." *Teaching British Women Playwrights of the Restoration and Eighteenth Century*, edited by Bonnie Nelson and Catherine Burroughs, Modern Language Association of America, 2010, pp. 275–84.

Halifax, George Savile, Marquess of. *The Lady's New-Year's Gift; or, Advice to a Daughter*. 3rd ed., Matt Gillyflower and James Partridge, 1688.

Hammond, Brean, and Shaun Regan. *Making the Novel: Fiction and Society in Britain, 1660–1789*. Palgrave Macmillan, 2006.

Hargrave, Jennifer L. "'To the Glory of the Chinese': Sinocentric Political Reform in Eliza Haywood's *The Adventures of Eovaai*." *Eighteenth-Century Studies*, vol. 49, no. 1, Fall 2015, pp. 31–50.

Harris, Mary Beth. "Upsetting the Balance: Exposing the Myth of Masculine Virtue and Desire in Eliza Haywood's *Philidore and Placentia*." *The Eighteenth Century*, vol. 58, no. 2, Summer 2017, pp. 195–218.

Harris's List of Covent-Garden Ladies. London, 1773. *ECCO*.

Harrow, Sharon. "Having Text: Desire and Language in Haywood's *Love in Excess* and *The Distressed Orphan*." *Eighteenth-Century Fiction*, vol. 22, no. 2, Winter 2009–10, pp. 279–308.

Harzewski, Stephanie. "The *Fantomina* Phenomenon: Eliza Haywood and the Formation of a Heroine." *The Eighteenth-Century Novel*, vol. 5, 2006, pp. 175–96.

Haywood, Eliza. *The Adventures of Eovaai, Princess of Ijaveo: A Pre-Adamitical History*. Edited by Earla Wilputte, Broadview Press, 1999.

———. "Affecting Masquerade Adventure." *Gentleman's Magazine*, Dec. 1754. Haywood, *Invisible Spy*, pp. 621–30.

———. *Anti-Pamela; or, Feign'd Innocence Detected.* Ingrassia, Anti-Pamela, pp. 51–227.

———. *The British Recluse.* Backscheider and Richetti, pp. 154–224.

———. *The City Jilt; or, The Alderman Turn'd Beau.* 1726. Haywood, *Three Novellas*, pp. 65–103.

———. *The Distress'd Orphan; or, Love in a Mad-House.* 1726. Haywood, *Three Novellas*, pp. 25–63.

———. Fantomina *and Other Works.* Edited by Alexander Pettit et al., Broadview Press, 2004.

———. *Fantomina; or, Love in a Maze.* Haywood, Fantomina *and Other Works*, pp. 41–71.

———. *Fantomina; or, Love in a Maze.* Edited by Jack Lynch, Rutgers U, andromeda .rutgers.edu/~jlynch/Texts/fantomina.html.

———. *The Female Spectator.* London, 1744–46. 4 vols.

———. *The Female Spectator.* Haywood, *Selected Works*, part 2, vols. 2–3.

———. *The Female Spectator: Being Selections from Mrs. Eliza Heywood's Periodical (1744–1746)*, chosen and edited by Mary Priestley, John Lane, 1929.

———. *The Female Spectator: Being Selections from Mrs. Eliza Haywood's Periodical, First Published in Monthly Parts (1744–6)*, edited with an introduction by Gabrielle M. Firmager, Bristol Classical Press, 1993.

———. *The History of Jemmy and Jenny Jessamy.* Edited by John Richetti, UP of Kentucky, 2005.

———. *The History of Miss Betsy Thoughtless.* Edited by Christine Blouch, Broadview Press, 1998.

———. *The History of Miss Betsy Thoughtless.* Introduced by Dale Spender, Pandora Press, 1986.

———. *Idalia; or, The Unfortunate Mistress.* London, 1723.

———. The Injur'd Husband *and* Lasselia. Edited by Jerry C. Beasley, UP of Kentucky, 1999.

———. *The Invisible Spy.* Edited by Carol Stewart, Pickering and Chatto, 2014. Chawton House Library Series, Women's Novels 18.

———. "The Lady's Revenge." *Selected Works*, vol. 2, pp. 58–74.

———. *Lasselia; or, The Self-Abandon'd.* Haywood, Injur'd Husband, pp. 103–49.

———. *A Letter from H[enry] G[oring].* London, 1750.

———. *Letters from a Lady of Quality to a Chevalier.* London, 1721.

———. *Love in Excess; or, The Fatal Enquiry (1719–20).* Edited by David Oakleaf, 2nd ed., Broadview Press, 2000.

———. The Masqueraders; or, Fatal Curiosity *and* The Surprize; or, Constancy Rewarded. Edited by Tiffany Potter, U of Toronto P, 2015.

———. *Memoirs of a Certain Island Adjacent to the Kingdom of Utopia.* 1725. Introduced by Josephine Grieder, Garland, 1972.

———. *The Mercenary Lover; or, The Unfortunate Heiress*. London, 1726.

———. *The Opera of Operas*. 1733. Haywood, *Selected Fiction*, pp. 171–220.

———. "Philidore and Placentia; or, L'Amour Trop Delicat." *Four Before Richardson: Selected English Novels, 1720–1727*, edited by William Harlin McBurney, U of Nebraska P, 1963.

———. *Poems on Several Occasions*. London, 1724.

———. *The Rash Resolve; or, The Untimely Discovery*. 1724. The Rash Resolve *and* Life's Progress, edited by Carol Stewart, Pickering and Chatto, 2013.

———. *Selected Fiction and Drama of Eliza Haywood*. Edited by Paula R. Backscheider, Oxford UP, 1999.

———. *Selected Works of Eliza Haywood*. Edited by Kathryn R. King and Alexander Pettit, Pickering and Chatto, 2001. 8 vols.

———. *Selections from* The Female Spectator. Edited by Patricia Meyer Spacks, Oxford UP, 1999.

———. *The Tea-Table; or, A Conversation between Some Polite Persons of Both Sexes*. 1725. Haywood, Fantomina *and Other Works*, pp. 73–106.

———. *Three Novellas*. Edited by Earla Wilputte, Michigan State UP, 1995.

———. *A Wife to Be Lett: A Comedy*. 1724. Haywood, *Selected Fiction*, pp. 1–82.

Henderson, Tony. *Disorderly Women in Eighteenth-Century London: Prostitution and Control in the Metropolis, 1730–1830*. Longman/Pearson, 1999.

Hicks, Stephen J. "Eliza Haywood's Letter Technique in Three Early Novels (1721–27)." *Papers on Language and Literature*, vol. 34, no. 4, 1998, pp. 420–36.

Highsmith, Patricia. *The Price of Salt*. W. W. Norton, 2004.

Hill, Aaron, and William Bond. *The Plain Dealer: Being Select Essays on Several Curious Subjects*. 2 vols., London, 1734. *ECCO*.

Hiner, Amanda, and Patsy S. Fowler, editors. *New Approaches to Eliza Haywood: The Political Biography and Beyond*. Special issue of *Journal for Early Modern Cultural Studies*, vol. 14, no. 4, Fall 2014.

Hitchcock, Alfred, director. *Marnie*, Universal Pictures, 1964.

hooks, bell. "Theory as Liberatory Practice." 1994. Mann and Patterson, pp. 8–14.

Houston, R. A. Literacy in Early Modern Europe: Culture and Education, 1500–1800. Longman, 1989.

Howell, Thomas Bayly. *A Complete Collection of State Trials and Proceedings for High Treason and Other Crimes and Misdemeanors*, vol. 19, Longman, 1816.

Hudson, Nicholas. "Formal Experimentation and Theories of Fiction." Keymer, *Oxford History*, pp. 330–47.

———. "Literature and Social Class in the Eighteenth Century." *Oxford Handbooks Online*, Apr. 2015, dx.doi.org/10.1093/oxfordhb/9780199935338.013.007.

Hultquist, Aleksondra. "Bringing Order to the Passions: Eliza Haywood's Fiction, 1719 and 1748." *Spaces for Feeling: Emotions and Sociabilities in Britain, 1650–1850*, edited by Susan Broomhall, Routledge, 2015, pp. 79–94.

———. *Equal Ardor: Female Desire, Amatory Fiction, and the Recasting of the Novel, 1680–1760*. 2008. U of Illinois, Urbana, PhD dissertation.

———. "Haywood's Re-appropriation of the Amatory Heroine in *Betsy Thoughtless.*" *Philological Quarterly*, vol. 85, nos. 1–2, 2006, pp. 141–65.

———. "Marriage in Haywood; or, Amatory Reading Rewarded." Carlile, *Masters*, pp. 31–46.

Hume, David. *Essays Moral, Political, and Literary*. Edited by Eugene F. Miller. Liberty Classics, 1985, pp. 563–68.

Ingrassia, Catherine, editor. Anti-Pamela; or, Feign'd Innocence Detected *and* An Apology for the Life of Mrs. Shamela Andrews. Broadview Press, 2004.

———. *Authorship, Commerce, and Gender in Early Eighteenth-Century England: A Culture of Paper Credit*. Cambridge UP, 1998.

———, editor. *The Cambridge Companion to Women's Writing in Britain, 1660–1749*. Cambridge UP, 2015.

———. Introduction. Ingrassia, Anti-Pamela, pp. 7–43.

———. "'Queering' Eliza Haywood." Hiner and Fowler, pp. 9–24.

Italia, Iona. *The Rise of Literary Journalism in the Eighteenth Century: Anxious Employment*. Routledge, 2005.

Jennings, Kristine. "The Sign of a Woman: Femininity as Fiction in *The History of Miss Betsy Thoughtless*." *Studies in the Literary Imagination*, vol. 47, no. 2, Fall 2014, pp. 39–58.

Johnson, Barbara. *The Critical Difference: Essays in the Contemporary Rhetoric of Reading*. Johns Hopkins UP, 1980.

Johnson, Samuel. *A Dictionary of the English Language*. 2nd ed., vol. 2, London, 1755–56. *ECCO*.

———. *The History of Rasselas, Prince of Abissinia*. Edited by J. P. Hardy, Oxford UP, 1988.

———. *The Rambler*, no. 4. 1750. *Samuel Johnson: Selected Writings*, edited by Patrick Cruttwell, Penguin, 1968, pp. 149–53.

Johnson, Samuel [of Cheshire]. *The Blazing Comet: The Mad Lovers; or, the Beauties of the Poets*. London, 1732. *ECCO*.

Jones, Robert W. "Eliza Haywood and the Discourse of Taste." *Authorship, Commerce, and the Public: Scenes of Writing, 1750–1850*, edited by E. Clery et al., Palgrave Macmillan, 2002, pp. 103–19.

Jones, Vivien, editor. *Women and Literature in England, 1700–1800*. Cambridge UP, 2000.

Keen, Paul, editor. *The Age of Authors: An Anthology of Eighteenth-Century Print Culture*. Broadview Press, 2014.

Kern, Jean. "The Fallen Woman, from the Perspective of Five Early Eighteenth-Century Women Novelists." *Studies in Eighteenth-Century Culture*, vol. 10, 1981, pp. 457–68.

Keymer, Thomas, editor. *Oxford History of the Novel in English: Prose Fiction in English from the Origins of Print to 1750*. Vol. 1, Oxford UP, 2018.

King, Kathryn R. "The Afterlife and Strange Surprising Adventures of Haywood's Amatories (with Thoughts on Betsy Thoughtless)." *Masters of the Marketplace:*

British Women Novelists of the 1750s, edited by Susan Carlile, Lehigh UP, 2011, pp. 203–18.

———. "Henry and Eliza: Feudlings or Friends?" *Henry Fielding in Our Time: Papers Presented at the Tercentenary Conference*, edited by J. A. Downie, Cambridge Scholars, 2008, pp. 215–32.

———. "New Contexts for Early Novels by Women: The Case of Eliza Haywood, Aaron Hill, and the Hillarians, 1719–1725." *A Companion to the Eighteenth-Century English Novel and Culture*, edited by Paula R. Backscheider and Catherine Ingrassia, Blackwell, 2005, pp. 261–75.

———. "Patriot or Opportunist? Eliza Haywood and the Politics of *The Female Spectator*." Newman and Wright, pp. 104–21.

———. "The Pious Mrs. Haywood; or, Thoughts on *Epistles for the Ladies* (1748–1750)." Hiner and Fowler, pp. 187–208.

———. *A Political Biography of Eliza Haywood*. Pickering and Chatto, 2012.

Kirby, Vicki. "Natural Convers(at)ions; or, What if Culture Was Really Nature All Along?" *Material Feminisms*, edited by Stacy Alaimo and Susan Hekman, Indiana UP, 2008, pp. 214–36.

Koh, Adeline. "Introducing Digital Humanities Work to Undergraduates: An Overview." *Hybrid Pedagogy*, 14 Aug. 2014, www.digitalpedagogylab.com/hybridped/introducing-digital-humanities-work-undergraduates-overview. Accessed 1 Apr. 2017.

Kramnick, Jonathan Brody. "Locke, Haywood, and Consent." *ELH: English Literary History*, vol. 72, no. 2, Summer 2005, pp. 453–70.

Kukkonen, Karin. "The Minds behind the Mask: Reading for Character in the Masquerade." *Neophilologus*, vol. 98, no. 1, Jan. 2014, pp. 161–76.

Kvande, Marta. "The Outside Narrator in Eliza Haywood's Political Novels." *SEL: Studies in English Literature, 1500–1900*, vol. 43, no. 3, 2003, pp. 625–43.

———. "Printed in a Book: Negotiating Print and Manuscript Cultures in *Fantomina* and *Clarissa*." *Eighteenth-Century Studies*, vol. 46, no. 2, Winter 2013, pp. 239–57.

Lanser, Susan S. "Of Closed Doors and Open Hatches: Heteronormative Plots in Eighteenth-Century (Women's) Studies." *The Eighteenth Century*, vol. 53, no. 3, Fall 2012, pp. 273–90.

Larsen, Nella. *An Intimation of Things Distant: The Collected Fiction of Nella Larsen*. Edited by Charles R. Larson, Anchor Books, 1992.

Leavy, Patricia, and Adrienne Trier-Bieniek. Introduction. *Gender and Pop Culture: A Text-Reader*, edited by Adrienne Trier-Bieniek and Patricia Leavy, Sense Publishers, 2014, pp. 1–25.

Lee, Sidney. "Mrs. Eliza Haywood." *Dictionary of National Biography*, edited by Leslie Stephen and Sidney Lee, vol. 25, London, 1891, pp. 313–15. *Wikisource*, en.wikisource.org/wiki/Haywood,_Eliza_(DNB00).

Lidinsky, April. "'Reacting to the Past' to Be Proactive in the Present: Feminist Roots of High-Impact Practices." *Feminist Teacher*, vol. 24, no. 3, 2014, pp. 208–12.

Lipsedge, Karen. *Domestic Space in Eighteenth-Century British Novels*. Palgrave Macmillan, 2012.

Loar, Christopher F. "The Exceptional Eliza Haywood: Women and Extralegality in *Eovaai*." *Eighteenth-Century Studies*, vol. 45, no. 4, Summer 2012, pp. 565–84.

———. *Political Magic: British Fictions of Savagery and Sovereignty, 1650–1750*. Fordham UP, 2014.

Lubey, Kathleen. "Eliza Haywood's Amatory Aesthetic." *Eighteenth-Century Studies*, vol. 39, no. 3, Spring 2006, pp. 309–22.

———. *Excitable Imaginations: Eroticism and Reading in Britain, 1660–1760*. Bucknell UP, 2012.

Luhning, Holly. "Writing Bodies in Popular Culture: Eliza Haywood and *Love in Excess*." *Women, Popular Culture, and the Eighteenth Century*, edited by Tiffany Potter, U of Toronto P, 2012, pp. 150–67.

Mackie, Erin. *Rakes, Highwaymen, and Pirates: The Making of the Modern Gentleman in the Eighteenth Century*. Johns Hopkins UP, 2009.

Mandell, Laura. "Gendering Digital Literary History: What Counts for Digital Humanities." Schreibman et al., pp. 511–23.

Mann, Susan Archer, and Ashly Suzanne Patterson, editors. *Reading Feminist Theory: From Modernity to Postmodernity*. Oxford UP, 2016.

Marshall, Ashley. *The Practice of Satire in England, 1658–1770*. Johns Hopkins UP, 2013.

Martina, narrator. "Chapter 05." *Wuthering Heights*, by Emily Brontë. *LibriVox*, librivox.org/wuthering-heights-by-emily-bronte. Accessed 13 Apr. 2017.

Maurer, Shawn Lisa. "The Periodical." Ballaster, *History*, pp. 156–72.

McDowell, Paula. "Women and the Business of Print." V. Jones, pp. 135–54.

McKeon, Michael. *The Origins of the English Novel, 1600–1740*. Johns Hopkins UP, 1987.

Merritt, Juliette. *Beyond Spectacle: Eliza Haywood's Female Spectators*. U of Toronto P, 2004.

———. "Reforming the Coquet? Eliza Haywood's Vision of a Female Epistemology." Newman and Wright, pp. 176–92.

Milhous, Judith, and Robert D. Hume. "J. F. Lampe and English Opera at the Little Haymarket in 1732–3." *Music and Letters*, vol. 78, no. 4, Nov. 1997, pp. 502–31.

Mills, Jennie. "Rape in Early Eighteenth-Century London: A Perversion 'So Very Perplex'd.'" *Sexual Perversions, 1670–1890*, edited by Julie Peakman, Palgrave Macmillan, 2009, pp. 140–66.

Milton, John. *Paradise Lost*. *Norton Anthology of English Literature, Volume I*, edited by Stephen Greenblatt and M. H. Abrams, 8th ed., W. W. Norton, 2006, pp. 1832–2055.

Moody, Jane, and Daniel O'Quinn, editors. *The Cambridge Companion to British Theatre, 1730–1830*. Cambridge UP, 2007.

Moore, Judith. *The Appearance of Truth: The Story of Elizabeth Canning and Eighteenth-Century Narrative*. U of Delaware P / Associated UP, 1994.

———. "Elizabeth Canning and Mary Squires: Representations of Guilt and Innocence in Legal and Literary Texts, 1753–1989." *Lewd and Notorious: Female Transgression in the Eighteenth Century*, edited by Katharine Kittredge, U of Michigan P, 2003, pp. 197–209.

———. "Whose Story Is This, and Who May Tell It? Medical Evidence versus 'Common Capacity' in the Framing of the Elizabeth Canning Case." *Writing British Infanticide: Child-Murder, Gender, and Print, 1722–1859*, edited by Jennifer Thorn, U of Delaware P / Associated UP, 2003, pp. 218–35.

Morrison, Leslie. "Serialized Identities and Novelistic Character in Eliza Haywood's *Fantomina* and *Anti-Pamela*." *Eighteenth-Century Fiction*, vol. 30, no. 1, Fall 2017, pp. 25–44.

Mulvey, Laura. "Visual Pleasure and Narrative Cinema." 1975. Thornham, pp. 58–69.

N. H. *The Ladies Dictionary, Being a General Entertainment of the Fair-Sex: A Work Never Attempted Before in English*. London, 1694. *EEBO*.

Nelson, T. G. A. "Stooping to Conquer in Goldsmith, Haywood, and Wycherley." *Essays in Criticism*, vol. 46, no. 4, Oct. 1996, pp. 319–39.

Nestor, Deborah J. "Virtue Rarely Rewarded: Ideological Subversion and Narrative Form in Haywood's Later Fiction." *SEL: Studies in English Literature, 1500–1900*, vol. 34, no. 3, Summer 1994, pp. 579–98.

Newman, Donald J. "*The Female Spectator*: A Bibliographic Essay." Newman and Wright, pp. 212–41.

Newman, Donald J., and Lynn Marie Wright, editors. *Fair Philosopher: Eliza Haywood and* The Female Spectator. Bucknell UP, 2006.

Nixon, Cheryl L., editor. *Novel Definitions: An Anthology of Commentary on the Novel, 1688–1815*. Broadview Press, 2009.

———. "Regulating the Unstable Family: Eliza Haywood's Fiction and the Development of Family Law." Hiner and Fowler, pp. 49–78.

Noggle, James. "Unfelt Affect." *Beyond Sense and Sensibility: Moral Formation and the Literary Imagination from Johnson to Wordsworth*, edited by Peggy Thompson, Bucknell UP, 2015, pp. 125–43.

Nowviskie, Bethany. "On the Origin of 'Hack' and 'Yack.'" *Debates in the Digital Humanities 2016*, edited by Matthew K. Gold and Lauren F. Klein, U of Minnesota P, 2016, dhdebates.gc.cuny.edu/debates/text/58. Accessed 13 Apr. 2017.

Nussbaum, Felicity. "Drama." Ingrassia, *Cambridge Companion*, pp. 118–34.

———. "Speechless: Haywood's Deaf and Dumb Projector." Saxton and Bocchicchio, pp. 194–216.

Oade, Nathanael. *The Indulgent Parents, and Rebellious Children: Being a True Narrative of the Unparallel'd Rebellion of the Sons of Mr. Nathanael Oade, Senior.* S. Popping, 1718. *ECCO*.

Oade, Thomas. *A Full Reply to a Late Pamphlet, intituled,* The Indulgent Parents, *Publish'd by Mr. Oade, Senior.* W. Boreham, 1718. *ECCO*.

———. *The Unnatural Parent; or, The Origin and Progress of the Unhappy Differences between Mr. Oade and His Sons.* J. Roberts, 1718. *ECCO*.

Oakleaf, David. "'Shady Bowers! And Purling Streams!—Heavens, How Insipid!': Eliza Haywood's Artful Pastoral." Saxton and Bocchicchio, pp. 283–99.

O'Brien, Karen. "Woman's Place." Ballaster, *History*, pp. 19–39.

O'Driscoll, Sally. "Outlaw Readings: Beyond Queer Theory." *Signs*, vol. 22, no. 1, Autumn 1996, pp. 30–51.

Orr, Leah. "The Basis for Attribution in the Canon of Eliza Haywood." *The Library*, vol. 12, no. 4, Dec. 2011, pp. 335–75.

———. *Novel Ventures: Fiction and Print Culture in England, 1690–1730.* U of Virginia P, 2017.

Pamela Censured. 1741. *Project Gutenberg*, 16 Sept. 2010, www.archive.org/stream/pamelacensured33735gut/33735.txt.

Parker, Kate. "'The Battle without Killing': Eliza Haywood and the Politics of Attempted Rape." *Eighteenth-Century Poetry and the Rise of the Novel Reconsidered*, edited by Kate Parker and Courtney Weiss Smith, Bucknell UP, 2014, pp. 27–48.

Parrish, Sonya Lawson. "'Obtain but Their Consent': Agency and Female Speech in Eliza Haywood's *Love in Excess* (1719)." *Spectacle, Sex, and Property in Eighteenth-Century Literature and Culture*, edited by Julie A. Chappell and Kamille Stone Stanton, AMS Press, 2015, pp. 68–82.

Parsons, Nicola. "Early Fiction." Ingrassia, *Cambridge Companion*, pp. 164–79.

Paulson, Ronald. *Popular and Polite Art in the Age of Hogarth and Fielding.* U of Notre Dame P, 1979.

"Perplexity." Johnson, *Dictionary*.

"Perplexity, *N.*" *Oxford English Dictionary*, Oxford UP, 2019, www.oed.com/view/Entry/141375.

"Perspectives: The Marymount University Fact Book 2016–2017." *Marymount University*, 2017, www.marymount.edu/marymount.edu/media/Planning-Institutional-Effectiveness/Online-Version-Fact-Book-16-17.pdf. Accessed 13 Apr. 2017.

Phillips, Natalie M. *Distraction: Problems of Attention in Eighteenth-Century Literature.* Johns Hopkins UP, 2016.

Pope, Alexander. *The Dunciad. The Poems of Alexander Pope: A One-Volume Edition of the Twickenham Edition*, edited by John Butt, Yale UP, 1963, pp. 317–60.

———. *The Dunciad, Variorum. With the Prolegomena of Scriblerus.* A. Dod, 1729.

———. "Epistle to a Lady," *Alexander Pope: Selected Poetry*, edited by Pat Rogers, Oxford World's Classics, 1996.

———. *The Rape of the Lock.* Greenblatt, *Norton Anthology*, pp. 2513–31.

Porter, Roy. *English Society in the Eighteenth Century.* Penguin, 1990.

Potter, Tiffany. "'A God-like Sublimity of Passion': Eliza Haywood's Libertine Consistency." *The Eighteenth-Century Novel*, vol. 1, 2001, pp. 95–126.

———. *Honest Sins: Georgian Libertinism and the Plays and Novels of Henry Fielding.* McGill-Queen's UP, 1999.

———. "The Language of Feminised Sexuality: Gendered Voice in Eliza Haywood's *Love in Excess* and *Fantomina.*" *Women's Writing*, vol. 10, no. 1, 2003, pp. 169–86.

———. "Life in Excess: Eliza Haywood and Popular Culture in *The Masqueraders* and *The Surprize*." Haywood, The Masqueraders, pp. 3–52.

Powell, Manushag N. "Eliza Haywood, Periodicalist(?)." *Journal for Early Modern Cultural Studies*, vol. 14, no. 4, Fall 2014, pp. 163–86.

———. "*Jonathan Wild*, a Novel for All Classrooms." *Approaches to Teaching the Novels of Henry Fielding*, edited by Jennifer Preston Wilson and Elizabeth Kraft, Modern Language Association of America, 2015, pp. 163–70.

———. "New Directions in Eighteenth-Century Periodical Studies." *Literature Compass*, vol. 8, no. 5, May 2011, pp. 240–57.

———. "Parroting and the Periodical: Women's Speech, Haywood's *Parrot*, and Its Antecedents." *Tulsa Studies in Women's Literature*, vol. 27, no. 1, Spring 2008, pp. 63–91.

———. *Performing Authorship in Eighteenth-Century English Periodicals*. Bucknell UP, 2012.

Price, Kenneth. "Social Scholarly Editing." Schreibman et al., pp. 137–49.

Rabin, Dana Y. "Seeing Jews and Gypsies in 1753." *Cultural and Social History*, vol. 7, no. 1, 2010, pp. 35–58.

Raven, James. *British Fiction, 1750–1770: A Chronological Check-list of Prose Fiction Printed in Britain and Ireland*. U of Delaware P, 1987.

"Reacting to the Past." *Barnard College*, reacting.barnard.edu.

Reeve, Clara. *The Progress of Romance, through Times, Countries, and Manners*. London, 1785. 2 vols.

Richardson, Samuel. *Familiar Letters on Important Occasions*. Edited by J. Isaacs, Dodd, Mead, 1928.

———. *Pamela; or, Virtue Rewarded*. Edited by Thomas Keymer and Alice Wakely, Oxford UP, 2001.

Richetti, John. "Histories by Eliza Haywood and Henry Fielding: Imitation and Adaptation." Saxton and Bocchicchio, pp. 240–58.

———. *Popular Fiction before Richardson*. Clarendon, 1992.

———. "Prose Fiction in the Early Eighteenth Century: Behn, Haywood, Defoe, Swift." *A History of Eighteenth-Century British Literature*, Blackwell, 2017, pp. 153–79.

Rigilano, Matthew J. "Embodying the Invisible: Materiality and Subjectivity in Cavendish, Manley, and Haywood," *The Eighteenth Century*, vol. 57, no. 1, Spring 2016, pp. 71–93.

Rogers, Pat. "Fielding on Society, Crime, and the Law." *The Cambridge Companion to Henry Fielding*, edited by Claude Rawson, Cambridge UP, 2007, pp. 137–52.

Sambrook, James. *The Eighteenth Century: The Intellectual and Cultural Context of English Literature, 1700–1789*. 2nd ed., Longman, 1993.

Sample, Mark. "The Digital Humanities Is Not about Building, It's about Sharing." *Defining Digital Humanities: A Reader*, edited by Melissa Terras et al., Ashgate, 2013, pp. 255–58.

Savage, Richard, editor. *Miscellaneous Poems and Translations: By Several Hands*. London, 1726. *ECCO*.

Saxton, Kirsten T. "Telling Tales: Eliza Haywood and the Crimes of Seduction in *The City Jilt; or, The Alderman Turn'd Beau*." Saxton and Bocchicchio, pp. 115–42.

Saxton, Kirsten T., and Rebecca P. Bocchicchio, editors. *The Passionate Fictions of Eliza Haywood: Essays on Her Life and Work*. UP of Kentucky, 2000.

Schellenberg, Betty. "The Professional Female Writer." Ingrassia, *Cambridge Companion*, pp. 37–54.

Schofield, Mary Anne. "Exposé of the Popular Heroine: The Female Protagonists of Eliza Haywood." *Studies in Eighteenth-Century Culture*, vol. 12, 1983, pp. 93–103.

Schreibman, Susan, et al., editors. *A New Companion to Digital Humanities*. Wiley, 2016.

Seager, Nicholas. "The 1740 *Roxana*: Defoe, Haywood, Richardson, and Domestic Fiction." *Philological Quarterly*, vol. 88, nos. 1–2, 2009, pp. 103–26.

Sherman, Stuart, and Stephen Zwicker. "The Restoration and Eighteenth Century." *The Longman Anthology of English Literature, Volume 1C: The Restoration and the Eighteenth Century*. Longman, 2010, pp. 1981–2009.

Simpson, Antony E. "The 'Blackmail Myth' and the Prosecution of Rape and Its Attempt in Eighteenth-Century London: The Creation of a Legal Tradition." *The Journal of Criminal Law and Criminology*, vol. 77, no. 1, Spring 1986, pp. 101–50.

———. "Popular Perceptions of Rape as a Capital Crime in Eighteenth-Century England: The Press and the Trial of Francis Charteris in the Old Bailey, February 1730." *Law and History Review*, vol. 22, no. 1, Spring 2004, pp. 28–70.

Skinner, Gillian. "Women's Status as Legal and Civic Subjects: 'A Worse Condition than Slavery Itself'?" V. Jones, pp. 91–110.

Solinger, Jason D. *Becoming the Gentleman: British Literature and the Invention of Modern Masculinity, 1660–1815*. Palgrave Macmillan, 2012.

Sontag, Susan. *On Photography*. Farrar, Straus and Giroux, 1977.

Speck, W. A. *Literature and Society in Eighteenth-Century England, 1680–1820: Ideology, Politics and Culture*. Longman, 1998.

Spedding, Patrick. *A Bibliography of Eliza Haywood*. Pickering and Chatto, 2004.

———. "Eliza Haywood Texts, Links, etc." *Patrick Spedding: Research Notes / Informal Writing*, 9 Feb. 2011, patrickspedding.blogspot.com/2011/02/eliza-haywood-biography-texts-links-etc.html.

———. "Measuring the Success of Haywood's *Female Spectator* (1744–46)." Newman and Wright, pp. 193–211.

———. "Shameless Scribbler or Votary of Virtue? Eliza Haywood, Writing (and) Pornography in 1742." *Women Writing, 1550–1750*, edited by Jo Wallwork and Paul Salzman, Meridian, 2001, pp. 237–51.

Spencer, Jane. "Drama." Ballaster, *History*, pp. 145–55.

———. *The Rise of the Woman Novelist from Aphra Behn to Jane Austen*. Blackwell, 1986.

Starr, G. A. *Defoe and Casuistry*. Princeton UP, 1971.

Staves, Susan. "British Seduced Maidens." *Eighteenth-Century Studies*, vol. 14, no. 2, Winter 1980–81, pp. 109–34.

———. "Fielding and the Comedy of Attempted Rape." *History, Gender, and Eighteenth-Century Literature*, edited by Beth Fowkes Tobin, U of Georgia P, 1994, pp. 86–112.

———."Women Writers ≠ Women Novelists." *Tulsa Studies in Women's Literature*, vol. 26, no. 1, Spring 2007, pp. 87–95.

Steele, Richard. *Tatler*, no. 225, 16 Sept. 1710. *The Tatler*, edited by J. J. Woodward, Philadelphia, 1831.

Sterling, James. "To Mrs. Eliza Haywood on Her Writings." *Secret Histories, Novels, and Poems*, by Eliza Haywood, 6th ed., vol. 1, London, 1725, pp. 7–8.

Stewart, Carol. "Eliza Haywood's *The Fortunate Foundlings*: A Jacobite Novel." *Eighteenth-Century Life*, vol. 37, no. 1, 2013, pp. 51–71.

———. Introduction. *Invisible Spy*, by Eliza Haywood, Pickering and Chatto, 2014. Chawton House Library Series, Women's Novels 18.

———. Introduction. The Rash Resolve *and* Life's Progress, Pickering and Chatto, 2013.

"Strange, *Adj.* and *N.*" *Oxford English Dictionary*, Oxford UP, 2019, www.oed.com/view/Entry/191244.

Straub, Kristina. *Domestic Affairs: Intimacy, Eroticism, and Violence between Servants and Masters in Eighteenth-Century Britain.* Johns Hopkins UP, 2009.

Stuart, Shea. "Subversive Didacticism in Eliza Haywood's *Betsy Thoughtless*." *SEL: Studies in English Literature, 1500–1900*, vol. 42, no. 3, Summer 2002, pp. 559–75.

Sussman, Charlotte. *Eighteenth-Century English Literature, 1660–1789*. Polity, 2012.

Sutherland, Kathryn. "Writings on Education and Conduct: Arguments for Female Improvement." V. Jones, pp. 25–45.

Svensson, Patrik. "Sorting Out the Digital Humanities." Schreibman et al., pp. 476–92.

Swenson, Rivka. "Optics, Gender, and the Eighteenth-Century Gaze: Looking at Eliza Haywood's *Anti-Pamela*." *The Eighteenth Century*, vol. 51, nos. 1–2, Spring-Summer 2010, pp. 27–43.

Swift, Jonathan. *Hints towards an Essay on Conversation*. U of Adelaide Library, 2008.

———. "The Lady's Dressing Room." *Norton Anthology of English Literature, Volume I*, edited by Stephen Greenblatt and M. H. Abrams, 8th ed., Norton, 2006.

Tauchert, Ashley. *Against Transgression*. Blackwell, 2008.

Thomason, Laura E. *The Matrimonial Trap: Eighteenth-Century Women Writers Redefine Marriage*. Bucknell UP, 2014.

Thompson, E. P. *Customs in Common*. Merlin Press, 1991.

Thompson, Helen. "Eliza Haywood's Philosophical Career: Ingenuous Subjection and Moral Physiology." *Ingenuous Subjection: Compliance and Power in the Eighteenth-Century Domestic Novel*, by Thompson, U of Pennsylvania P, 2005.

———. "Plotting Materialism: W. Charleton's *The Ephesian Matron*, E. Haywood's *Fantomina*, and Feminine Consistency." *Eighteenth-Century Studies*, vol. 35, no. 2, Winter 2002, pp. 195–214.

Thorn, Jennifer. "'A Race of Angels': Castration and Exoticism in Three Exotic Tales by Eliza Haywood." Saxton and Bocchicchio, pp. 168–93.

Thornham, Sue, editor. *Feminist Film Theory: A Reader*, New York UP, 1999.

Three Centuries of Drama: English, 1701–1750. Microform. Readex Microprint, 1953–55.

Tierney-Hynes, Rebecca. "Fictional Mechanics: Haywood, Reading, and the Passions." *The Eighteenth-Century*, vol. 51, nos. 1–2, Spring-Summer 2010, pp. 153–72.

Todd, Janet. *The Sign of Angelica: Women, Writing, and Fiction, 1660–1800.* Virago Press, 1989.

Towsey, Mark. "Women as Readers and Writers." Ingrassia, *Cambridge Companion*, pp. 21–36.

Traub, Valerie. *The Renaissance of Lesbianism in Early Modern England.* Cambridge UP, 2002.

Trethewey, Natasha. *Bellocq's Ophelia.* Graywolf Press, 2002.

Turner, Cheryl. *Living by the Pen: Women Writers in the Eighteenth Century.* Routledge, 1992.

"Unaccountable." Johnson, *Dictionary*.

"Unaccountable, *Adj.* and *N.*" *Oxford English Dictionary*, Oxford UP, 2019, www.oed.com/view/Entry/208992.

"University of St. Thomas." "A-Plus Schools for B Students," *U.S. News and World Report*, 2019, www.usnews.com/best-colleges/rankings/national-universities/a-plus.

Warner, Marina. *Stranger Magic: Charmed States and the* Arabian Nights. Vintage, 2012.

Warner, William B. "The Elevation of the Novel in England: Hegemony and Literary History." *ELH: English Literary History*, vol. 59, no. 3, Autumn 1993, pp. 577–96.

———. "Formulating Fiction: Romancing the Reader in Early Modern Britain." *Cultural Institutions of the Novel*, edited by Deidre Lynch and William B. Warner, Duke UP, 1996, pp. 279–305.

———. *Licensing Entertainment: The Elevation of Novel Reading in Britain, 1684–1750.* U of California P, 1998.

———. "Novels on the Market." *The Cambridge History of English Literature, 1660–1780*, edited by John Richetti, Cambridge UP, 2005, pp. 87–106.

Warren, Robert. *Practical Discourses on Various Subjects: Proper for All Families.* 2 vols. Robert Warren, 1723. *ECCO*.

Waters, Mary. "Periodical Writing." Ingrassia, *Cambridge Companion*, pp. 226–41.

Watt, Ian. *The Rise of the Novel: Studies in Defoe, Richardson and Fielding.* U of California P, 1957.

Westrup, Jack, et al. "Aria." *Oxford Music Online*, doi.org/10.1093/gmo/9781561592630.article.43315. Accessed 13 May 2017.

"What Is *18thConnect*?" *18thConnect: Eighteenth-Century Scholarship Online*, Center of Digital Humanities Research, Texas A&M University, www.18thconnect.org/about. Accessed 13 Apr. 2017.

Whicher, George Frisbie. *The Life and Romances of Mrs. Eliza Haywood*. Columbia UP, 1915.

"Wikipedia Editors Survey: Results from the Editor Survey, April 2011." *Wikimedia Commons*, Apr. 2011, upload.wikimedia.org/wikipedia/commons/7/76/Editor_Survey_Report_-_April_2011.pdf. Accessed 13 Apr. 2017.

"Wikipedia:Template Messages." *Wikipedia*, 17 March 2019, en.wikipedia.org/wiki/Wikipedia:Template_messages. Accessed 26 Mar. 2019.

"Wikipedia:WikiProject Countering Systemic Bias." *Wikipedia*, 28 Nov. 2015, en.wikipedia.org/wiki/Wikipedia:WikiProject_Countering_systemic_bias. Accessed 13 Apr. 2017.

Williams, Kate. "Women Writers and the Rise of the Novel." Ballaster, *History*, pp. 113–25.

Wilner, Arlene. "The Mythology of History, the Truth of Fiction: Henry Fielding and the Cases of Bosavern Penlez and Elizabeth Canning." *The Journal of Narrative Technique*, vol. 21, no. 2, Spring 1991, pp. 185–201.

Wilputte, Earla. "Eliza Haywood's *Poems on Several Occasions*: Aaron Hill, Writing, and the Sublime." *Eighteenth-Century Women: Studies in Their Lives, Work, and Culture*, edited by Linda V. Troost, vol. 6, AMS Press, 2011, pp. 79–102.

———. "Haywood's Tabloid Journalism: *Dalinda; or, The Double Marriage* and the Cresswell Bigamy Case." Hiner and Fowler, pp. 122–42.

———. *Passion and Language in Eighteenth-Century Literature: The Aesthetic Sublime in the Work of Eliza Haywood, Aaron Hill, and Martha Fowke*. Palgrave Macmillan, 2014.

———, editor. *Three Novellas*. Michigan State UP, 1995.

———. "'Too Ticklish to Meddle With': The Silencing of *The Female Spectator*'s Political Correspondents." Newman and Wright, pp. 122–40.

———. "Wife Pandering in Three Eighteenth-Century Plays." *SEL: Studies in English Literature, 1500–1900*, vol. 38, no. 2, Summer 1998, pp. 447–64.

Wilson, Kathleen. *The Sense of the People: Politics, Culture and Imperialism in England, 1715–1785*. Cambridge UP, 1998.

Wolf, Amy. "*The Female Spectator* and the New Story of Eliza Haywood." *Eighteenth-Century Life*, vol. 33, no. 1, 2009, pp. 74–82.

Woolf, Virginia. *A Room of One's Own*. 1929. Harcourt Brace Jovanovich, 1957.

———. "A Scribbling Dame." *Times Literary Supplement*. 17 Feb. 1916, vol. 735, p. 78. *Times Literary Supplement Historical Archive*, Gale Group, www.gale.com/c/the-times-literary-supplement-historical-archive.

"The Worrying Consequences of the Wikipedia Gender Gap." *MIT Technology Review*, 19 Apr. 2012, www.technologyreview.com/s/427626/the-worrying-consequences-of-the-wikipedia-gender-gap. Accessed 13 Apr. 2017.

Young, Iris Marion. "Throwing Like a Girl: A Phenomenology of Feminine Body Comportment, Motility, and Spatiality." 1980. Mann and Patterson, pp. 194–200.

Zirker, Malvin R., editor. An Enquiry into the Causes of the Late Increase of Robbers *and Related Writings*. Wesleyan UP, 1988.

Žižek, Slavoj. "Fantasy as a Political Category." *The Žižek Reader*, edited by Elizabeth Wright and Edmond Leo Wright, Blackwell, 1999, pp. 87–100.